Ariel's Ecology

Ariel's Ecology

Plantations, Personhood, and Colonialism in the American Tropics

Monique Allewaert

 University of Minnesota Press
Minneapolis
London

An earlier version of chapter 1 was previously published as "Swamp Sublime: Ecologies of Resistance in the American Plantation Zone," *PMLA* 123, no. 2 (March 2008): 340–57.

"Beau sang giclé" by Aimé Césaire was originally published in Aimé Césaire, *The Collected Poetry* (Berkeley: University of California Press, 1983); reprinted by permission of the University of California Press.

Published by the University of Minnesota Press
111 Third Avenue South, Suite 290
Minneapolis, MN 55401-2520
http://www.upress.umn.edu

Library of Congress Cataloging-in-Publication Data

Allewaert, Monique.
   Ariel's ecology : plantations, personhood, and colonialism in the American tropics / Monique Allewaert.
   Includes bibliographical references and index.
   ISBN 978-0-8166-7727-6 (hc : alk. paper)—ISBN 978-0-8166-7728-3 (pb : alk. paper)
   1. Human ecology—Southern States—History—18th century.   2. Human ecology—Caribbean Area—History—18th century.   3. Human beings—Effect of nature on—Southern States—History—18th century.   4. Human beings—Effect of environment on—Caribbean Area—History—18th century.   5. Human beings—Effect of environment on—Psychological aspects.   6. Plantation life—Southern States—History—18th century.   7. Plantation life—Caribbean Area—History—18th century.   I. Title.
   GF504.S68A55   2013
   304.20975'0903—dc23   2013010129

Printed in the United States of America on acid-free paper

The University of Minnesota is an equal-opportunity educator and employer.

Contents

Tempest in the Plantation Zone

Sea Breathing

Full fathom five thy father lies,
Of his bones are coral made;
Those are pearls that were his eyes;
Nothing of him that doth fade
But doth suffer a sea-change
Into something rich and strange.

—William Shakespeare, *The Tempest*

Perhaps the most well-known lines of William Shakespeare's colonial play *The Tempest* (1609), Ariel's lyric account of the transformation of the European traveler Alonso's body might seem the spun stuff of fantasy. After all, Ariel sings it to enchant Alonso's son Ferdinand so as to further Prospero's plan of dividing the Europeans shipwrecked on the island. Yet Ariel's lyric also offers a series of truths about how life in the colonies will affect the agency and integrity of human and nonhuman bodies. Any potential for human agency seems to vanish into the passive tense of Ariel's song, which breaks men's bodies into parts so as to make men and other creatures into media through which a mysterious sea change effects its inexorable difference. However, what Ariel describes is not the disappearance of human agency but an emerging minoritarian colonial conception of agency by which human beings are made richer and stranger through their entwinement with the operations of corals and, over the course of the play, other colonial climatological forces as well as plant and animal bodies. Ariel, a figure for the elemental natural world that he personifies and for the subaltern human beings whom he approximates in his indentured servitude, anticipates the conjunction of the colonial natural world and colonized human beings. If this conjunction constitutes a sort of decomposition, it also makes possible a form of personhood that was particularly visible to subaltern beings in the colonies.[1]

Ariel describes cavitations, expansions, and transformations of the human body that are at once literal and figurative and that render the possibility that bones and eyes are not simply parts of human structures because they also move with the sea breathings of corals and mollusks.[2] This is not simply to say that human bodies were influenced by colonial environments. In fact, Ariel describes a body that is pulled into parts and yet holds open the apparently paradoxical possibility that personhood is not vanished by this disaggregation but instead changed. I begin with Ariel's song because it crystallizes the argument I will make in this book. In the American tropics, bodies were often experienced as disorganized and disorganizing, and, what's more, it seemed possible that parts once organized into bodies might well evince autonomy outside of this organization. This transformation of human and other bodies was a key anxiety of Anglo-Europeans writing in and about the American colonies, and it was endured and revalued by those persons claimed as property in the colonies, particularly by Afro-American persons.[3] In this book, I will argue that this rendering of the body in parts did not signal the end of personhood but the origin of a minoritarian and anticolonial mode of personhood that was largely developed by Afro-Americans. At stake in tracing this minoritarian personhood is a recalibration of the conceptions of the body, of personhood, and of agency that Americanists as well as ecocritics have relied upon.

The genealogy of the body, personhood, and agency I will develop in this book is quite distinct from other emerging colonially inflected understandings of bodies. For instance, John Locke, who invested in colonial projects including the slave trade and who drafted the Carolina Constitution, emphasized the individuation, discreteness, and identity (or self-sameness) of any living body. Locke believed that regardless of the "constantly fleeting particles of matter" leaving and joining any vegetable or animal body, this body remained identical to itself over time because the succession of matter and actions that composed it would always be "vitally united to the same organized body."[4] For Locke, identity depends on the organization of matter into an individual body. In his account, the key function of a vegetable or animal body is to maintain its organization of parts because it is this organization, as well as this body's (and consciousness's) capacity for organization (and not the matter or the actions of the body per se), that produces the body as a single, self-identical, and particular consciousness that persists despite the diverse materials, things, temporalities, and places that press upon and pass through it.[5] If we were to stay within this Lockean genealogy, Ariel's account of Alonso's movement with seas, corals, mollusks, and pearls would signal his death, for what Ariel imagines is the disaggregation of the organized body such that it can no longer be understood as a specific identity but seems to have no identity at all.

Certainly Ferdinand anticipates this Lockean reading when he interprets Ariel's song as evidence of Alonso's death. Indeed, my argument that Ariel presages a conception of the body as a disorganizing, fundamentally diversifying entity is not proposed by the great seventeenth- and eighteenth-century philosophers and legal thinkers whose ideas would prove so central to colonial and then U.S. politicians' understandings of the body, the person, and the social contract, whether ecclesiastic or secular. Although hardly of a piece, philosophers from Hobbes to Descartes to Montesquieu to Blackstone, like Locke, understood the person and the social compact to depend on the identity of a body over time. In nearly every materialist tradition of the era, whether recirculating classical materialisms or the new sciences of the seventeenth and eighteenth centuries, the body is conceived as an organized and organizing system.[6]

However, the tropics produced a different materialist tradition in which the body (animal or vegetable) is invaded, rendered in parts, and otherwise deranged. This disaggregation was almost always experienced as catastrophic by human beings, whether by Anglo-European travelers who worried that their vigor and morality were threatened by effects of tropical heat, matter, and economic structures or by Afro-American slaves and maroons who were coded as bodies whose destruction by climatic and economic structures was legally justified by metropolitan and colonial law. That tropical climates and economic forms produced disaggregated bodies was indeed catastrophic. However, it also indicates that the Americas gave rise to an alternate materialism of the body. Here, it was as though disaggregation and dispersal, which classical and enlightenment materialisms conceived as, properly speaking, a property of matter, became a property of the body.[7]

Even if this minoritarian conception of the body and the person was not a central axis of European philosophical and legal traditions, it was a shadow cast by enlightenment thought, and it changed the intellectual and political terrains of a number of locations that were influenced by colonialism. It emerges in Ariel's lyric, which is not a lie and describes a man who is not dead. It emerges, in part, from the fact that Locke's insistence on the self-identity of the body and the person opens the possibility of an oppositional account of bodies and persons founded not on identity but on diversification. This possibility of diversification is raised in a number of eighteenth-century texts, including Benjamin Franklin's early work *Dissertation on Pleasure and Pain* (1725) as well as Denis Diderot's *Rêve d'Alembert* (1769, 1830), both of which speculate on the autonomy of parts.[8] And this possibility emerges in the debates waged by metropolitan thinkers as well as provincial ones about whether a human being, or any animal or plant body, would in the colonies become a different kind of organization of matter and thus a different kind of being.

This final possibility was laboriously documented from the earliest decades of American colonialism. Colonial travelers and natural historians charted the quantitative differences between colonial climates, soils, astrological phenomena, and plant and animal life and the European versions of the same, paying particular attention to how these differences affected humans and other animals in the colonies.[9] Belief that the properties of the matter that composed a place shaped the persons in that place undergirded still-circulating humeral theories. For example, Robert Burton's *Anatomy of Melancholy* (1621) theorized the effects of air, wetness, and heat on human beings' temperaments. In the more classical Enlightenment philosophies and sciences, Charles Montesquieu's *Spirit of the Laws* (1748) argued that the particularities of place, especially climactic phenomena, affected persons and shaped political forms. Montesquieu's theorization focused on the effects of cold, temperate, and hot climates on persons and governments, paying little attention to the effects movements between climates had on persons and governments. However, movement between climates and continents was precisely what colonial mercantilism and incipient capitalism depended on, and this meant that human beings, animals, insects, plants, and microbes were all constantly being brought into contact and changed "by the power of transplantation," as J. Hector Crèvecoeur later put it.[10] Caribbean and North American intellectuals, naturalists, and politicians were particularly concerned about the impact of tropical climates on Anglo-Europeans as they moved from the temperate climates supposedly more suited to them to the tropical and subtropical climates supposedly better suited to Africans and Native Americans.

Jim Egan has shown the profound anxiety Anglo-European colonists had about the effects of colonial climates on their persons: "of all the objections to colonization offered by English writers from the sixteenth century onward, none proved more resilient than those focused on climate."[11] Focusing on James Grainger's *The Sugar Cane* (1764), Egan charts a colonial Anglo-British attempt to shift the grounds of identity away from climate, which could produce degenerations of "white" British bodies, to the experiences of sympathy and exchange—which were coded as distinctly British but were, crucially, imagined as a Britishness founded on dematerialized practices through which the body produced protections against the incursions of climate. Through experiences of sympathy and exchange that "dematerializ[ed] the effects of climate," Britons might "become consumers of climate" and not determined by it.[12] The key difference between my analysis and Egan's is that I argue that this work of dematerialization typically failed, leaving traces of the materiality and climatological transformation it was trying to suppress. Developing a related point, Chris Iannini shows that American naturalists like M. L. E. Moreau de St. Mery and Thomas Jefferson, who argued for the Enlightenment credentials of white Creoles, also evinced the effects that metropolitan scientists like the Comte de Buffon and Abbé Raynal associated with American climates. Raynal's extension of Buffon's thesis of American degeneracy to Creole "human beings" proposes that tropical climes "contribute[d] to a kind of moral degeneracy with symptoms including excessive passion, sensuousness, and indolence" that left Creoles "susceptible to supernatural belief and incapable of sustained rational thought."[13] This same heat and humidity that seemed to slow animal life and stupefy reason increased the generation and decay of plants, which developed, spread, and moved faster in the tropics and subtropics. This not only allowed long, sometimes multiple, growing seasons for cash crops but also caused human habitations left untended to vanish into the spread of vegetable life. The insects that also proliferated in tropical humidity found their way into animal bodies, from which they consumed and then, unwittingly, gave over to the diseases they sometimes carried, especially yellow fever. The insects also found ways into plant bodies, some of which would consume the insects in turn, such as Venus flytraps.

According to Anglo-European travelers and scientists as well as Afro-American artifact makers and storytellers, the movement of human beings from one place to another as well as the effects of the fast-growing plants and ever-present insects produced transformations of the human body and psyche that are akin to what critics have called *creolization,* by which is meant not simply birth in the colonies but, as Sean Goudie proposes, "admixtures, or syncretisms, between Old and New World 'races' and cultures."[14] Most theorists suggest that creolization is ultimately a cultural claim about how the divergent traditions brought into contact by colonialism forged identities and practices that were not equivalent to any of the traditions from which they had emerged. However, the countergenealogy I derive from Ariel's lyric suggests that we might understand creolization not simply as a cultural phenomenon but also as a material and even ontological phenomenon that described how the substances and agencies that interacted in and thus composed a given place, as well as the economic conditions particular to this place, produced bodies and forms of personhood in which diversification became primary.

One of the consequences of this creolized ontology is that the integrity of the human being as such was threatened. This threat was nowhere more evident than in Anglo-Europeans' categorization of Africans and Afro-Americans as not entirely human, or as what I call *parahuman.* Parahumanity, a term and concept I theorize in chapter 3, describes the slave and maroon persons who seventeenth- through nineteenth-century Anglo-European colonists typically proposed were not legally or conceptually equivalent to human beings while at the same time not being precisely inhuman. They were thus beside the human—they were *para*human.[15] As was already clear in *The Tempest*'s account of the Algerian-descended Caliban, colonial texts typically understood African-descended human beings as constituting a kind of interstitial life between humans, animals, objects, and sometimes even plants. The customary move of abolitionists as well as anticolonial and postcolonial critics has been to condemn this colonial valuation of Afro-Americans as not precisely human in order to rehabilitate Africans and Afro-Americans to the category of the definitively human. To be sure, colonial racism and exploitation were despicable. However, instead of simply disparaging this valuation of Afro-Americans as parahuman, I will consider how accounts of the body, the person, and the political change if we trace the knowledges and possibilities that emerged from the minoritarian position adumbrated by Ariel and most fully instantiated by Afro-Americans who were excluded from the fold of the human and forced into the position of parahumanity.

By exploiting this key conceptual ambiguity in colonial scientific, legal, and political categories, I aim to trace the knowledge, beliefs, and strategies of resistance produced by those who were not counted as humans. Colonial typically conceived of Africans as a not-definitively-categorizable form of life. Moreover colonial organizations of labor power, particularly the plantation form, required that slaves (often of African descent) become deeply familiar with the properties of nonhuman animal and plant life. This meant that Africans in the diaspora, whether slave or maroon (self-emancipated slaves), had especially deft imaginings of the forms of power and agency that developed at the interstices between human and nonhuman life. This, I will argue, was linked to Afro-American fetish production, to the Creole tales' accounts of the proximity between human and other animal lives, and to botanico-religious cosmologies like Obeah, Vodou, and Santeria. These diasporic religions developed by slaves and maroons evince traces of African cosmologies (particularly Yoruba, Dahomey, and Congolese), Native American cosmologies (particularly Arawak), as well as European cosmologies (particularly Catholicism in Spanish and French colonies like Cuba, Haiti, and Martinique). They all centrally foreground botanical medicine and healing.[16]

In fact, Anglo-Europeans were quite aware that subaltern persons' relations with the colonial natural world could result in incipiently political alliances. Consider that Caliban's repudiation of Prospero echoes Ariel's lyric disaggregation of the colonial body while vesting it with revolutionary potential: "All the infections that the sun sucks up / From bogs, fens, flats, on Prosper fall, and make him / By inchmeal a disease."[17] I join Caliban's curse with Ariel's lyric to suggest that Africans in the Atlantic diaspora gained power through their recognition and exploitation of human and parahuman beings' relations with nonhuman forms. Existing colonial, anticolonial, and postcolonial analyses of the play have tended to divide Ariel from Caliban, but attending to the environmental fantasies that circulate in the play reveals that from the earliest moments of colonization Anglo-Europeans imagined a tenuous and revolutionary alliance between tropical elemental forces and subaltern persons. Afro-Americans who gained power by exploiting this more-than-human relation did not simply resist Anglo-European colonialism but also undercut its central assumptions about the organization of human and nonhuman forms, whether organic or not. The rock-bound Caliban as well as the curses he inveighs counter the rather common colonial assumption that human beings were qualitatively distinct from a natural world that they could claim and codify as property. Moreover, Caliban's attention to the power and disruption that might emerge from bogs, fens, flats, and other natural phenomena figured nonhuman bodies, organic or not, as vectors for subaltern resistance, thus challenging the colonial assumption that any body that was not definitively human was an exchangeable product.[18]

Following through on the conceptions of the body and the person sounded by Ariel's lyric expands the strategies for critiquing capitalism. Capitalism and critiques of capitalism tend to presume that human bodies, like other bodies and forms, were originally qualitatively distinct (and were thus used for and to some specific end) but that this distinction was undermined by the money form, which could transform any quality into a numeric quantity that might be exchanged and might thus potentially be equivalent to any other form. The rise of capitalism is then often described as though it occasioned a fall from a prior cosmology in which qualitative distinctions were primary, leading to the emergence of a new cosmology characterized by quantitative distinctions that are imagined to be no differences at all because they make all that is solid and specific dissolve into air. Ariel's lyric challenges this elevation of the qualitative over the quantitative. More precisely, Ariel's lyric provides the ground for challenging capitalism within the realm of the quantitative by treating quantity as an expression of a physical, rhythmic, and fundamentally relational singularity that exceeds and also disrupts the money form's claim that a quantity is a flatly numeric measure. In Ariel's ecology, there is no medium of exchange like the money form that remains conceptually outside of the process of relation. Instead, everything including that which is conventionally understood as a medium—for instance, the sea—is bound up in processes of touching and proximity. Here, one entity touches upon and intensifies or exhausts or even decomposes another: this first entity's relation to the second is that of touching, of constituting, of perhaps in turn being constituted by it, all of which precludes exchanging one for the other. What this suggests is that relation, far from being a synonym for exchange, names a process through which bodies and parts punctuate themselves against larger fields that they also decompose. Relation, then, describes an enmeshment that is not a merging and that forecloses the possibility of exchange.

In the pages that follow, I will argue that the literal and figurative disaggregation of the human body in the American tropics requires that we conceive agency as what we might now call an ecological phenomenon. My objectives in tracing this minoritarian conception of agency are primarily political, philosophical, and ecocritical concerns that I will elaborate more fully in this introduction. As such, I am not first and foremost focused on intervening in debates concerning the intellectual history of the eighteenth and nineteenth centuries. That said, my analysis of the agency of eighteenth- and early nineteenth-century travelers, maroons, and slaves diverges from traditional periodizations of the eighteenth and nineteenth century and also diverges from the traditional sources used to document this period.

The eras of exploration and discovery as well as the Enlightenment understood to have developed from them are often described as having been shaped by human beings' preoccupation with uncovering, mapping, measuring, and (in most cases) instrumentalizing the natural world, all of which supposedly allowed human beings to perform synthesizing operations through which they attained their fullest potential. Romanticism is in turn often described as resulting from human beings' attempts to reunite themselves with a natural world (including themselves) from which they had become estranged in the preceding ages of reason and revolution.[19] The ecological personhood that I theorize veers from both the conventional Enlightenment and Romantic understandings of the relation of the human to the nonhuman for the simple reason that both presume, prima facie, the separation of human beings from the natural world. The most pronounced characteristic of Ariel's lyric and of the artifacts I will discuss in the pages to come is that such a separation was not possible. Thus, the artifacts I discuss cannot be folded into conventional understandings of the Enlightenment (because they did not imagine a natural history grounded on the division of human beings from nonhuman forces), and they cannot be folded into conventional understandings of Romanticism (because, having never claimed such a division between humans and the natural world, they did not need to go about undoing it). This means that the American tropics, including the plantation spaces whose commodity production fueled the Enlightenment's quantifying projects and Romanticism's fantastical visions, also witnessed the emergence of a disaggregated conception of the body that enables an understanding of the person that cannot be reduced to either of these periodization's understandings of the human, nature, or politics.

Bodies and Persons

Images and conceptions of the body have long been central to understandings of personhood and politics, and Ariel's description of a body pulled into parts that do not all contribute to a larger whole anticipates a form of personhood and a form of politics. Drawing on analyses of the incursions (boundary crossings), combinings (boundary transformations), and disaggregations (boundary deformations) of the bodies of slaves, maroons, and Anglo-European travelers, I trace the emergence of a person that is to the side of Locke's liberal conception of the person and at the same time not equivalent to the subject, or the citizen subject, that has been the prime mover of most twentieth- and twenty-first century Americanist criticism. In shifting from the subject to the person, I follow on Nancy Ruttenburg's work, which first proposed this terminological shift might be central to a genealogy of nonliberal democracy.[20]

The value of the term *person* is not primarily that it is a more legitimately eighteenth-century term to use in the context of the postrevolutionary Americas. After all, the term *subject* had a perfectly common political meaning in the eighteenth century, and it still circulated in the colonies and former colonies, even if it was not the term most commonly used by politicians and in political writing in the former North American colonies. One advantage of the term *person* is that it applies to a range of entities that were neither subjects nor citizens. In this sense, the term allows the inclusion of those outside of the official political life of the Age of Revolution while not rehabilitating them to normative political terms and positions. What's more, the term *person* can describe an entity on the verge of entering a political community as well as an entity that is inside of a political community. In the *Second Treatise on Government,* Locke makes clear the prepolitical status of the person, explaining that when "anyone unites his Person, which was before free, to any Commonwealth; by the same he unites his Possessions . . . and they become, Persons and Possessions, subject to Government."[21] As this formulation suggests, the person can exist both before its instantiation in governmental forms and after this instantiation. I emphasize the position of the person on the precipice of prepolitical and postpolitical forms so as to suggest that, even if Americanist criticism has overwhelmingly imagined that persons—including dispossessed persons—desire entry into the dominant political form of the U.S. republic, an entry through which the person becomes a citizen, we might also consider that those persons who would only be prejudicially included inside of dominant governmental forms might well have desired and even produced the conditions for other governmental forms.

The term *person* has been central to Anglophone politics and philosophy since Thomas Hobbes's *Leviathan* (1651) drew on the Latin meaning of *persona* as a disguise for the stage to propose a *person* as an entity with a capacity to act or represent, whether on one's own behalf (natural persons) or on behalf of others (artificial persons).[22] Moving from Hobbes's classically inflected and performative account of the person, Locke conceives persons as "intelligent agents, capable of a law, and happiness, and misery," which is to say, agents that manifest the *consciousness* that was Locke's key concept. Locke's account of the body as an organization that persists over time is the prelude to and analogue for his account of consciousness, which he defines as a collection of substances, parts, actions, and memories that are organized into a "vital union."[23] By the eighteenth century, the term *person* had gained even greater currency. William Blackstone's *Commentaries on the Laws of England* (1765–79) proposed the *person* as the most basic quasi-political actor in a state and further explained that the term could be used to designate aliens and denizens as well as subjects and citizens. In the U.S. Constitution (1789), *person* is the term most consistently used to designate legal and political agents, including slaves designated obliquely as persons, or more precisely as three fifths of a person, in Article 1, Section 2. Blackstone's *Commentaries* indicates that by the mid-eighteenth century the term *person* had come to be associated with the form of the organic human body, which is to say a body whose parts worked together to produce a whole whose generative power depended precisely on its holism. If in Locke the body and the person endowed with consciousness are formally analogous but distinct, Blackstone all but conflates the body with the person. A natural person is an individual and organic human body that appears "such as the God of nature formed us," but an artificial person is the product of human laws and is conceptualized through the somatic metaphors of the *corporation* or *body politic*, which imaginatively endow the artificial person with the bounded, centralized, and organized form Blackstone saw as the fundamental characteristic of the natural person.[24]

To some degree, Blackstone's use of the organic human body as a key political symbol follows on contract theory, which used the metaphor of the organized body to imagine that all the agents composing a social contract worked together to form a single entity such that multiplicity and difference might be imaginatively converted into unanimity and unity. However, Blackstone suggests that the organic human body is not only or even primarily the symbol of the social contract. Nor is it a small-scale analogue for what occurs at the supposedly higher levels of consciousness as it was for Locke. Rather, Blackstone presumes that the body is the vessel through which the person achieves basic rights from life to property.[25] In laying out what he calls "the right to personal security," Blackstone argues that in English law the "limbs of a man are of such high value" that a person may justifiably commit homicide if they are threatened. Indeed, Blackstone focuses his account on the rights of persons to own property, but the only right that trumps property is that of preserving the life and organicism of the body for which no form of property can offer "suitable atonement."[26]

Blackstone understands *persons* as first and foremost human bodies whose power derives from the subsumption of parts into wholes. However, the U.S. Constitution uses the term *person* as its most generic term for political or quasi-political agents, applying it to both citizens and slaves, even if the latter are defined as quantitatively lesser persons. Here we arrive at a key impasse. While Blackstone's common law presumes organic persons, the United States' founding legal document admits partial persons. Although the Constitution does not imagine Afro-Americans as literally partial persons, counting slaves as three-fifths of persons betrays a historical truth since slaves often were rendered in parts. This impasse reveals that the dominant enlightenment conception of the person as an organic body modeled on the human form is shadowed by a minoritarian enlightenment conception of the person as a partialized body. Under the regime of plantation colonialism that extended into the United States, Afro-American persons did not always possess bodies in which all parts were present and contributed to the functioning of the whole. Instead, the slave and maroon body could be justifiably amputated. This was both a legal mode of punishment, as in the French *Code Noir,* and more often an extralegal punishment. As I discuss at length in chapter 3, parahuman bodies—missing parts from ears to arms to legs to heads—gave rise to images and stories that evince Anglo-European anxiety and guilt about the brutalization of Afro-American persons and were also crucial to Afro-American resistance. The agency of the missing parts was not generally an explicit theme in Anglo-European writing about the broken parahuman body of the slave or maroon, but it was taken up in Afro-American cultural practices that understood that the missing or extracted parts of any body would retain some of the powers of the body from which they came, even though they could not reproduce that body. This raises the possibility that a part could exist separately from the whole that it had composed and that, although it recalls this whole, it does not replicate it.

The difficulty of conceiving a slave person as an organic body might well have contributed to Blackstone's belief that modern slavery was legally and philosophically incoherent. To be sure, Blackstone objected to slavery because it trespassed models of contract founded on the principle of mutual exchange and it violated a person's right to habeas corpus. However, it also foregrounded the existence of persons whose bodies did not evince the organicism he deemed necessary to any body, whether the natural body of the human being or the artificial body of the corporation that was modeled on this natural body. It is easy to imagine how Blackstone would account for the slave's broken and fragmented body: it would be an artificial body, and not the good artificial body of the corporation but the monstrous artificial body produced by the slave driver who willfully departed from the "God of nature's" order by fragmenting parts that should be consolidated into a unity. It is also possible to resolve the impasse between the organic human body of Blackstone's legal person and the broken parahuman body of the slave person, whose brokenness is uncannily (although certainly not deliberately) announced by the U.S. Constitution's description of slaves as three fifths of persons.

One might simply argue that colonial slavery and its sanctioned mutilation of Afro-Americans' and sometimes Native Americans' and poor white laborers' bodies was irrational, primitive, and contravened an otherwise rational theory of personhood and property relations. The problem with this argument is that it imagines slavery as an anomaly that needed only be abolished for justice to be secured, for human bodies to be conceived as properly organic, and for contradictions to be resolved. However, slavery was not anomalous or external to the seventeenth-, eighteenth-, and nineteenth-century political and philosophical traditions of the so-called West but existed inside of them. And the effects of person are not secondary but primary. All of which is to say that I am less interested in resolving the impasse the person poses to Blackstone's theory than in showing how this impasse allows an opening in then regnant and still circulating understandings of the body and the person.

The mode of personhood presaged by the body in parts changes the genealogy of the power and agency associated with the person. Colonial monarchical and liberal traditions both tend to imagine that the person has a single origin that marks the beginning of an identity that persists over time. However, for slaves and maroons, scenes of origin proliferated. One of the key particularities of Afro-Americans in American plantation zones, whether slave or maroon, was that the mythologies of a definitive and single origin that were central to liberal theories of personhood were simply not possible. Slaves generally did not know their birthdates and often had only partial knowledge of their parentage. Not only did maroons not generally know their birthdates, they also produced understandings of time and history that were not based on marking birth as a dated event. Richard Price's excavation of maroon histories cites a number of twentieth-century maroon historians, and not one of these historians seems to have indicated his or her birth date or even a birth year, so Price begins his account of each historian's genealogy with the approximative "circa."[27] To be sure, maroons were orthogonal to both slave and colonial cultures and did not have access to the technologies of print and literacy through which calendric time has typically been maintained from the seventeenth century to the present. Nonetheless, as Price's work documents, they clearly did have concepts of time and history and were aware of those used by plantation societies. Which is to say, if the birth dates that marked the single, genetic origins that were important to colonial cultures were deemed important to maroons, they might have found a technology to mark birth as a dated event, and yet they did not.

Entry into a maroon community, whether at birth, childhood, or adulthood, meant passing into a social form that had developed to challenge the plantation form; this is true even if maroon communities that gained full autonomy from colonial states sometimes did so by promising colonial governments that they would turn over slave runaways. Maroon communities often gave rise to alternative social formations, practices of personhood, and conceptions of resistance. If maroons were in transversal relation to the scene of genesis as a single and singular event, they nonetheless existed at the interstices of three different relations of power and agency: in relation to the plantation form, to a power structure dedicated to the rejection of certain aspects of the plantation form, and to autochthonous social structures emerging outside the plantation form. At least three different cosmologies inform these multiple geneses. First, the plantation form was founded on the division of persons from property but positioned Afro-Americans in a nether space between persons and property; in so doing, it opened up a space for its own subversion. Second, the act of marronage, which arose in response to and as a rejection of the plantation form and its organization of both labor and life, was partly reactive to the plantation form. For this reason, maroon communities that remained in the shadow of plantations sometimes repeated or even sustained the valuations of property and life that subtended plantation economies (for example, some maroon communities would hand runaway slaves back to plantation interests). Third, maroon communities, partly because they were generally not involved in commodity production and partly because they were often in more sustained contact with Native Americans and Native American cosmologies as well as with resignified fragments of African cosmologies, did not presume this same division between human persons and properties, whether artifacts, animals, plants, or land. In the case of marronage, then, it is not clear if the social structure in relation to which agency emerged would be the plantation form, which was certainly the hegemonic power in the eighteenth- and early nineteenth-century American tropics, or the sometimes implicit and sometimes explicit challenge to the plantation form that resulted in marronage, or the forms of autonomous culture forged in marronage, which often featured a stronger interest in the power and autonomy of nonhuman life-forms than was typical in Anglo-European colonial cultures. All these genealogies and operations of power shaped maroons' understanding of human agency in the American tropics.[28]

This means that Afro-American slaves who were systematically denied access to knowledge of their birth and their genetic parentage, as well as maroons who exited from the plantation scene to produce genealogies and modes of agency that emerged from the interstice of at least three forms of genesis, tended away from mythologies comprising a single origin endlessly repeated as well as the modes of personhood that presume a single originary matrix. Instead, they developed mythologies that proliferate origins. To elaborate this point through a canonical example, consider Frederick Douglass, who opened his *Narrative* (1845) by noting his ignorance of his age or birthday. As a number of critics have noted, Douglass begins by noting his ignorance of his own origins, but he nonetheless presents his master's whipping of his Aunt Hester as a primal scene, for it is in watching this event that he comes to know what it is to be a slave. Yet, as these critics have also argued, Douglass's battle with the slave-breaker Covey is also a primal scene, this time tracing how a "slave became a man." Although these competing and contradictory scenes of origin might be given dialectical interpretations (and often are), what interests me is that they indicate that there can be no genesis of the slave-subject, properly speaking, because the slave whose nonbirth (date) is closed out of the rectilinear time of the nation-state is expressly not a citizen. The emergence of the slave as a "man" not only cannot reverse the fact that the Afro-American slave emerged from a matrix that enforced his nonorigination, it also occurs below the threshold of citizenship that is equated with subjectivity. After all, in American colonies and the early U.S. nation-state, black men and women had limited civil or political rights, and even if free they were always vulnerable to being revalued as property. The exception to this state of affairs was the postcolonial state of Haiti, where starting in 1805 blackness was rhetorically universalized and thereby made a precondition of citizenship. I will discuss this form of citizenship in more detail in chapter 5.[29]

Yet, although Douglass's narrative reveals the nonarrival of subjectivity, it also traces multiple geneses of Afro-American personhood. In fact, Douglass's production of three distinct versions of his autobiography might not simply be interpreted as the result of his rebellion against white abolitionists from whom he became increasingly autonomous but also as evidence of a tendency of Afro-American cultural production to proliferate origins, tracing a number of routes through which a person's agency could be occluded or expressed.[30] Because I want to emphasize that these different stories of origin are not simply repetitions of a first and primary story of origin through which the subject emerges, it is important to note that Douglass's account of originary events shifts across the three autobiographical works. The final autobiography, *Life and Times of Frederick Douglass* (1892), for instance, does not include the scene of Aunt Hester's whipping.

Douglass glancingly acknowledges the relation of Afro Americans to an agential natural and artifactual world as part of this expansion of personhood. He recounts a brief period of petit marronage (short-term as opposed to long-term or permanent marronage) during which another slave gave him a fetish root to protect him from the violence of the plantation form. When he subsequently returned to the plantation, he fought and defeated the slave-breaker Covey, after which he was never again subjected to the physical violence of slavery. Douglass does not assign this change in his situation to the intervention of the root, which he describes as a piece of African superstition, but he nonetheless keeps this sequence of events in place, keeping in sight a cosmology and practice that used powerful plants and fetishes to wage resistance.[31] If Douglass fleetingly acknowledges the power of the natural world and fetishistic practice in his account of the expanding origins and agencies of parahuman persons, later Afro-American writers more explicitly develop this point. Consider Zora Neale Hurston's attention to the cultural forms emerging from the "wombs of folk culture," a formulation that renders wombs pluralized, decorporealized, and decorporealizing matrixes.[32] Or Édouard Glissant's figuration of the slave ship as a "womb abyss," and Wilson Harris's account of the "womb of space" in which the relations between the cultures and life-forms brought into relation by colonialism give rise to unexpected continuities and disjunctions that put an end to conventional ideas of either beginning or ending.[33]

These invocations of multiplying geneses, including geneses forged through relations with nonhuman agencies, require a theorization of personhood that traces the multiple events through which personhood accrues and, sometimes, dissolves. Attending to this multiplicity requires recognizing repetitions across multiple origins. If we cede this multiplicity, the experience of ambivalence, so central to psychoanalytic and poststructuralist accounts of agency, becomes something different. Instead of describing the position of being caught between opposing impulses born of a foundational matrix, it might be conceived as a negotiation of a series of oppositions and impulses that emerge across divergent and sometimes contradictory (non)origins. This multiplicity, although not in any simple sense libratory or utopian, cannot be understood as the product of the dialectically opposed forces and desires that give rise to double binds.

Ecomaterialism

The body, which I conceive as an organization of matter and parts and also fantasies about this organization of matter and parts, is the prima facie site through which personhood is produced and negotiated as well as where the overlapping economic, biological, and social systems that compose place are produced and negotiated. I mean this as an explicitly ecocritical conception of the body. In focusing on experiences and fantasies of the body in the American tropics and subtropics, I aim to contribute to the emerging subfield of postcolonial ecocriticism,[34] which emphasizes that subaltern persons, far from being unacquainted with environmental concerns and thus in need of being integrated into the burgeoning environmental movement of the twenty-first century, have long been among those most directly impacted by the environmental crises that accelerated with the development of colonial capitalism. For this reason, in many cases it was subaltern persons and those in close proximity to them who forged the first responses to the conjoined problems of economic and environmental exploitation. (It is not, then, insignificant that the Greek root *oikos* can refer to both the economic and the environmental.) My focus on the tropicalized body as well as on parts disaggregated from this body joins postcolonial ecocriticism to the new materialist studies' explorations of minoritarian understandings of matter, which recalibrate critical understandings of bodies, agencies, mediation, and connection.[35] In drawing on the work of the new materialists, ecocriticism might be conceived not simply as an account of nature or of place (or a repudiation of nature and place) but as an interrogation of how the corporeal and noncorporeal, organic and inorganic materials and parts that compose beings and places emerge.

This ecomaterialist theorization of the body in the plantation zone stands to make a series of linked interventions to Americanist and ecocritical scholarship. First, this personhood anticipates an American studies and an ecocriticism based on a body opened to the systems and substances that compose its outsides, whether those be assemblages like fetishes, or the industrial and legal technologies that compose the disciplinary structure of the plantation form, or the more subtle but nonetheless significant movements of particulate matter. In so doing, this mode of personhood moves away from the aesthetics and ethics of sympathy that have been common to both early American studies and ecocriticism. The closely related discourses of sympathy and interest depend on the fantasy of the bounded body that may, through the working of sympathy, be motivated to care for another.

The surface of the skin figures centrally in late eighteenth- and early nineteenth-century sentimental discourses. Consider, for instance, the blushing that is so regularly noted in early American writing, from Thomas Jefferson's complaint that Africans cannot blush to Sarah Wentworth Morton's evocation of the white abolitionist's blush for the crimes of slavery. This figuration emphasizes that the sentimental body is a bounded one. The sentimental body's insides (here, typically abstracted and psychologized as feelings) are sometimes made visible on its exterior but do not trespass this exterior. I cannot think of a single example of a sentimental text in which blushing culminates in bleeding: the blood that evinces sentimental feeling remains just beneath the surface of the skin. Sentimental writings' imagination of the skin as a sheath and a screen carefully manages the more disruptive consequences of recognizing that the body is an interface with, and a media for, its outsides. If the bounded body is the implicit metaphor undergirding sentimental discourses,[36] the disaggregated and opened body I trace in the pages that follow challenges this sentimental fantasy by looking to the practices and fantasies through which a person's body can be understood to extend into and be transformed by its outsides. These bodies, often black, that were, according to eighteenth- and nineteenth-century natural historians, incapable of blushing evince an imbrication with their outsides that registers a terrifying vulnerability to the events and forces on its outsides.

Despite the terror this openness evokes, it offers grounds for an ethics of relationality, by which I mean an engagement in which a body is recognized as a medium that extends into (and is extended into by) media that are proximate to it, and sometimes even into media that are not proximate to it. This process of mediation can strengthen, weaken, or eliminate that body, but in all cases it continually transforms and diversifies that body. It is, by my account, no accident that it is in radical abolitionist texts such as William Earle Jr.'s *Obi, or The History of Three-Fingered Jack* (1800) that the conventionally sentimental scene of crying produces effects that eliminate the conception of skin as a boundary and surface to realize the body as a medium. As I note in chapter 4, the maroon's tears culminate in a violent expulsion of the insides of body, here no longer abstracted as feelings but concretized as blood.

The significance of this tropical experience and fantasy of the body is not merely that it departs from sentimental experiences and fantasies of the body, but that it indicates a response to the brutalization of the human body in the Atlantic world that is not grounded on a desire for the constitution of the body as an enclosed and organic form. This is not only a claim about the shapes bodies take but also about psychology, insofar as I am suggesting that this form of personhood is not melancholically cathected to organizations of the body and the person that were impossible in the American tropics. My point is not that an interest in disaggregation and the non-melancholic psychology that I associate with it indicate a proto-poststructuralist position emerging in the eighteenth- and nineteenth-century tropics. Quite the contrary: although poststructuralist accounts of the body are formed on and against historically prior modernist accounts of the body, my claim is that this tropical understanding of the body is formed simultaneously with, and thus is not predicated on, the understanding of the body as an enclosed and organic form. This conception of the body as an organic form was then emerging in biology, aesthetics, and philosophy; eventually it would become dominant (and influence modernist conceptions of the organic), but it was not yet dominant in the late eighteenth century. Finally, this conception of the body does not imagine that parts of bodies—or of political communities—must necessarily be subordinate to the wholes that they compose. This, by implication, allows an American mythos in which plurality and diversity provide the originary and centrifugal motion, and in so doing pose a challenge to older American and ecocritical mythologies based on dialectics (the machine and the garden or virgin land) as well as those based on centripetal motion (the errand and the jeremiad).

Methods

The ecomaterialist conception of the body developed here contributes to the new American colonial studies' decentering of the United States by upending modes of personhood grounded on the production of whiteness and the priority of the human being, which, as we will see, were linked productions.[37] If this puts my book squarely within the new American colonial studies, the majority of these studies do not focus on agency and personhood as such. Srinivas Aravamudan's analysis of tropical residents' (or *tropicopolitans'*) contestation of enlightenment cosmopolitanism is an important precedent. Attending to the agency that develops from subaltern actors' redeployments of and tropings on dominant enlightenment ideologies, Aravamudan traces a postcolonial agency that is visible in "acts of reading, transculturation, and hybridity as well as from those of separation, opposition, and rejection [of literary culture]."[38] As Aravamudan suggests, the critical effort to trace postcolonial agency demands an archive that is not entirely composed of print and manuscript sources, which were not widely available to and were sometimes not desired by subaltern agents. Further elaborating on Aravamudan's insight, Susan Scott Parrish proposes that analyses of early Afro-American cultures require recognizing that "the talking woods more than the 'Talking Book' functioned as the 'ur-trope' of Anglo-African experience."[39] This agency that develops across literate and differently literate communities makes it possible to trace formulations of personhood and community that are not equivalent to those that critics have traditionally associated with the period, which have tended to focus on how the rise of literacy and the proliferation of print cultures shaped the modern subject and modern nationalism.[40]

My focus on cultural productions that developed outside of official literacy, even if they often did pass into manuscripts and printed texts, requires an archive that is different from that customarily used by scholars of the eighteenth and early nineteenth centuries, who, when they have focused on agency, have documented the forms of subjectivity, citizenship, economic power, and civic engagement that resulted from participation in cultures of literacy.[41] The archive I use here draws on print, manuscript, and nonwritten source materials. Because I draw on a number of different media and genres, including travelogues, botanical texts, medical texts, novels, engravings, drawings, and oral stories, my study makes no claims about any particular communications medium or genre. Nor do I focus my attention on media or genre theory more generally. Literary critics have convincingly shown that the genres that emerge at a given moment embed within their forms the contest between emergent, dominant, and declining social structures.[42] However, my aim here is not to tell the story of then-regnant modes of socialization or of their contestation with emerging or older dominant modes. Instead, I attempt to tell a story about modes personhood that were not and never became dominant and thus have no generic form or communication media to claim as their own. No doubt, this investigation could be supplemented by an investigation of the *extrageneric*, a topic that seems ripe for study in the early American period when so much of what was written is not obviously entirely within any one particular genre.[43] This extrageneric body of writing suggests that a number of early Americans desired experiences of self and community that were not those of the novel, the sermon, the jeremiad, the travelogue, or the lyric.

In part I of the book, I focus on Anglo-European natural historians who documented the effects of tropicalization. Across the two chapters that make up part I, I document these natural historians' understandings of the relation between organic and inorganic matter, their theorization of form and system, and their conception of planetary relations. In chapter 1, "Swamp Sublime," I show how the Philadelphia-based naturalist William Bartram's travels in the American tropics gave rise to an ecological mode of personhood that he associates with Afro-Americans but that also indicates his own departure from the normative citizen subjectivity of literate early American men. This argument launches my effort to situate Bartram within a minoritarian enlightenment tradition (which I will reference throughout with the lowercase) attentive to tropical and subtropical regions' disordering of the colonial projects that they also sustained. Chapter 2, "Plant Life," continues this focus on minoritarian enlightenments by investigating an American strand of vitalist materialism produced by Benjamin Rush, Alexander Humboldt, and Benjamin Barton as well as Bartram. Across their work, I trace a belief that plants contributed to the Americas' especially agential and potentially dangerous atmospheres. Plants and the diseased matter they passed into American atmospheres indicate the capacity of the part and the particulate to assert its autonomy from the systems in which they participate. This account of the autonomy of parts challenges the mechanism of dominant enlightenment natural historical and political thought, testifying to a genealogy of form and system that does not require the submission of parts to larger wholes.

In the second part of the book, where I turn from a relatively privileged colonial and early national elite to focus on the forms of body and personhood that Afro-Americans produced in the American tropics. In chapter 3, "On Parahumanity," I argue that the term *parahuman* might describe American slaves' categorization as neither human nor animal. In Afro-American oral stories, this experience of parahumanity testifies to modes of self that did not simply critique the category of the human that was unevenly available to them but also suspended it. That parahuman stories suspend the dominant Enlightenment tendency to pose the human being as the apotheosis of natural historical and cultural processes challenges criticism that understands the Enlightenment (here understood in the singular) as the moment that witnessed the ascendency and ubiquity of the modern conception of the human. This also makes clear that Afro-Americans' experiences of the body contributed centrally to forging minoritarian enlightenment traditions. Chapter 4, "Persons without Objects," continues this focus on alternative conceptions of the body and personhood. Its central argument is that the fetish artifacts produced by

Afro-Americans presume a dispersed body that is important, first, for its conception of the person's constitutive relation to her outsides and, second, for offering a decentered account of systems, including that of the person.

The principal artifacts of chapters 3 and 4 are the oral stories and fetishes produced by Afro-Americans. In the late eighteenth century, both were mainly documented by Anglo-European naturalists and slaveholders such as Matthew (Monk) Lewis, who recorded stories from the many slaves he owned and is a primary source for chapter 3. To deepen the investigation of oral stories and fetishes beyond the accounts of these obviously compromised sources, I consider why these cultural forms are generally occluded in early black writing in English and draw on accounts of oral stories and fetishes from later periods.

Although my collation of sources that are not historically and geographically of a case is unusual in early American scholarship, I am not the first Americanist or Atlanticist scholar to propose a temporally and geographically disjointed archive. Scholars of the Atlantic diaspora have pioneered historical methods that collate artifacts from earlier and later historical moments. Richard Price's work on maroon oral history, Annette Gordon-Reed's use of Jefferson's black descendants' oral stories, and Colin (Joan) Dayan's analyses of Haitian vodou's recollection of enslavement and resistance all influence my method here. Joseph Roach's investigation of cultural productions that emerge across geographically discrete nodes of circum-Atlantic networks is another critical precedent.[44]

In the book's third and final section, I consider how the minoritarian conceptions of the body and the person that I cull from both an Anglo-European elite and the Afro-American culture resonated for white women in North America. To do this, in chapter 5, "Involving the Universe in Ruins," I turn to Leonora Sansay's Haitian writings. *Secret History; or The Horrors of St. Domingo* (1808) and the later and often nonattributed novel *Zelica: The Creole* (1820) both focus on Anglo-European women traveling through revolutionizing St. Domingue, chronicling their transformation through the intervention of Afro-American cultural forms, including fetishes. This transformation indicates Sansay's interest in modes of agency that departed from those then available to women in the United States. It also suggests that white middle-class women, in addition to claiming the genre of the novel for their own ends,[45] also looked to Afro-American cultural production in claiming their own agency.

In the epilogue, I argue that the work of accessing minoritarian enlightenments requires a strategy of transversal reading that cuts across,
but not against, a work's stated interests, allowing the excavation of the set
of desires and fantasies that cannot be reduced to the more dominant interests that move through that same work. I am also, throughout, attempting a minoritarian mode of writing. My deliberately aestheticized way of
writing about Bartram, Phillis Wheatley, Sansay, and others, while faithful
to the historical record, emphasizes and makes much of details in their
oeuvres that are strange and remain unresolved—in fact, are often un-
treated—in literary criticism in order to open these figures to the American mythology I propose in this introduction.

Mythos

Édouard Glissant writes that the ball and chain gone green rolling on the
ocean floor folds the history and artifacts of slavery into the time of oceanic drift and vegetable growth.[46] When the ball and chain washes onto
the beach, it cannot tell the specific history of the life and death of the slave
it once bound. After all, the human body it once held has been consumed
by sea life, recalled but certainly not returned in the sea rhythms in which
it came to be enfolded. Yet this absence and opacity suggests a myth of history whereby it is possible to hold together noncontiguous historical moments, to open each to the other and to fill this opening with repetitions
and resonances that, as they accumulate, allow historically informed speculations about the artifacts and persons who vanished without being included in traditional historical archives.

If Glissant's opaque image offers a myth of history, it also participates
in the mythos of the body and person that I trace from Ariel. The image of
the ball and chain rolling in the sea's depths emphasizes the lost body and
person of the slave and thus might seem the inverse of Ariel's song, which
is not about the lost body but about the powers of disaggregated, composite—in short, creolized—bodies and persons. Yet the loss of the body and
the person was the ubiquitous threat of life in the tropics, and it was also
the condition under which creolization occurred. Glissant's invocation of
the lost body and Ariel's invocation of the disaggregated and transformed
body articulate two linked points in this colonial American mythology.
Entry into the colonies is figured and experienced as death, drowning, dismemberment, and irretrievable loss. This figuration and experience of

death, drowning, and dismemberment recalls that the colonies were what Orlando Patterson has called spaces of social death, which I would suggest was a condition that touched not just Afro-Americans but all persons moving through the colonies.[47] However, the economic, disciplinary, and agricultural systems that made the Americas cultures of social death were not simply sites of tragedy and loss. Bodies and persons pulled apart, trespassed, and brutalized in these regions produced modes of story (parahuman tales), artifactual creation (fetishes), and fantasy (of decomposing and recomposing bodies) that gave rise to a minoritarian mythos of the Americas in which the autonomy of parts engenders new fusings. In this mythos, diversification and diversity became the originary American story.

I

1

Swamp Sublime

Ecology and Resistance in the American Plantation Zone

Land Becomes Sea

In the description of Georgia's sea islands that opens the second part of his *Travels* (1791), William Bartram imagines that the marshlands that connect the mainland to these islands are part of a swampy archipelago that extends from Virginia to Mississippi to Vera Cruz.[1] This vision of geographical continuity either anticipates Manifest Destiny or, on the contrary, presages the dissolution of the North American continent: "Whether this chain of sea-coast-islands is a step, or advance, which this part of our continent is now making on the Atlantic ocean," Bartram muses, "we must leave to future ages to determine." The advancing continent seems initially to confirm a present-day scholarly tendency to read the writings of eighteenth-century Anglo-European elites as contributing to the imperialistic project of continental expansion. But as Bartram moves deeper into his meditation, the continent begins to dissolve. He reminds the reader that the tide-filled marshes that join the continent to the islands "were formerly high swamps of firm land," and any southern planter could confirm that draining these coastal marshes would yield "strata of Cypress stumps and other trees."[2] Land becomes sea, and only fossils and fragments remain to testify to these marshes' terrestrial past, as the southern terrain that Bartram exhaustively details in more than four hundred pages moves toward annihilation.

My suggestion that Bartram's *Travels* is a watery meditation that threatens to dissolve into its own apocalyptic undertow departs from critical assessments that focus on the material history of the places through which Bartram moved or on his contribution to the ultimately imperialistic project of revolutionary nationalism, which required forgetting, or at least managing, Indian pasts and making nature into a well-regulated space ensuring the good order of the nation-state.[3] My reading of *Travels* resists the assumption that colonial and then national ventures were largely uncontested and hegemonic. With its watery future, the continent typifies the volatile tropical spaces that Bartram characteristically interprets cataclysmically.[4] In the southern lowlands, the "ruins of costly buildings and highways . . . overgrown with forests" and "habitations . . . mouldering to earth" complement the "heaps of white, gnawed bones of the ancient buffaloe, elk and deer, indiscriminately mixed with those of men, half grown over with moss."[5] As these passages indicate, his account of the tropics shows that supposedly uncultivated land bears traces of human history and politics even as the region's forests, vines, mosses, and sinks obscure this human history. Yet if Bartram's tropics always have a history, they also reveal the impossibility of separating human agents and histories from the liquefactions of the natural world.

Although Bartram focuses on dissolutions, I believe that we need not read *Travels* abyssally since it also yields an ecological conception of revolution that might recalibrate theorizations of resistance in the eighteenth-century plantation zone. I use the term *plantation zone* to designate a space that is tropical (or subtropical) and whose economy and political structures are shaped by the plantation form.[6] The entanglements that proliferated in the plantation zone compromised taxonomies distinguishing the human from the animal from the vegetable from the atmospheric, revealing an assemblage of interpenetrating forces that I call an ecology.[7] This ecological orientation departs from an eighteenth-century political and aesthetic tradition distinguishing persons—in particular white colonial subjects—from the objects and terrains they surveyed. In fact, Bartram's increasingly ecological orientation compromised his ability to function as a citizen-subject of an emerging U.S. print culture. Focusing on Anglo-European travelers and on African resistance, I argue that instead of simply producing subjects who gained power through an abstract and abstracting print culture, the plantation zone witnessed the emergence of persons who gained agency by combining with ecological forces.[8] This shift from subjectivity to personhood, which I locate in Bartram's as well as later botanists' and travelers' work and then trace in Afro-American cultural productions, testifies to an organization of life that is not dependent on the separation of subjects from an object world. This is not to say that human agents in the plantation zone enjoyed an idyllic intersubjectivity with animals, plants, and objects. Rather, the point is that at precisely the moment citizen-subjects were emerging in metropolitan centers, the plantation zone gave rise to an ecological practice closely linked to *marronage,* a process through which human agents found ways to interact with nonhuman forces and in so doing resisted the order of the plantation.

In *Travels,* Bartram intended not to chronicle the complex political history of the American tropics, to elegize loss, or to lose or find himself but rather to distinguish southern North America as a temperate region that contributed to the healthy "activity of the human faculties."[9] This project required a methodological commitment to framing the lowlands through the terminology used to describe eighteenth-century temperate regions. Accordingly, he records the terrain through which he passes in the nomenclature of Linnaean botany, always pausing to give a plant or animal a properly Latinate name, often spinning multiple-page lists of species that he finds in tropical hollows. Yet in spite of his effort to describe the southern lowlands as a temperate space, the tropical, the useless, and the cataclysmic continually set him off course.

He consistently describes this southern geography in terms that emphasize its tropical splendor. This tropicalization is underscored by the concatenation of Virginia, Mississippi, and Vera Cruz; by his attention to the region's connections to unambiguously tropical spaces, including Cuba and the West Indies; and by his recurrent complaints about the region's humidity. It is not enough to designate the terrains that fascinated him with the adjective *tropical.* Rather, Virginia, Mississippi, and Vera Cruz had all been colonies where heat-dependent crops—indigo, tobacco, sugar, coffee, and rice—were produced on lowland plantations fueled by slave labor. In short, the terrain depicted by *Travels* was characterized by a collation of interpenetrating forces that was regional (tropical) and linked to a particular economic and political configuration (the plantation). In this tropical and subtropical plantation zone, animals, persons, plants, artifacts and their histories, and even land were penetrating, fusing with, transforming one another. The region's heat-driven processes contributed to the growth of cash crops that sustained metropoles. But the proliferation of colonial regimes as well as the region's lush vegetation slowed down, encroached on, and transformed all human agents in this ecology. Many colonials disappeared into the tropics, and Bartram himself all but vanished during the five-year botanical journey that served as the basis of *Travels.*

Sometimes Bartram experienced his entanglement in the lowlands as a pleasurable loss of self. To the dismay of his successful father, the royal botanist John Bartram, William failed in every venture to which he turned his hand. This aptitude for failure might well have given him the impetus to disappear into tropical frontiers. It might also have been what made him so profoundly uncomfortable in eighteenth-century Philadelphia that he refused every invitation that would have brought him into the public. Although invited to work in one of Benjamin Franklin's print shops, he declined. Although elected a member of the prestigious American Philosophical Society, he apparently never attended a single meeting. Although included on the faculty at the University of Pennsylvania, he never taught a class. The significant point here is that Bartram's fascination with the tropics pulled him outside the emergent American public sphere. Eventually he did publish his *Travels*, but it was a slow production, and he had a tortured relation to his printed book.

In *Letters of the Republic* (1992), Michael Warner proposes that eighteenth-century print cultures and the publics resulting from them catalyzed the enlightenment revolutions that birthed the citizen-subject of modern nationalism.[10] The forms of subjectivity that developed through print culture required that persons give up private identities for public identity; it also required that they give over their private bodies to a print culture that was intensely material insofar as it proliferated presses, typefaces, and print artifacts and was disembodied insofar as it idealized the abstraction of particular persons into larger and themselves abstract public bodies.[11] The aim of representative men like Benjamin Franklin was to produce themselves as exemplary citizen-subjects who existed primarily in print and in relation to others who also circulated in print.

If Franklin is Warner's exemplar of the citizen-subject, Bartram offers a good test case through which we can trace the emergence of a mode of agency and personhood that is not equivalent to subjectivity and developed outside the metropolitan centers associated with print culture. Instead of an inscrutable proto-Bartleby who chooses against choosing in order to register his ambivalence about print and publicity, Bartram was something of a proto-Chandos: a man so entwined with the tropical ecology that the projects of representation, communication, and publicity became excruciating.[12] His account of swamps and the transformation of people who lived in them reveals a mode of action that pulls away from the public sphere as well as the revolutionary nationalism and modes of subjectivity that have become associated with it.

Plantation spaces possessed those who traversed them. The heat that changed the orientation and movements of bodies, the diseases that the atmosphere was thought to carry, and the bites that the region's insects and venomous snakes inflicted, all compromised bodily and metaphysical integrity. Bodies so penetrated could not be so easily abstracted into the corpora sustained by print culture; their penetration revealed a deformation of the human body that stalled representational processes that imagined the human and political body as synonymous such that one could provide the template for the other. This penetration, deformation, and breaking emphasized that in the American tropics the human body, instead of giving itself over to print cultures, was also pulled into sprawling and overlapping biological, economic, and social systems.

There was perhaps no space more paradigmatically tropical and more threatening to colonials than the swamps in which Bartram spent a good part of five years. Although swamps were frequently part of a plantation's grounds and, as he notes, were most often used for rice cultivation, they also compromised the order and productivity of imperial ventures, from explorations to plantations. Often described as unnavigable terrains—Bartram called them "inextricable"—swamps stymied colonial armies and cartographers.[13] Cabeza de Vaca's early account of the Spanish exploration of Florida emphasizes the "great difficulty and danger" of the wetlands, where Indians kept them under continual attack.[14] Two centuries later, the members of William Byrd's surveying team imagined Virginia's Dismal Swamp as an alluring "terra incognita," but this fantasy disappeared once they entered the swamp and found themselves lost, sunk, and sick.[15] Byrd juxtaposes this account of his surveying team with an encounter between himself and a community of mulattoes who claimed to be free but who he suspects are escaped slaves. Significantly, swamps sheltered diasporic Africans who, in refusing slave status, repudiated the prevailing organization of Virginia's plantation economy.[16] If swamps were intractable for Anglo-Europeans, colonials such as Cabeza de Vaca and Byrd regarded them as navigable terrain for Africans and American Indians.

The tropical swamps that sheltered runaways and maroons and that were folded with difficulty into colonial and then national taxonomies ranged across the tropics.[17] These difficult to map and (in the Anglo-European imagination) Africanized spaces pulled colonials into a hum of life and decay that compromised efforts to produce state, economic, and scientific order. Swamps also confounded Anglo-European efforts to mine American landscapes to produce commodities, to further science, and to fulfill conventional aesthetic categories—ranging from the picturesque to the sublime. Instead of making economic, objective, or aesthetic use of swamplands, Anglo-Europeans were repeatedly sucked into their dense networks.

When he described lowland plants as "vegetating," Bartram named the process by which a sentient force acts in an ecology that acts on and through it. Many colonial writers, including Bartram's admirer François René de Chateaubriand, described how people, like plants, entered into vegetative states in the plantation zone.[18] The entanglements occasioned by swamps complicated colonial efforts to make clear distinctions between human beings and the natural world. In the opening pages of *Travels*, plants manifest agency. Observing a Venus flytrap, Bartram asks, "Can we . . . hesitate a moment to confess, that vegetable beings are endued with the same sensible faculties or attributes, similar to those that dignify animal nature; they are organical, living, and self-moving bodies, for we see here . . . motion and volition."[19] The plants in Erasmus Darwin's *The Botanic Garden* (1791) had sensations, but Bartram pushed this idea farther, insisting that "vegetable beings" also have "volition." He maintains that animals, unlike plants, "have the powers of sound, and are locomotive," but this distinction weakens in the next paragraph, when he describes plants' power of "transplanting or colonising their tribes almost over the surface of the whole earth."[20] Taxonomizing in the tropics proved a vexing endeavor because human beings are revealed to be entwined with vegetable life.

In the introduction to *Travels*, Bartram lavishly describes a spider's killing and eating of its prey and contemplates the growth of a vine.[21] The cessation of movement and imperviousness to chronometric time necessary for making such observations offers some sense of what eighteenth-century colonial writers meant when they gave the verb *vegetating* to people. More significantly, in the process of making these recordings, Bartram's body becomes not simply a corollary for but also a part of the movements of the tropics. Recording the growth of a vine, Bartram slides toward the metaphysical:

> [We see] climbers . . . invariably leaning, extending, and like the fingers of the human hand, reaching to catch hold of what is

nearest, just as if they had eyes to see with; and when their hold is fixed, to coil the tendril in a spiral form, by which artifice it becomes more elastic and effectual than if it had remained in a direct line, for every revolution of the coil adds a portion of strength; and thus collected, they are enabled to dilate and contract as occasion or necessity requires.[22]

This meditation on the vine's capacity to join itself with "what is nearest" might at first seem a simple anthropomorphism: the extensions of vines resemble the extensions of hands, and plants, like hands, seek community. Anthropomorphism, however, domesticates the foreign by making it human; Bartram's "as if" suggests a movement that falls short of putting plants and people into correspondence.[23] This vine does not work in the way that human beings do: it works better.

In *Travels,* Bartram suggests that human lives are bound up in the lives of plants and, moreover, that those who would survive in the tropics must learn from plants how to move with the southern ecology. The tendril that pulls a person into its spiraling motions joins the human will to that of plants, producing a knowledge that changes human actions. These grasping vines' desire for conjunction and collectivity with other tropical forces depends on the stretching outward of parts. The gracefully collectivizing movements result in huge strength: "humoring the motion[s] of . . . limbs and twigs," the webby hold of the cirri ensures that they are not "liable to be torn off by sudden blasts of wind or other assaults."[24] No simple parasite that lives off another thing that is independent in itself, the vine joins what it encloses in its delicate hold. Agencied appendages moving outward, binding and combining—this is what enables life in the tropics.

The combinatory power endemic to the tropics also poses hazards. For one, Bartram fears being consumed by the region. The most obvious referent for this fear is tropical disease, and he does record a bout with an illness that permanently damaged his eyesight. Even more to the point, the combinings that proliferated in the plantation zone destroyed the integrity of structures, whether of bodies, vines, buildings, or histories. After praising the adaptive capacity of the wild pine, Bartram notes that the regions' trees become colonizing powers: "peach trees, figs, pomegranates, and other shrubs, grow out of the ruinous walls of former spacious and expensive buildings."[25] The transformative power of the tropics' vegetable life often allows for increased strength, but these transformations also profoundly change human habitations, bodies, and patterns of thought, as I shall discuss in further detail in chapter 2.

Transformed by the tropics' ecology, Bartram was unable to mime the stance of objectivity that structured colonial subjects' scientific practices, and this compromised his ability to produce the useful knowledge that would redeem southern North America as a temperate zone. But if he veered from the project of compiling useful knowledge, his travels through the lowlands might still prove of aesthetic use. Given his laborious revisions of the manuscript as well as his turn to the rhetoric associated with the sublime, he clearly had aesthetic ambitions.

The eighteenth-century discourse of the sublime, most famously developed by Edmund Burke's *Philosophical Enquiry into the Origin of Our Ideas of the Sublime and the Beautiful* (1757), emphasized the philosophical significance of aesthetic pursuits. In Burke's account, experiencing the sublime required courting the useless, because "whenever strength is only useful . . . then it is never sublime."[26] But if theories of the sublime argued for the importance of the ostensibly useless, they also hewed closely to the expectation that the perceiving subject would remain distinct from the object world. Burke insists that sublime spectacles should give subjects only the idea of danger, for "when danger . . . press[es] too nearly," it is "incapable of giving any delight" and is, instead, "simply terrible."[27] In eighteenth-century aesthetic theory, the subject of sublime experience was required to remain distinct from sublime objects. Theories of the sublime thus confirmed the basic assumption of a dominant (but certainly not the only) strain of enlightenment naturalism: that the subject stand apart from the object world that he or she would master.[28]

If the sublime is a subjective experience evoked by spectacles that seem dangerous in their magnitude or power, swamps are quintessentially sublime spaces: they are vast geographies that defy measurement. Yet tropical swamps not only seemed dangerous, they were dangerous. Bartram suggests that human beings in the plantation zone are truly in peril, and here the possibility of the Anglo-European sublime vanishes: white men who move through swamps do not gain ground firm enough to sustain conceptualizations that will confirm that their (subjective) capacities for empiricism, reason, or aesthetic appreciation are greater than the threat of the swamps. In swamps, the subjective and objective converge, making clearly delimited human subjectivity impossible. This impossibility is especially evident when, attacked by alligators, mosquitoes, heat, and his own exhaustion, Bartram admits that he is "deprived of every desire but that of ending my troubles as speedily as possible."[29] His inability to produce a subjectivity that bounds sublime scenes is dramatically evident in this moment when he fantasizes ceasing to be, but it is most consistently evident in his sentences; even when he means to evoke order, they are swimming productions that seldom manage to frame a point. His turn to the sublime devolves into an impassioned fusion of human, animal, and vegetable life, and here the aesthetic project of colonialism is as deeply compromised as its scientific one.[30]

Snakes, diseases, and vines might penetrate people's bodies, and the lushness of vegetable life might possess their minds. However, the most visceral threat to white colonials in the plantation zone came from the diasporic Africans who were "compelled to labour in the swamps and lowlands."[31] Bartram understood that there was reason to fear the Africans, who were sometimes a majority population in the American tropics. In 1765, he persuaded his father to buy him property in the Florida wetlands and slaves to work this property so that he could start a rice and indigo plantation. Henry Laurens, a family friend, reported that Bartram was the only "human inhabitant within nine miles," by which he meant the only white man, and he also suggested that Bartram's miserable failure as a planter resulted from his difficulty in managing his slaves, whom Laurens described as inept and rebellious. Only two of his slaves could "handle an axe," and one of these was "exceedingly insolent," so much so as "to threaten his life."[32] Although Bartram takes pains to emphasize plantations' idyllic good order, he also notes the brawn of male slaves as well as their skill with "gleaming axes."[33]

Swamps threatened colonials' efforts to separate themselves from the natural world, but it was rebellious Africans who most clearly made swamps revolutionary. Toward the conclusion of *Travels*, the danger posed by Africans in plantation societies comes to the fore. After leaving a South Carolina plantation, Bartram was riding along sandy ridges, contemplating the cavitation of reefs and land, when he

observed a number of persons coming up a head, whom I soon perceived to be a party of Negroes. I had every reason to dread the consequence. . . . [and] had reason to apprehend this to be a predatory band of Negroes. . . . I was unarmed, alone, and my horse tired; thus situated every way in their power, I had no alternative but to be resigned and prepare to meet them. . . . I mounted and rode briskly up; and though armed with clubs, axes and hoes, they opened to right and left and let me pass peaceably. Their chief informed me whom they belonged to, and said they were going to man a new quarter at the West end of the bay; I however kept a sharp eye about me, apprehending that this might possibly have been an advanced division, and their intentions were to ambuscade and surround me; but they kept on quietly.[34]

Bartram emphasizes that he is powerless—"unarmed, alone" and "resigned"—before the "power" of Africans whom he fears might kill him. The power of these Africans comes from their alliance with the land: "axes and hoes" are as much weapons as clubs are. Moreover, the Africans have a chief—a term that Bartram occasionally uses to mean a political leader outside a specifically Indian context and that indicates the autonomy of this band of Africans. In the span of a clause, the possibility of African *marronage* disappears, as the chief names himself and his companions as belonging to a master. Nonetheless, the possibility returns with doubled force when Bartram then imagines that this group is an "advanced division" of a larger army of African militants who mean to "ambuscade" him.

In this passage, Bartram wavers, uncertain whether to cast these Africans as slaves or maroons. These two sorts of diasporic African identity were markedly different: slaves had a relation to a master, for whom they were required to labor; maroons refused this relation and vanished into the swamps or mountains, sometimes forming large and still-extant communities.[35] Although eighteenth-century Anglo-Europeans typically imagined that slaves were submissive, they saw maroons as militants. The distinction between the states of slavery and *marronage* shrinks in this passage. Bartram's oscillating description of these Africans as slaves or maroons suggests that he thinks all slaves may refuse the weight of mastery. Moreover, Bartram expects that both slaves and maroons have a particularly proximate relation to tropical terrains, and he also expects that this proximity has military significance.

After this episode, Bartram vanishes Africans into the tropics' background, but the African agency that surfaces and then disappears from *Travels* does not remain sublated. Sometime after completing *Travels*, Bartram wrote an antislavery tract on the back of one of his father's plant catalogs (Figures 1 and 2). In this never published polemic, he states that only

Figure 1. Antislavery tract by William Bartram. Courtesy of the Historical Society of Pennsylvania.

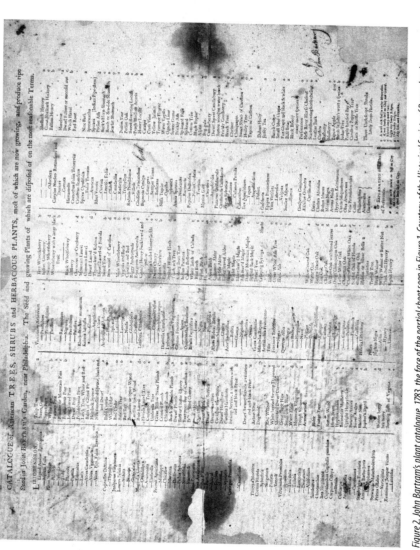

Figure 2. John Bartram's plant catalogue, 1783, the face of the partial sheet seen in Figure 1. Courtesy of the Historical Society of Pennsylvania.

total abolition can stop a cataclysm in which the Africans "will be masters and . . . enslave or exterminate their masters and oppressors."[36] Africans, he supposes, can produce an annihilation more immediate than the slow destruction of swamp or ocean. His argument in favor of abolition indicates that he imagines maroons as potent revolutionaries. If *Travels* testifies to an ecological cycle that consumes the history and subjectivity of white men, this unpublished tract suggests that Africans will somehow be able to use this ecology to destroy plantation societies unless state powers act first and abolish slavery.

In calling for a political and juridical solution (the abolition of slavery), Bartram comes close to taking on the mantle of citizen-subject. However, instead of presenting the tract to the public, he hid it among his father's effects. The artifact is emblematic of Bartram's disappearing subjectivity: it is written on the reverse of a catalogue that testifies to his father's legacy. Bartram's marks show through on the pages of his father's catalogue, but his resistance as well as the African resistance Bartram takes as his subject is contained by his father's colonial taxonomies. In a letter to a South Carolina friend, Bartram requests that his regards be conveyed to the "Black People," for "these acknowledgement[s] at least, are due from me to them, although they are Negroes and Slaves."[37] No doubt there are many reasons why a white man who owned slaves might imagine himself in debt to black persons. One of Bartram's debts, the one I discuss in the remainder of this chapter, is a glimmering awareness that an ecological relation between persons and place had political purchase. His account of the tropics chronicles the loss of the continent, of human memorials, of the subject, and of the recognizably political. Yet the immersion of persons in place was neither a drowning nor a glimpse of the end of time. Bartram may have gleaned that there was a positive, political content to this relation, but he was not able to offer it.[38]

Revolutionary Natures

Nature was often vested with revolutionary significance in the late eighteenth century, as Ronald Paulson has argued.[39] The increasingly antirevolutionary Burke describes the French Revolution as an explosion of primal forces that produced overly natural people who, like "savages" or "Maroon slaves," "rudely" stripped away "all the decent drapery of life" to reveal a barren terrain.[40] According to Burke, the revolutionary taste for the natural culminated in a horrid literalism that cast persons and landscapes in the harsh light of reason: "In the groves of [the revolutionaries'] academy, at the end of every visto, you see nothing but the gallows."[41] The problem with revolution was not only that it was primitive but also that it produced a new scenery that could not be safely observed because it could annihilate an observer. To push Burke's point, the practice and rhetoric of revolution breached the distinction between a social realm, which was the province of the human, and a natural realm, which was the province of primal forces, animals, and objects. Revolution brought about a too close association of the human and the natural, and this association deeply compromised a tradition in which nature was organized as a series of landscapes that were distinct from the human beings who valued them. Burke's suggestion that groves became gallows invokes a future without landscape.

The pressure revolutionary rhetoric put on the assumption that persons were distinct from nature and its objects was particularly felt in plantation societies, not only because of the pull of vines and swamps but also because of the classification, by race slavery, of certain persons as objects. "Savages," maroons, and naturalists were all aware that the distinction between persons and objects foundered in the tropics. This foundering, which Burke feared and Bartram chronicled, contributed to the shift from a landscape perspective to an ecological practice—from nature as an object of appreciation to nature as an assemblage of forces.

My belief that the possibility of landscape was weakened in the eighteenth-century plantation zone and gave rise to an ecological perspective is not common among critics who write on this subject. Édouard Glissant, for one, argues that the landscape writing that flourished in the eighteenth-century tropics indicates a "propensity to blot out the shudders of life, that is, the turbulent realities of the Plantation, beneath the conventional splendor of scenery."[42] White colonialists who attended to landscape, he suggests, contributed to a deeply obfuscating representational structure that hid the region's perpetual unrest.

Glissant is surely right to point out that rhapsodic accounts of tropical landscapes contributed to the production of white colonial subjectivities, and he is also right to point out that Africans were often elided from or carefully managed in colonial encomiums to landscape. However, Bartram's failure to produce himself as a subject separate from the southern lowlands, his failure to prioritize Linnaean taxonomies over other ventures, and his failure to fully dismiss the violence that emerged from swamps requires an elaboration of Glissant's analysis.[43] First, Bartram's failures indicate that Africans and the turbulence of the plantation zone did sometimes break into Anglo-European representations of tropical scenery and, when they did, confounded efforts to hold apart fantasies of tropical scenery and the realities of entanglement and brutal fragmentation. Second, this break in the landscape tradition reveals a genealogy of diasporic resistance. Glissant proposes that slaves and maroons did not typically occupy themselves by representing landscape, which is certainly true as most Africans in the diaspora had little if any access to the eighteenth-century print culture that enabled representational projects. Nor did Africans have much incentive to contribute to a landscape tradition that covered over the brutality of life on plantations.

However, Anglo-European texts like Bartram's indicate that diasporic Africans were hardly indifferent to tropical ecologies. Drawing on these texts as evidence is suspect: they are often the same works that attempt to produce a tropical splendor that covers over the brutality of the plantation zone. Yet Anglo-Europeans believed that Africans were better able to manipulate this ecology than they were. In historical fact and in these Anglo-Europeans' accounts, the Africans who were brutally and problematically allied with tropical terrains used the knowledge they had gained from this ecology in pragmatic and literal ways. The tropics in which plantations were typically located by the close of the eighteenth century did not offer an abstract nature that could be made into symbols for revolution; rather, their ecology contributed to revolution.[44]

Those who lived in the colonies—white Creoles, slaves, maroons, and Indians—all realized that knowledge of ecology was not only necessary for survival but also had military significance. Emilia Viotti da Costa writes, "Long before the Americans and French had risen in the name of freedom, slaves had struggled for their freedom in the colonies of the new world."[45] Viotti da Costa's suggestion that African struggles for freedom inspired Anglo-European revolutions is no doubt accurate. But Africans fighting for freedom provided more than ideological currency for eighteenth-century revolutionaries. They were a military precedent, aphorized centuries later by Che Guevara's dictum that revolutionary action requires "a perfect knowledge of the ground."[46] To be sure, Anglo-European writers' association of African rebellion with tropical ecologies often cast Africans as primitives in an effort to minimize the military acumen of slaves and maroons. For instance, historians have sometimes suggested that the slave and mulatto victory in Saint-Domingue can be attributed to Africans' greater immunity to yellow fever, thus implying that they were simply vectors for a disease that acted through them and were not themselves agents in the devastation of France's colonial empire.[47]

Despite such efforts to minimize the significance of Africans' knowledge of the ground, white Creoles were well aware that slaves and maroons used the ecology of the tropics to their advantage in the perpetual warfare that developed from race slavery. In 1769, Edward Bancroft wrote a natural history of Guiana in which he noted that the cassava root produces a "speedy and fatal poison" that "by the inattention of the Slaves" was "frequently drank by the sheep, hogs, and poultry on the Plantations."[48] Although he dismisses this destruction as the result of simple inattention, Bancroft also notes slaves' uses of plants and understands that this botanical knowledge was applied to sabotaging the order of colonial plantations: for instance, "the female Slaves who intend to procure abortion" used the orco plant to "lubricat[e] the uterine passages."[49]

Although travel writers, slaves, and maroons paid attention to the utility of tropical vegetation, they also recognized that the tropics were more than a collection of inert things to be ground into poisons or otherwise instrumentalized. As Bartram's meditation on vines makes clear, the tropical ecology was an animate force whose combinatory power could provide strength, and was imagined to do just that for African agents, but could also consume—and was imagined to do just that to Anglo-European agents. In *Narrative of a Five Years Expedition against the Revolted Negroes of Surinam* (1796), John Stedman claims that the "trembling" surface of lowland swamps frequently gave way to "Chasm[s]" in which a man "must in[e] vitably perish, if not extricated by immediate help."[50] These precarious surfaces required that troops walk with great care and in single file. And while Bartram may have been able to make his way through lowland swamps, Stedman repeatedly notes such passage was decidedly disadvantageous for a large colonial army. He also believes that African militants understood how tropical forces could be synthesized with human movements. For instance, he praises Surinamese maroons' tactic of embedding infrastructures in swampy terrain that European troops considered an unnavigable morass.[51] Knowing that in some places swamps had firm bottoms, maroons placed felled logs underwater, to mark paths that could be traversed swiftly. Wim Hoogbergen writes that after struggling to find a way through Surinam's swamps, Colonel Louis Henri Fourgeoud found a "floating bridge of tree trunks hidden between the bushes." Fourgeoud decided that this passageway was "so narrow that they could not possibly use it," for it would require that his troops pass slowly and in single file, thus making them vulnerable because "the path was constantly kept under fire by the Maroons."[52]

The tropics' animate vegetation and shifting ground were by necessity home and battlefield for its stateless agents and facilitated guerilla operations against colonial powers. The belief that Africans and Indians were particularly able to manipulate the zone registers in the engraving *March thro' a Swamp or Marsh in Terra-Firma*, which William Blake produced in the early 1790s as an illustration for Stedman's *Narrative* (Figure 3). In the engraving's right foreground, a cypress tree's limbs rise into looping vines, themselves draped with Spanish moss; in the left foreground, a black ranger chest-deep in a swamp leads white troops forward. But the soldiers do not look to their guide. Arms akimbo, eyes moving in every direction, they hold their guns above their heads—a positioning that creates a series of strong diagonal lines that stand out sharply against the softer diagonal lines of the rain of the background. An Anglo-European figure in front points outside of the frame of the engraving. Directionless, the soldiers' confused movements are discordant with those of the rain, the trees, and their fellows.

But the suggestion that Anglo-Europeans are disaggregated by the plantation zone is only part of the story offered by Blake's engraving. In the far left of the background's driving rain, African maroons align their bodies with the delicate curves of palm trees, from which they attack these troops. One maroon unloads a fusillade that falls in the same lines as the rain. Toward the back of the middle ground, white troops point their guns skyward to stop this attack, but they aim away from the maroons above them, failing to find targets. The same swampy terrain that enmires Blake's white troops accommodates his African figures, one of whom walks imperviously through the quagmire, cargo balanced on head. Africans are represented as having a special relation to and knowledge of the tropics, and maroon warfare is represented as an extension of this ecology: the sway of a tree fulfills the sway of a body, and a shower of rain yields a shower of bullets. Blake's engraving crystallizes the colonial fear that detached subjectivity was impossible in plantation spaces, where white men struggled against an ecology that was often militarized.

March thro' a swamp or Marsh in Terra-firma.

London. Published Dec.r 2.d 1793. by J Johnson, St Paul's Church Yard.

Figure 3. March thro' a Swamp or Marsh in Terra-Firma, *engraving by William Blake, 1794. Note the upper far left corner where maroons in the palm trees shoot down on English troops. Courtesy of the John Carter Brown Library at Brown University.*

Blake's attention to the deftness with which Africans navigated the plantation zone underscores a point that Stedman and Bartram also understood: Anglo-European colonists, unfamiliar with this ecology, were at a significant disadvantage against the Africans, Indians, and poor whites who were forced to labor there and who used the knowledge and skills they had gained from this labor to disrupt the order of the plantation. The relation of persons to place in the tropics was not inherently racialized. Diasporic Africans, Indians, poor whites, and colonial naturalists all found ways of working with this ecology and not in simple opposition to it. Given these agents' disparate but sometimes overlapping goals, a variety of resistant practices could emerge from the zone. But although the relation of persons to place was not necessarily racial, eighteenth-century Anglo-Europeans generally did see it as shaped by a racial logic: Africans knew that swamps could be made into motile, invisible infrastructures, knew which plants offered up poisons and which offered food, and knew the hollows and dark spots that provided shelter and concealment.

Representations that bound Africans to swamps worked to delegitimize ecological knowledge by making it into a sign of primitivism. These representations of Africans also reveal the persistent belief that the relation of persons to place differed in the plantation zone from what it was in Britain, on the Continent, and in the northern American colonies. Attending to Anglo-Europeans' representations of Africans in the southern lowlands is precisely what enables us to trace a shift from a landscape-focused concept of nature to an ecological one.[53] If American plantations evinced a mode of being in which bodies were fragmented and human consciousness was enmeshed with plants, histories, economies, and mythologies, it was diasporic Africans who were associated with this mode. These representations make clear that Anglo-Europeans viewed Africans as revolutionary agents despite and because of their fragmentation by the brutalities of the diaspora. In Anglo-European travelers' accounts, the strength that Africans gained from their ability to move with ecology was not simply a biological fact or a Faulknerian testimony to endurance. Rather, the portents of annihilation that break open Bartram's meditations on landscape and the murderous intent that amasses in the background of Blake's engraving reveal the awareness that those who could manipulate ecology possessed a transformative power associated then and now with revolution.

As my turn to revolution suggests, the relation of persons to place bears on conceptualizations of political resistance in eighteenth-century plantation societies. Recent accounts of revolution in the tropics, including Michel-Rolph Trouillot's *Silencing the Past* (1995), Susan Buck-Morss's "Hegel and Haiti" (2000), and Sibylle Fischer's *Modernity Disavowed* (2004), devote significant attention to the Haitian Revolution and the modernities it produced.[54] These theorists all emphasize that the creation of a free black republic dedicated to opposing racism and imperialism radically challenged the political and philosophical assumptions that grounded contemporary revolutionary states. Conceptualizing ecological resistance makes clear the extent to which resistance in the tropics (not just in Saint-Domingue) challenged the politics and philosophy associated with revolution. To develop this point, it is worth briefly turning to Buck-Morss, who also proposes that resistance in the tropics allows for a new understanding of revolution. What she gains by her argument, however, is a partially redeemed Western metaphysics as well as a revolutionary event purged of the contradictions and false universalisms that plagued the political philosophy of the age of revolution. This gain differs from that of an ecological account, which departs from the dialectic between subject and object that often grounds theorizations of revolution.

Buck-Morss criticizes an Enlightenment philosophy that proliferated metaphors of slavery while failing to account for literal, historical slavery. However, she argues that Hegel was not blind to historical slavery. Rather, he was aware of the Haitian Revolution and drew on it when developing his master–slave dialectic. By Buck-Morss's argument, these slaves' self-emancipation inspired Hegel's belief that

> freedom cannot be granted to slaves from above. The self-liberation of the slave is required through a "trial by death" . . . the goal of *this* liberation, *out* of slavery, cannot be subjugation of the master in turn, which would be merely to repeat the master's "existential impasse," but, rather, elimination of the institution of slavery altogether.[55]

In Buck-Morss's argument, the tropical rebellion that has been sublated by Western political philosophy points to a way outside of the "existential impasses" and toward a democratic community not founded on the struggle between lord and bondperson. Slaves in the tropics offer the only successful model of revolution, for they show the possibility of a collective that is not founded on vertically organized relations and thus make revolutionary liberty into a truly universal value.

Although powerfully and admirably reparative, Buck-Morss's reading raises a series of problems. First, it puts Afro-American resistance in the service of what is essentially an Anglo-European metaphysical tradition. Second, it passes over the eighteenth-century revolutionary tradition's addiction to hierarchy, an addiction that partly explains the preponderance of metaphors of slavery in the political writings of the time, which often motivated Anglo-European scientific and aesthetic projects and plagued eighteenth-century democratic revolutions.[56] Third and most significant, Buck-Morss's analysis assumes that the quintessential actor of tropical revolution is a slave become subject: "slaves . . . achieve self-consciousness by demonstrating that they are not things, not objects, but *subjects* who transform material nature."[57] This reading returns us to Warner's print-culture thesis, for here again the end point of eighteenth-century revolution is the production of subjects, and, as Buck-Morss makes clear, the work of subjects is to transform the object material of nature. To be sure, the production of citizen-subjects was a preoccupation in centers of revolution from Cap François to Philadelphia to Paris. But, as we have seen, the tropics also yielded a practice that ended the political fantasy that subjects remained distinct from an object world that was simply acted on.

My point is not that Buck-Morss is wrong but that there is more to be gained by an ecological account of resistance. Glissant's theory of relation elaborates on that advantage.[58] Written two hundred years after Bartram wrote his *Travels*, Glissant's *Poetics of Relation* (1990) is also a meditation on land's turning to sea. *Poetics* opens into the "ochre" terrain of an African continent that yields to the abysses of the diaspora. But if the focus is aqueous, Glissant never entirely yields the terrestrial; he conceives the spaces joined by the African diaspora as a "land-sea."[59] An alluvial trope in which solidities become fluidities that still maintain a residue of materiality, the land-sea returns in his concluding chapter, which begins on a beach. The "devastated mangrove" swamps that lie behind the beach and "tie" it to the island inspire a new vision: the beach is "quivering," in fact "burning," and then gives way to swamp and sea.[60]

The close of Glissant's *Poetics* recalls Bartram's arrangement of land, swamp, and sea. In both, the first is becoming the last. But for Glissant a swamp does not presage apocalypse: it is an animate force that "resists" and, in doing so, reveals depths that "allow us to take off like *marrons.*"[61] By Glissant's analysis, swamps offer occasion for twentieth- and twenty-first-century *marronage* that has broad political and philosophical significance. Swamps are "depths [that] navigate a path beneath the sea in the west and the ocean in the east," and this path promises that "though we are separated, each in our own Plantation, the now green balls and chains have rolled beneath from one island to the next, weaving shared rivers that we shall open up when it is our time and where we shall take our boats."[62] Remnants of slavery weave land into rivers but do not bind the tropics to the slave past, because the future Glissant offers is that of *marronage,* and maroons are ecological actors who cannot be bound by the history and artifacts of slavery. In what follows, I will trace how this conception of marronage impinged upon early Americans' experiences and imaginations of their bodies and personhood.

Before pressing farther, it is important to make clear what might be gained by moving from the drowned subjectivity of Bartram's swamps to Glissant's "we," which holds together human beings, terraqueous powers, and artifacts. Most obviously, looking to tropical ecologies offers ways to build stories about places and actors that archives documenting the citizen-subjects of print culture cannot. Moreover, conceiving of human agency as a collaborative force that requires joining with planetary flows contributes to a theory of revolution in which death—of the subject or the moment—need not be understood as the limit of any agent or event. This shift from thinking of the plantation zone as a space of endings allows us to abandon the elegiac orientation that crippled Bartram, and it avoids the agon of dialectical approaches that tend to reinscribe some center and, in so doing, restage the deprivation of margins where possibility is always attenuated. To be sure, eighteenth-century Anglo-Europeans saw swamps as monstrosities that stalled the subject-making work of the sublime. But the swamping of the sublime gives way to an aesthetics that suffuses persons through places to open the way for a reimagining of the terrain of the political.

2

Plant Life

Tropical Vegetation, Animate Matter, and Cosmopolitical Form

Plants and Politics

One of the most animate protagonists of Alexander Humboldt's labyrinthine *Personal Narrative* [*Relation historique*] (1814) is tropical vegetation powerful enough to overpower human life.[1] During his 1799–1804 travels through Tenerife, Venezuela, Columbia, Cuba, Ecuador, Peru, Mexico, and finally the United States, where he spent time in Philadelphia and Washington, D.C., Humboldt experienced the vegetation of tropical and subtropical regions as a pervasive force whose exuberant range and dense mesh contravened botanists' taxonomical projects. "If you carefully transplanted all the orchids, all the epiphytes that grow on one single American fig tree," Humboldt writes, "you would manage to cover an enormous amount of ground. The . . . lianas that trail along the ground climb up to the tree-tops, swinging from one tree to another. . . . As these parasitical plants form a real tangle, a botanist often confuses flowers, fruit and leaves belonging to different species."[2]

Even more than Bartram, whose work the polyglot Humboldt certainly knew, the Berlin-born Humboldt emphasized the cultural devolutions occasioned by life in the American tropics. Humboldt points out that heat and humidity give rise to plant and insect life that destroys paper, libraries, and archives, which means that, because the Spanish had destroyed Native Americans' "quipus and symbolic paintings," there are few traces of history in the tropics where time seems swallowed into the "eternal greenness" of a vegetable present.[3] The botanic, insect, climatic, and geologic intensity of the tropics could decompose the literary works and historical archives through which colonial cultures asserted their dominance. What's more, Humboldt (perhaps influenced by Thomas Jefferson's argument, in *Notes on Virginia,* that heat and humidity are the conditions of vitality) proposed that tropical heat and humidity give rise to an extreme diversity of life-forms and that this diversity could destroy human beings.[4] The tropics' vegetable diversity might be "picturesque," but Humboldt also believed that it contributes to an atmosphere in which "organic matter is produced more rapidly, and where the same organic debris fills the air with putrid and deleterious miasmas."[5] The "same winds that are loaded with the perfume of flowers, leaves and wood" are "charged with the gases emanating from rotting animal and vegetable substances" that transmit "the germs of disease into [travelers'] organs."[6]

Humboldt's belief that Anglo-Europeans were threatened by tropical plants and atmospheres as well as the agential and disease-ridden matter they produced indicates an awareness of ecological strife that qualifies his faith in the success of Spanish, French, British, and American colonial projects. This awareness of ecological and (insofar as libraries and books are decomposing) cultural strife undercuts critical accounts of Humboldt's work that project backward the anodyne inclusiveness of his late work *Kosmos* (1845–62) to argue that Humboldt's comprehensive effort was to reveal a harmonious natural world, whether that harmony is seen as the necessary ground for his imperialist fantasies, his faith in the totalizing view of nature available to the scientist-philosopher (*Naturphilosophie*), or his understanding of the necessarily beneficial workings of the web of living forces.[7] Moreover, this belief that tropical plant life contributes to the production of animate matter is one of the key claims of an American branch of eighteenth-century nonmechanistic and often vitalist materialism that will be my focus in this chapter.

Vitalist materialism was a late eighteenth-century movement in natural history that preceded the study of biological organisms that Foucault conceives as vitalism proper and names as one of the girders of modernity's biopolitical organization of power.[8] Vitalist materialism and the animism that preceded and sometimes inflected it (eighteenth-century animism is the belief in an immanent and divine anima that is not reducible to, yet not generally separable from, matter) suggested that atoms and other invisible particles and fluids (for instance, the "seeds" of disease as well as phlogiston or mesmeric fluid) possess agency that is not dependent on their organization into bodies. Although vitalist materialists such as Humboldt often did focus on organized bodies, they also attended to particles and fluids including the Americas' disease-ridden organic matter, which moves outside of and between organized bodies. This meant that they did not consider the organized body as such to be the sole locus of agency. Significantly, this American branch of vitalist materialism raised the possibility that any part—whether a unit of matter or an organized form like a plant or an animal that contributes to some larger system—possesses agency and autonomy, even outside of the systems in which it participates. Parts, then, possess attributes that cannot be reduced or subordinated to the larger systems in which they participate. Here, synecdoche, the formal term to describe a symbiosis of part and whole such that each anticipates the other, gives way to a relation in which the part is recognized as a singularity that contributes to the production of wholes.

Attending to this mostly forgotten eighteenth-century natural history, which moves through the work of Humboldt and Bartram as well as the writings of the physician and founding father Benjamin Rush, redresses a certain closing down of political possibility that occurred in Philadelphia in 1789 when the U.S. founding fathers chose Constitution over revolution. This closing of political possibility has inadvertently been repeated in a good deal of twentieth-century literary criticism, which, by focusing on these founding fathers and their political desires, has often told a story of the submission of individuals to a mechanistic and deterministically conceived U.S. nationalism. The vitalist materialism that circulates through late eighteenth- and early nineteenth-century natural history suggests a subterranean, never fully acknowledged genealogy of matter, form, and system that developed in part from tropical and subtropical botany. In subsequent chapters I will focus primarily on the modes of agency that developed in tropical peripheries brought into the circuit of Atlantic exchange through plantation economies; however, in this chapter I show that the American vitalism that developed from tropical botanizing, which had institutional footholds in postrevolutionary Philadelphia, carried the potential for an alternative scientific and political practice. This suggests that while early American political forms would go on to follow a generally conservative course that has been ably documented by historians and literary critics, they need not have been as normative, as mechanized, and as nationalized as they have seemed to later generations of critics.[9]

American Vitalism

Toward the close of "Lectures on Animal Life" (1799), the Philadelphia-based physician, scientist, and occasional political essayist Benjamin Rush proposed that governments must not forget that the "humble but true origin of power" is "the people." This contention of something like popular sovereignty might seem surprising from Rush who, in the January before the Philadelphia Convention (May to September 1787, during which leaders of the emerging United States moved from a confederation to a constitutional government) proposed strong limits to the now-independent colonists' constituent power, arguing that the people only possess power "on the days of their elections," after which power returns to their rulers, whom they must obey.[10] Although Rush's political philosophy has often been deemed moderate or even conservative by subsequent generations of Americanist critics, his scientific works such as "Lectures on Animal Life" bear traces of nonmechanistic materialisms, including vitalism, associated with radical politics, particularly in the works of the French philosopher Denis Diderot and the English theologian, philosopher, and scientist Joseph Priestley.[11] Rush links these dissident political and scientific positions as he moves immediately from his somewhat uncharacteristic support for popular sovereignty to a theorization of the nature of matter:

> It is not necessary to be acquainted with the precise nature of that form of matter, which is capable of producing life, from impressions made upon it. . . . It is immaterial . . . whether this matter derive its power of being acted upon wholly from the brain, or whether it be in part inherent in animal fibres. The inferences are the same in favour of life being the effect of stimuli, and of its being as truly mechanical, as the movements of a clock from the pressure of its weights, or the passage of a ship in the water, from the impulse of winds, and tide.[12]

Colleen Terrell argues that passages like these indicate Rush's thoroughgoing mechanism, which would seem a perfectly plausible assessment.[13] After all, in claiming that the animation of matter is "truly mechanical" and that matter is passive until activated by the "impressions made upon it" by other already animate forces, Rush distinguishes his understanding of matter from that of animists and vitalists like George Stahl, William Cullen, Robert Whytt, and John Hunter. Instead of granting that the vital principle is activated in all matter, Rush insists that matter and other seeds possess a "capacity of life" that must be activated by forces pressing upon them. Here Rush comes close to rehearsing the standard mechanist position that matter is dead substance only put into motion by exterior forces that are themselves first activated by a transcendent and divine will (or, in some mechanists' accounts, a force exterior and transcendent to matter, such as gravity) that remains outside the system and that guarantees that the operations of the system work with unbending regularity.[14] Punning on *immaterial*, Rush suggests that the origin of matter's capacity to generate life is inconsequential because this origin is not inherent to matter but, as his pun would have it, of an immaterial and divine origin. Yet the sentence that Rush develops from this pun makes a quite different claim, for it suggests that matter's germinal power is not at all immaterial because it is a property inherent to "brains" or "fibres." That brain matter or fibrous matter might hold germinal power invokes a materialist cosmology in which agency is a power implicit in all matter, even if its germination requires the impression of stimuli.[15] Moreover, while the agency of brain matter or fibrous matter is imagined to work in the service of organizing power and life into the form of organic bodies, Rush leaves open the possibility that certain forms of matter might also disorganize bodies.

As the passage develops, Rush's metaphors begin to move away from the body. Rush anatomizes the animal body into the potentially agencied components of brains and fibers. His next sentence puts machines together again when it turns to the "movements of the clock," evoking the machine whose synthesis of parts provided seventeenth- and eighteenth-century mechanists with their favorite example. Yet he invokes the clock only to jump to another example, the ship, which pulls away from standard mechanistic accounts. Unlike the clock, which mechanists tended to imagine as a self-contained and contextless machine that works through the immaterial and omnipresent force of gravity, the ship is a machine whose movement depends on visible and contingent forces such as tides and winds, which, as Humboldt's account of the dangers of tropical winds suggests, carry agential animal and vegetable matter. The ship is not simply an independent, well-organized machine but rather one composed of and pressed upon by a number of other material forces. In fact, it is not the clock but the ship that is the more apt metaphor for Rush's conception of bodies and other systems. Instead of mechanism's contextless machines, Rush attends to densely contextualized systems, or ecologies, that produce life, death, and the movements of matter. His environmentalism retains the possibility that certain seeds of matter can be activated by a range of causes and give rise to unpredictable motions that decompose systems, whether that of the body, the city, or the polis. Thus, while Rush refuses vitalism's generally agential matter, his environmentalism keeps in circulation one of its central tenants: the power of the part or particulate to disorder the system.

There is in fact good reason to read Rush not as a doctrinaire mechanist but as influenced by vitalist materialism. As a teenager, Rush was apprenticed to the Philadelphia physician John Redman, who introduced him to the writings of the Dutch physician, chemist, and botanist Herman Boerhaave. Boerhaave has often been described as a doctrinaire mechanist, but Jonathan Israel's account of the Spinozism running through enlightenment sciences and philosophies designates him a crypto-Spinozist for his interest in materialisms that countered mechanistic deism.[16] Upon completing his apprenticeship and an undergraduate degree at Princeton, Rush traveled abroad to study medicine at Edinburgh, which, along with Montpellier in France, was the leading center of eighteenth-century vitalism.[17] While at Edinburgh, Rush studied with William Cullen, who "launched a direct attack upon . . . medical mechanistic assumptions," a position that struck many as a refusal of transcendental influence, which is to say as an avowal of atheism, and which led the university's provost to warn Cullen that he was jeopardizing both the university and his own academic career.[18] In lectures given during Rush's residence at Edinburgh, Cullen "rejected the mechanistic concept of dead matter and offered a system founded upon the existence of active, directional forces in nature."[19]

After studying with Cullen, Rush traveled to London to study with David Hartley, a Christian monist who proposed that spirit and consciousness are not separate from matter. Hartley's theory of association was appropriated by Unitarian dissenters, most famously by Priestley who would become Rush's friend after he immigrated to Philadelphia. In 1775, Priestley republished parts of Hartley's *Observations on Man* (1749) along with three introductory essays in which he tried to simplify the more esoteric aspects of Hartley's thought and neutralize its seemingly blasphemous claims about the agency of matter. For Hartley, "vibrations in the brain," themselves influenced by vibrations in the air and other fluidized media, were the probable "cause of all our ideas."[20] Plants' and animals' behaviors were equally produced by vibratory influence, and Priestley notes that Hartley's thesis supported the work of those who imagined that plants "hav[e] some degree of sensation."[21] The vibrations that gave rise to plant and animal behaviors as well as abstract concepts such as time and space also joined organic bodies to their environments. As is the case with

Rush's ship, Hartley's theories do not allow that a machine can be understood as separate from its contexts. Indeed, the notion of context is revised in Hartley's theory, for it does not allow that some parts of a scene could serve as background for a prioritized foreground but instead implies a series of quantifiable, yet interlocked, vibratory bodies and forces.

Hartley's theory raised a series of scandals. First, it posited that there was no force outside of the world because God and his will were expressions of vibrating matter and thus entirely in the world. Second, there were no principles or instincts that could be taken as given. Rather, all principles and behaviors were born of experience, and this meant that new organizations of existing matter might give rise to new principles, behaviors, and organizations. Third, the smallest and least significant bit of matter was no longer brute and dead but potentially motile and significant. Finally, this thesis countered central tenets of Christianity. As Priestley explains, in Hartley's system "*immateriality*, as far as it has been supposed to belong to man, would be excluded altogether."[22] Priestley insisted that this thesis was not as blasphemous as it seemed; he proposed that it should only concern those "who maintain that a future life depends upon the immateriality of the human soul" and that it could "not at all alarm those who found all their hopes of a future existence on the Christian doctrine of *a resurrection from the dead.*"[23] Yet here Priestley's defense runs into another quandary: given that Hartley associates spirit and life with material vibrations and not necessarily with human beings as such, it might well be the case that any form of life could be raised from the dead. To counter this criticism that more doctrinaire Christians might make of Hartley's system, Priestley finds himself compelled to argue that plants will not be raised from the dead, although he can only sustain this point by moving from the scientific explanations through which he has built his argument and turning to points of Christian theology, pointing out that God has only promised resurrection to humans and not to plants.[24]

Hartley, Priestley, and other natural historians who speculated on the agency of matter developed antinomian Christian doctrines that were sometimes misrepresented as atheism, and they were also linked to political radicalism. This was not simply because atheists' supposed nihilism made them more liable to support political upheavals. If vibrating matter had the potential for directional movement, it opened the possibility that matter and the parts and bodies it composed were autonomous and might not unfailingly contribute to the workings of larger wholes but could instead express their own potentially deviant impulses. A cosmology in which God was expressed immanently and in which matter and parts of bodies were self-existing might imply an anarchy of forms, and not simply an anarchy of the natural forms that were natural historians' primary focus but also the political forms that often were analogized as being like the natural form of the organized (human) body.

That deviant materialisms could lead to an anarchy of form is suggested in Benjamin Franklin's early work *A Dissertation on Liberty and Necessity, Pleasure and Pain* (1725), a quasi-Epicurean treatise composed in Franklin's characteristic satirical mode.[25] In the *Dissertation*, Franklin evokes and mutates mechanism's familiar clock metaphor, raising the possibility of a maker who produced a

> curious Machine or Clock, and put its many intricate Wheels and Powers in such a Dependence on one another, that the whole might move in the most exact Order and Regularity, [but] had nevertheless plac'd in it several other Wheels endu'd with an independent Self-Motion, but ignorant of the general interest of the Clock; and these would every now and then be moving wrong, disordering the true Movement, and making continual Work for the Mender.[26]

Here Franklin raises the possibility of the "Self Motion" of the parts of a machine and replaces a transcendent maker with a "Mender" who cobbles together working machines in a chaotic physical universe. But Franklin quickly withdrew from these sorts of mutations of more doctrinaire mechanistic natural science. Ever pragmatic, Franklin understood that most early eighteenth-century establishment figures aligned nonmechanistic materialisms with both atheism and radical revolution; in the *Autobiography* (1791), he names the *Dissertation* as one of his errata.

Franklin's effort to distance himself from nonmechanistic natural history suggests the potentially negative social and political effects that might result from openly avowing deviant materialisms, which speculated a world in which all parts and all constituents might have the power to act of their own volition. The potential for disorder in such a system is high, and though Franklin's thought was consistently innovative and often bore traces of radical positions, his tendency was to move away from the most radical political and scientific positions of his thought to argue for a middle path that had the virtue of creating order out of chaos.

Like Franklin, Rush recognized the risks of claiming heterodox natural-historical positions, and he too was generally deeply pragmatic, and in the *Lectures* disavows vitalism and epicureanism. Nonetheless, his work often bears traces of the vitalist materialism he first learned in Edinburgh and London and that sometimes inflects his own thought, particularly his writings on yellow fever, a disease that had become an epidemic in the mid-Atlantic and particularly affected Philadelphia, the first capital of the United States, where Rush worked and lived.

Rush argued that yellow fever is an indigenous American disease that develops from the tropical and semitropical climates common to American locales from Saint-Domingue to Saint Vincent, to Jamaica, to South Carolina, to mid-Atlantic colonies like Pennsylvania. Anticipating Humboldt's argument about the agential vegetable matter carried by tropical air, Rush proposed that hot and humid climates that can cause a "preternatural quantity of oxygen in the atmosphere"[27] that causes the "impregnation" of atmospheres with disease. This highly oxygenated air causes matter collecting in gutters, sinks, swamps, and marshes to give off "exhalation[s]" that pass into and disordered human and other animal bodies.[28] Rush believed that any region could give rise to disease, so, contrary to critics' charges, he did not mean to suggest the Americas are any more or less likely to experience contagious diseases than other regions of the globe. Yellow fever was simply a contagion that emerged in American environments whereas the bubonic plague was a contagion that developed in European ones. Although he insisted that every manifestation of a contagious disease, whether American or not, emerges from a unique alignment of proximate causes, his general formula was that hot and humid American climates give rise to putrefaction that causes stagnant water and other fluid media to exhale the disease, sometimes to the point that the disease becomes contagious.[29]

Rush's account of dense exhalations comes close to imagining a shapeless material force born from American air and plants and emanating from swamps, gutters, and marshes, but he was not particularly interested in tracing the monstrous effects of agenced matter. Instead, he attempted to determine how human "reason and labor" can combat the production of the exhalations that cause yellow fever. In so doing, he produced a cosmology that is distinct from Hartley's, for here human reason, if it is the product of material forces, is also posited as distinct from the matter that composes it. "Climates . . . are not necessarily sickly," Rush insists, going on to explain that the "sun would seldom smite by day, nor the moon by night, were pains taken to prevent the accumulation and putrefaction of those matters which occasion malignant bilious fevers."[30] To this end, he advocated public health measures that would focus on the elimination of stagnant waters whether naturally occurring (swamps and marshes) or not (gutters and cellars) as well as the removal of any putrid matter that could give rise to yellow fever. All of these measures were meant to improve air quality, for he imagined the America's highly oxygenated and thus matter-carrying air was the vector of the disease. Rush's treatments of yellow fever in human bodies attempted to stop the "preternatural motion in animal matter"—quite literally, in Hartley's terms, the bad vibrations that passed into humans living in the Americas' vegetable air.[31] He prescribed emetics, purgings, cold-water enemas, and bloodlettings, all of which aimed to alter the material and chemical composition of the human body, thus countering the effects of miasmatic exhalations and bringing the body toward vibratory rhythms that verge on equilibrium.[32]

Although Rush was the most famous North American physician of his time, the theorization of matter, vibration, and agency that subtends his writings on yellow fever hurt him professionally. By the end of the 1790s, Rush was combating a series of factions, from doctors who opposed his continued reliance on bloodletting to Federalists who lambasted his contention that yellow fever was an indigenous (as opposed to an exclusively West Indian) disease, claiming this thesis was not only wrong but also bad for business. Rush's environmentalist understanding of disease and of bodies hurt him for two reasons. First, it emphasized the agency of matter in the production of environments; even though he proposed a quasi mechanism whereby human reason was not determined by material forces, his account of the impregnation of atmospheres with matter that could derange human bodies was a heterodox position. Second, his accounts of broadly American environmental forces understood the West Indies and the continental United States to share and be shaped by similar material conditions, which was controversial for U.S. citizens who were increasingly motivated to distinguish the United States from West Indian cultures. In 1797, King's College (Columbia University) attempted to appoint Rush as its chair in medicine. What should have been an unimpeachable and prestigious appointment to the College was derailed when the Federalist and West Indian–born Alexander Hamilton, who was on the King's College board of trustees, intervened to block Rush's candidacy.[33]

Familiar with the similar fates of his friends Priestley and Thomas Paine, Rush was well aware of the costs of avowing radical natural histories and politics, and he never openly did. Thus, in the "Lectures" delivered at the century's close, Rush camouflaged his influence by vitalist materialism in puns and jumped metaphors. Nonetheless, Rush was well aware that his scientific writings might be seen as germinating a latent radicalism. At the end of the "Lectures," Rush proposed that crafting these lectures was akin to "wad[ing] across a rapid and dangerous stream," and he concluded that he would leave it to his students to determine whether he had "gained the opposite shore with my head clean, or covered with mud and weeds."[34] Coyly suggesting that his students must decide if his lectures preserve mechanism's sanctification of spirit and its belief in the deadness of matter, which would leave him with a clean head, or if they sanctioned vitalism's materialization of mind along with the rest of the physical world, in which case he emerged covered in mud, Rush refused to name his position.[35]

It is worth further elaborating the reasons why this vitalist materialism was controversial. As we have seen, this was partly because vitalist materialism eliminated a transcendent God, and while this was not by any means equivalent to atheism (in fact, Hartley, Priestley, and other vitalist materialists were deeply religious), it was often interpreted as atheism. Moreover, it verged on offering a scientific basis for an anarchy of forms. As Peter Hanns Reill's and Elizabeth Williams's intellectual and scientific histories of France, Germany, and Scotland, show, vitalist materialists posited a motile, flexible matter that contributed to a world in which movement and change were continual. Vitalists' belief that matter is inherently motile is evident in their common conception that substances are also fluids or have fluid-like properties. For instance, the German chemist Carl Scheele defined phlogiston (a substance first discovered by the animist George Stahl and that most eighteenth-century natural historians believed existed in all life-forms) as a "substantialized principle" that "had the ability to penetrate all bodies" and was thus uncontainable though it could be eliminated from combustible bodies through fire.[36] Celebrated French chemist Antoine Lavoisier's caloric had many affinities with the phlogiston it supposedly replaced, including a fluid-like capacity to saturate all other substances.[37] If fluidized substances were always moving outside of the bodies that they also composed and if these substances' movements could also change these bodies, then no body was ever inert or self-identical. Indeed, no material body was ever emphatically solid (even if its nonsolidity was not

generally visible to human eyes), and no material body could be definitively fixed because its animate matter was always connecting it with other
substances. Again, Reill elucidates this point: "Late-eighteenth-century
naturalists, when accepting the linkage between active, striving force and
substance, envisioned nature as continually in movement, never static,
never at rest, always forming and reforming itself through combination,
dissolution, and new combination."[38]

Vitalist materialists' belief in a fluidized matter unendingly intersecting
and even combining with other material bodies to form new compounds
raised several conundrums. First, how could any body or machine remain
the same over time? As the author of the *Port Folio's* essay on vegetable life
warns, "identity cannot be predicated [for] . . . any living organized body,
for any assignable moment of time."[39] More fundamentally, how was it even
possible to identify a determinate body in this flux? In short, vitalism threatened a strong nonidentitarianism, or to put it more bluntly, it proposed an
ontology in which *combining* and not *being* was the first principle. The implications of this ontology include that identity over time is not possible, that
there is no absolute separation of organic and inorganic forms (which means
that humans, animals, vegetables, and minerals cannot be conceived as entirely categorically distinct), and that unexpected combinations of matter,
including monstrous combinations, are always possible. This potential of
vitalist materialist thought was particularly threatening in the Americas.
Eighteenth-century thinkers believed the "warmer climates" of the Americas
caused vegetable life to more spectacularly manifest plants' "acknowledged
power of animality [motion, volition, and perception]."[40] The exuberance of
plant life was not simply a spectacle that natural historians might dispassion-
ately observe because this plant life was believed to combine with and charge
American air and water so as to make it a vector through which human
bodies were decomposed and reformed in ways presaged by Ariel's lyric.

In the main, eighteenth-century vitalists did not generally address and
work through the nonidentitarian implications of their thought, which
would require rethinking the relation of the agents in a system when any
given part is never self-identical.[41] Instead, they introduced concepts and
drew on methodologies that neutralized the nonidentitarian ramifications
of their theories. For instance, vitalist chemists developed elaborate concepts of elective affinity and rapports, both of which promised that even if
an infinite number of material combinations were possible, the number of
likely combinations was dramatically smaller.[42] In addition to winnowing

the number of likely combinations, elective affinity presumed the physical proximity of the material agents brought into relation, with more proximate agents more likely to combine than more distant ones, thereby suggesting that controlling the arrangement of material forces in an environment delimited the possible combinations. This belief that controlling an environment could in turn control material combinations was part of the reason for the strong environmental focus of natural historians influenced by vitalist materialist leanings, including Rush. Closely linked to the vitalist concept of elective affinity was the proposal that the natural world tended toward and desired "harmony and equilibrium."[43] Although all combinations were in theory possible, the principle of harmony promised that monstrous combinations were unlikely.

Analogy

More than anything else, vitalist materialists' use of analogical logic neutralized its nonidentitarianism. Reill proposes analogy as the characteristic methodology of enlightenment vitalism, proposing that, unlike mechanist mathematical methods that strive for universal laws, analogy strives to reconcile the diversity of individual cases with the unity of nature. Dahlia Porter moves toward a similar point in her argument that Erasmus Darwin's *Loves of the Plants* (1791) uses analogy to transform Linnaeus's "vast collection" of natural historical types into a system of relation.[44] Like analogical systems more generally, Darwin promises that any thing or concept placed in one category is like, and at the same time distinct from, things and concepts placed in other categories. In presuming this combination of likeness and difference, analogy promises, first, that the entities brought into relation are self-identical and, second, that these entities are not simply thrown into a catalogue in which any sort of combination is possible but are carefully arranged in an interlocking series governed by a mimetic logic in which the workings of one life-form reveal the workings of another without allowing one case to be reducible to the next.

Although Reill suggests that analogy was a particularly vitalist methodology, it is more apt to describe analogy as a typically eighteenth-century methodology that had migrated from Christian religious thought to natural history, bringing with that migration many of the habits of its early and explicitly religious application. That analogy was not a uniquely vitalist methodology is evident if we consider the case of Linnaeus. Linnaeus was a mechanist, and the eminent French vitalist the Comte de Buffon's primary antagonist. In fact, Linnaeus uses analogies quite extensively, especially in his celebrated and widely known account of plant sexuality. The account of plant sex in the *Philosophia Botanica* (1751) begins by claiming that "in the beginning of things, a single sexual pair of every species of living [being] was created" and concludes by looking onto the scene of plant sex, which scandalized some precisely because it so explicitly proposed that plant sex could be understood as analogous to human (hetero) sex: "the Calyx is the *bedroom,* the Corolla is the *curtain,* the Filaments are the *spermatic vessels,* the Anthers are the *testicles,* the Pollen is the *sperm,* the Stigma is the *vulva,* the Style is the *vagina,* the [vegetable] Ovary is the [animal] *ovary,* the Pericarp is the *fertilized ovary,* and the Seed is the *egg.*"[45] The analogies to be drawn between plant and animal sex are evidently multiple, as Linnaeus offers a series of further likenesses, proposing that the calyx that he has just identified as the plant's "bedroom" might "also be regarded as the *lips of the cunt* or the *foreskin.*"[46]

If analogy was a broadly eighteenth-century methodology that, more than the mathematical models of earlier materialists, recognized the singularity and diversity of life-forms, analogy was also an especially effective tool for neutralizing the more unsettling consequences of vitalist materialist thought: namely, that no entity is identical to itself because it is constantly in relation to and has the potential to combine with the other bodies with which it composes an environment. As Gilles Deleuze has proposed, analogical thought presumes the identity or the self-sameness of each of the terms that it puts into relation.[47] Thus, if vitalist materialist thought verged on proposing the non-self-identity of all life-forms, the analogical method returned identity; concept and method, in short, worked to different ends, or, more aptly, method worked to blunt the radicalism of concept.

Porter does not attend to the analogical method's production of identity, but this point undergirds her analysis. Focusing particularly on Darwin's construction of an analogical relation between human and plant sexuality, she proposes that "the relations between stamen and pistil are *like* those between man and woman."[48] The Darwinian analogy Porter identifies here presumes a series of identities. First, it proposes distinct but analogous modes of plant and animal being, thus shifting attention to the formation of discrete kingdoms and away from the constitutive relation between those entities segregated into kingdoms. It further proposes that these categories of identity are divided into subcategories of genital being that can be mapped onto both plant and animal life, both of which similarly manifest maleness and femaleness. Finally, it proposes that the joining of male and female genital beings within a species category is the most salient sort of combination enacted by any being as this conjunction allows the perpetuation of a species.[49]

Darwin's invocation of Linnaeus's analogy imposes three sorts of controls on vitalist materialism.[50] First, even as it recognizes a diversity of beings, it imposes identity on any given being. Second, it proposes that one primary identity (almost always the human being, in eighteenth- and early nineteenth-century natural history) provides the template through which other identities can be understood, thus closing down the possibility that one kind of life-form behaves in ways that are incomprehensible to another; in short, natural historical analogy closes down the possibility of anything being completely formally and conceptually distinct from the human being. Third, it shifts attention from, if it does not altogether deny, the interactions that occur through crossings and mixings of kingdoms or species. Analogy, that is, tends to emphasize the tabulation of identities and the submission of parts to wholes and not the environments composed through the relation of matter and forms.

If analogy performed a conservative function in vitalist materialism, by the late eighteenth-century a growing body of botanists were retreating from the analogical method that dominated eighteenth-century scientific and philosophical thought. This withdrawal from analogical logic informs Rush's jump from clock to ship, which, instead of arranging metaphors in the mimetic and scalarized relations common to analogy, evokes a catachrestic relation that brings to the fore two wholly different systems, that of the clock that is undisturbed by the volatility of matter or environments and that of the ship that works at the intersection of moving matter and environments. This movement from analogy is particularly strong in turn of the century botanical writing.[51] Botanists' particular aversion to analogy probably indicates a desire to move plant life out of a relation in which it was subordinate to animals, particularly the human animals that were posited as the quasi-divine forms that were the implicit ground for analogical series. The result of this shift from analogy allowed the development of a vitalist materialism that more closely approached its strongly anti-identitarian ramifications and that disorganized the relation of parts to wholes.

One of the strongest American critics of botanical analogies was Rush's protégé and eventual successor at the University of Pennsylvania, Benjamin

Barton. The Philadelphia-born and Edinburgh-educated Barton worked, often with Bartram's assistance, to produce the *Elements of Botany* (1804), a work that, like Bartram's *Travels,* was so devoted to particularity that it stops short of offering either a coherent system or method. But even though Barton offers no system or method of his own, he is quite hostile to Linnaeus's reliance on the analogical method. He frequently interrupts his diffuse descriptions of vegetable life, properties, and habitats to critique the "illustrious Swede" for being overly "fond of analogies," complaining that Linnaeus's "favourite subject of the analogies which subsist between animals and vegetables" leads him to incorrectly conceptualize the anatomy, organic functions, and environmental sensitivity of plant life.[52]

Botanists' turn from the analogical method dates from at least 1785 when Thomas Percival, a Manchester physician and correspondent of Rush and Franklin who closely followed American botany, wrote *Speculations on the Perceptive Power of Vegetables.* In his tract, Percival uses the analogical method only to dissolve the analogies he puts into play: he begins by proposing that "several analogies of organization, life, instinct, spontaneity, and self motion" reveal that plants, like animals, experience perception and enjoyment, and he concludes by arguing for a plant animality in which "vegetables participate, in some low degree, of the common allotment of vitality."[53] In Percival's argument, then, the analogical method verges on eliminating the categories of the animal and the vegetable that natural history almost always held distinct. Whether deliberate or not, it is Percival's destabilization of the analogical method that most strongly challenges the Linnaean system of proliferating "gradations" that maintains the classical organizations of life-forms into a "scale of beings."[54] Arguing against both Linnaeus and "mere mechanism," which only acknowledge "external impulse," Percival proposes that plants' perceptivity and sensibility are evidence of an internal impulse that offers insight into an "animated nature."[55] It is not clear if Percival conceives this animation as a general power of everything that composes nature (which in this case would include matter and would indicate that Percival was a vitalist materialist) or if he means to suggest that anima is a principle that moves through but is external to the natural world (in which case, he might best be termed an animist, a school of thought closely linked to vitalist materialism and that understood anima as exterior to matter even if it always accompanied it). Either way, Percival's vitalism decomposes analogy and taxonomy. Eighteenth-century natural historians frequently found that life-forms that seemed to be vegetables were in fact animals, such as the coral, the sponge, or the anemone that Griffith Hughes calls the "Animal Flower" in *The Natural History of Barbados* (Figure 4).[56] Percival's argument, however, is not on the level of the specific plant but a far bigger claim that investigations of "exotic" plants will yield a more expansive account of the animacy of the natural world.

The destabilization of analogy in botanical thought is evident in *Elements*, a work that grew from an extensive, intense, and (despite their physical proximity) mostly epistolary relationship between Barton and William Bartram.[57] In 1791, Bartram wrote to Barton that he believed that "new [plant] species are emerging daily," articulating a faith in the diversity of life that also strongly resonates in *Elements*, whose unrelenting attention to the diversity of life-forms complicates taxonomical practices, whether that be the division between plant and animal kingdoms or the division of species within kingdoms.[58] In *Elements*, plants are sensible, highly mobile (they "swim upon the water" to "perform extensive migrations"), and dramatically changed by environmental factors, so much so as to verge on becoming new species.[59] Priestley's analyses of air and atmosphere fascinated Barton, who suggested that as botany developed further it should devote itself to the "relations which subsist between the atmosphere and vegetables."[60]

Instead of proposing that vegetables were in mimetic relation to the animal kingdom to which they were also subordinate, *Elements* documents combinations of matter, bodies, and environments. Barton proposes that tropical plants' large leaves developed as a trans-species phenomenon that, in addition to benefiting plants, benefited human beings, birds, and other tropical animals.[61] That a departure from the analogical method results in attention to cross-species interactions is particularly evident in Bartram and Barton's conceptualization of plant sexuality. Linnaeus recognized the existence of hermaphrodite flowers; however, he emphasized that such flowers had both male and female genitalia and that the "conjoining of the sexes is necessary" to reproduction, again emphasizing the scene of intraspecies genital reproduction.[62] In a letter to Barton, Bartram offers a quite different account of the hermaphroditism common to "American Species" of grapes, noting that their "Fruitfull [female] Vines, have Hermophrodite Flowers" while "the Flowers of the Male Vines have only five Stamens."[63] Read through the lens of Linnaean analogy, which

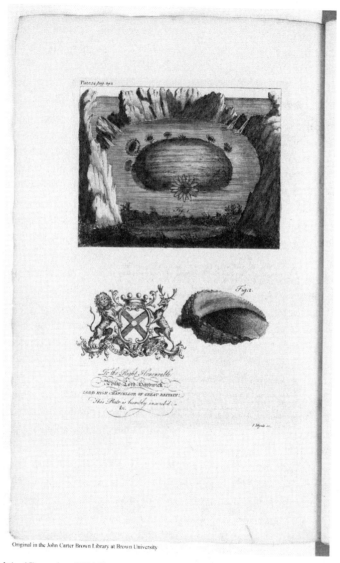

Figure 4. Animal Flower, *from Griffith Hughes,* The Natural History of Barbados, *1750. Hughes's image of the Animal Flower (or sea anemone) is typical of eighteenth-century natural historians' interest in life-forms that called into question the distinction between vegetable and animal life. Percival's* Speculations on the Perceptive Powers of Vegetables *(1785) goes a step farther than Hughes by defining animality in terms of its root,* anima. *By this definition, animality is an attribute of all vegetable life, a move that disorders the chain of being as well as the analogical relations through which life-forms within it were brought into relation. Courtesy of the John Carter Brown Library at Brown University.*

unbendingly posits a mimetic relation between plant and human sexuality, Bartram would seem to be evoking a world in which hermaphroditic female life-forms self-replicate while male life-forms proliferate genitalia that never intersect with females. The homoeroticism of this analogical scene may well be deliberate. However, Bartram's reading of sex slips this analogical scene to offer a different order of queerness. As the letter continues, Bartram proposes that hermaphrodite flowers reproduce not through the connection of genitals but through combining with other forces in their environments. In the 1802 letter, Bartram names wind as the agent through which hermaphrodite plants reproduce.

By the time Bartram's and Barton's correspondence found its way into print in the 1804 edition of *Elements*, Barton, probably familiar with the recent work of German botanists and pollination theorists Josef Kolreuter and Christian Sprengel, speculates that plant reproduction can occur through the intervention of bees.[64] In making this leap, Bartram and Barton were among the first wave of natural historians who supposed that species themselves were in transformative relations with other species.[65] Across their correspondence and the book that grew from it, Barton and Bartram developed an anti-analogical vitalism whose queerness comes from its refusal of the analogical order that posited that animals were like but not attached to plants, whether this attachment was erotic or not. Attending to the ways plants combine in and with the substances and bodies that compose their environments, Barton and Bartram develop the American vitalism that is evoked only to be disavowed by Rush's work. Disorganizing chains and hierarchies of being, they reveal the enmeshed and enmeshing life-forms, time scales, modes of existence, and biological processes that were so spectacularly evident in the American tropics.

Cosmos

Barton and Bartram's departure from the analogical method opened the possibility of a nonidentitarian natural history in which no body remains identical to itself over time because it is always altered by its relation with other bodies and forces in an ecology as well as the wayward movements of its component parts. This natural history anticipates what Isabelle Stengers terms the *cosmological* or *cosmopolitical*, by which she means a methodology that recognizes that any body or environment develops through ongoing negotiations among a broad array of material forces that operate on a cosmological in addition to a planetary scale. For Stengers, a cosmopolitical ecology is the "science of multiplicities, disparate causalities, and unintentional creations of meaning," and is notable for its turn from methods focused on the submission of parts to the larger totalities that they compose. As she puts it, a cosmopolitical ecology "doesn't understand consensus but, at most, symbiosis. . . . The 'symbiotic agreement' is an event, the production of new, immanent modes of existence, and not the recognition of a more powerful interest before which divergent particular interests would have to bow down."[66] Stengers makes clear that the relation among parts—or more aptly, singularities—that gives rise to the cosmos is not harmonious. This means that when a symbiosis or compromise is formed it always excludes and even violates some of the entities that compose it and that might resist it. As this suggests, any collectivity, whether the small-scale collective of the body or the large-scale collectivity of the environment or a political field, is also constraining, which means that any collectivity produces the conditions for different systems—indeed, its undoing.

The term *cosmological* was in use in the eighteenth century and would soon be given a meaning close to that which Stengers proposes by Humboldt, who, drawing on the tropical natural history he offered in the *Personal Narrative* and *Essay on the Geography of Plants,* began work on the multivolume *Kosmos,* which proposed that human and nonhuman beings together constituted an infinitely complex and contingent universe.[67] As we have seen in the earlier *Personal History,* written immediately after his return from the Americas, Humboldt suggested that vegetable bodies and vegetable-laden air trespassed on human beings and their history. This sustained attention to the contest among the intersecting material forces in an environment might lead us to expect that Humboldt's cosmology would attend to difference and contestation, but by the time he wrote his later work he understood the cosmos to describe a necessarily harmonious unity of complex systems. Reill, who proposes that Humboldt and his brother were paradigmatic enlightenment vitalists, draws on this claim to argue that enlightenment vitalism more broadly was characterized by a focus on harmony, which was believed to undergird the interrelation of complex systems and incompatible scales.[68] I agree with Reill's interpretation of Humboldt's later work; however, we have seen that Humboldt's earlier natural history was far less interested in harmony.

Although Humboldt's vitalism eventually results in a cosmopolitics that covers over the discord and disagreement that come from contemplating how the sometimes unpredictable movements of parts contribute to the production of larger systems, it is not the case that all late eighteenth-century vitalist materialism was equally committed to harmony. In addition to Humboldt's early work, the vitalist botany that we see developing from Barton and Bartram focuses intently on the contingent and unpredictable results of the relation of bodies and systems across the multiple scales that compose an environment, reopening the possibility of a vitalist materialism alive to dissent, difference, and the negative as well as the positive effects of contingency.

At first consideration, the devout Bartram might seem an unlikely source of a materialist cosmology. Yet, like the equally pious Hartley and Priestley, Bartram emphasizes an animated material world, and he holds this animacy as an expression of divinity in matter. In his unpublished manuscript "The Dignity of Human Nature" (which in fact often makes an argument precisely opposite its stated title), Bartram writes that "Divine Intelligence, penetrates & animates the Univers. This is the immortal Soul of Nature, of Living moving beings, of Vegetables, & is in the Elements."[69] Like Rush and subsequently Humboldt, he understands the vegetable world to contribute to this animation. Describing the vegetable profusion of Georgia's tropical spring, he writes that "the atmosphere was now animated with the efficient principle of vegetative life."[70] If Bartram participates in vitalist materialism, or at the very least in an animist materialism that is close to it, his thought evinces both the harmonious cosmology that Humboldt would eventually propose and the risk-attendant cosmology that lurks in Humboldt's earlier work and that Stengers theorizes. In the introduction to *Travels*, Bartram proposes that although humans might

> admire the mechanism of a watch, and the fabric of a piece of brocade, as being the production of art . . . nature is the work of God omnipotent; and an elephant, nay even this world, is comparatively but a very minute part of his works. If then the visible, the mechanical part of the animal creation . . . is so admirably beautiful, harmonious, and incomprehensible, what must be the intellectual system? that inexpressibly more essential principle, which secretly operates within?[71]

Admiring clocks and fabrics is not sufficient, Bartram suggests; truly perceiving nature requires recognizing the expansive, not humanly visible work of a still-acting God who is less an anthropomorphized being than a force, or "essential principle," moving through matter, bodies, and environments.

Bartram's meditation proceeds through a play on measure and scale: Bartram introduces the elephant, a large creature, only to displace it with the world, the apparent totality of the environment, which is then revealed not as a totality but as a miniature within more expansive systems. In skipping scales and miniaturizing both the elephant and the world, Bartram implies that any singularity—from an animal like the elephant to an environment like the earth—is a part of wholes larger and smaller than itself. Moving through these different systems and sliding scales, God is the infinitely extended and animating force of matter, machine, and environment that traverses and grounds all scales, revealing that creature and world are distinct expressions of the same force. Here, God functions in two senses. First, God is the totality of all creatures and environments—which is to say, God is the cosmos. Second, God is a vital force that "secretly operates within" every microcosmos.[72]

That Bartram's God is expressed in both the totality of all entities and in each part of this totality, or to refine my terms, the singularity of every *microcosmos,* raises the question of how Bartram conceives the relation of the cosmos to the microcosmos.[73] Do microcosmos reflect the cosmos that in turn encloses them, which is to say does any microcosmos testify to and repeat the majesty of the totality? Or do microcosmos act upon and change the cosmos that they compose, which is to say, does a microcosmos, in addition to testifying to the totality it composes, maintain autonomy from it, indicating the internal division and the autonomy of the components of any totality? The former position eliminates the diversity and with it the chaos that vitalist materialism evokes, first by stripping the microcosmos of any capacity to influence larger systems and second by suggesting that all forms ultimately only express the same transcendent unity anticipated by the larger cosmos. The latter position keeps open the possibility for diversity and chance by allowing that the unpredicted movements of microcosmos from atoms to plants to elephants through planets might shape the cosmos. Bartram's interest in diversity and contingency as well as his turn from the mimetic mode of analogy would suggest the latter, which would mean that both microcosmos and cosmos are continually changing and also changing one another such that neither can be conceived as a reflection of the other. Here, the part is in fact a singularity that maintains its autonomy from the wholes it also composes. However, in this passage as in most of his published work, Bartram promises that this process of reciprocal interaction is characterized by a harmony that would suggest the first position.

If Bartram's published work gestures toward a harmony, in his unpublished work he offers what Laurel Ode-Schneider terms a "darker" vision that is more fully attentive to the risks of vitalism and more proximate to Stengers's cosmopolitics.[74] Bartram's turn from a harmonious to a risky cosmology is most evident in his botanical drawings, which he began composing while quite young and which, by his early twenties, brought him the attention of London-based naturalists John Fothergill and Peter Collinson. They cautiously overlooked his propensity for failure and commissioned him to collect and illustrate American species and artifacts, especially plants. Fothergill and Collinson were producing natural historical taxonomies that aimed to include American plants, which often had pharmacological or commercial uses.[75] Bartram's assignment was to introduce tropical plants to metropolitan science, and thus he was asked to collect specimens that might be grown in European greenhouses and to provide faithful copies of American botanical species.[76]

In eighteenth-century botanical illustrations, plant species were often divorced from their contexts, either represented as one within a series that constitutes a category or as having limbs and roots attenuated (Figures 5 and 6). When larger contexts were evoked in eighteenth-century botanical illustration, it was generally to indicate scale so that the audience might be able to determine the relative size of the specimen collected or of a specimen in its environment. If this interest in scale was, in part, to allow Europeans who did not travel in the Americas to better understand and categorize American species and terrains with which they were unfamiliar, it also contributed to the comparative efforts of vitalists such as Buffon, who famously argued that the vital principle was less fully expressed in the Americas, giving rise to smaller and less energetic life-forms.[77] The expectation that botanical illustrations should indicate scale informs Peter Collinson's instructions to Bartram: Collinson asked that when Bartram depicted several kinds of a species on the same page he arrange them "from the very Smallest to the Largest."[78]

Despite what Collinson and Fothergill had requested, Bartram often did not eliminate contexts from his drawings. Nor did he consistently provide scalar arrangements. In fact, while Bartram was certainly capable of

Figure 5. Flora and Fauna of North Carolina, *John Brickell, 1743. Despite the diversity of life-forms collected here, the left side of Brickell's illustration groups together American quadrupeds, arranging them by size. The right side of the illustration groups together American ovoviviparous animals, including reptiles, birds, and insects. I suspect the muskrat is included on the right side because it did not fit on the previous page. Courtesy of the John Carter Brown Library at Brown University.*

producing scalar and decontextualized botanical illustrations and often did, his drawings for Collinson and Fothergill presented vertiginous, descalarized scenes attentive to the violence of tropical ecologies.[79] Consider *American Lotus, Venus Flytrap, Great Blue Heron* (ca. 1765–75) (Figure 7), one of the unpublished illustrations Bartram produced for Collinson and Fothergill, an illustration they admired but also criticized for being overly "imaginary." Bartram presents a field of gigantically outsized lotuses that seem to grow into the sky, recalling plants' relation to the trees that proliferated in the eighteenth-century tropics.[80] The immensity of these lotuses passes from arrangements of scale, evoking the power of tropical plant life that Humboldt would also note and that the Haitian poet René

ANDROMEDA PULVERULENTA.

Figure 6. Andromeda pulverulenta, *William Bartram, 1791. Bartram's drawing of the* Andromeda *follows a common botanical convention of depicting a specimen apart from its context. When context was included, it was expected to be to scale, as is typically the case in the work of Mark Catesby, one of Bartram's predecessors, who even when he plays with measure reproduces American ecologies in a scalar fashion. Courtesy of the John Carter Brown Library at Brown University.*

Depestre later called *végétations de clarté* ("plants of light," or, in Jack Hirshman's English translation, "vegetations of splendor"). At the drawing's far left, a great blue heron, a bird that can be as large as five feet high, is of a size with the flytrap, a plant usually no more than five inches in diameter. A leaf from a vine subtly moves out of the frame as though

Figure 7. American Lotus, by William Bartram, 1791. Here, Bartram departs from both the tendency to represent a specimen apart from contexts and the tradition of representing life-forms in an environment according to scale. Copyright Natural History Museum, London.

anticipating a moment when Bartram's jumped scales pass from page to world.

In an Atlantic culture in which size, scale, and comparison mattered quite a lot, Bartram's failure to give his patrons the scalar representations they requested is notable.[81] To be sure, Jonathan Swift and before him François Rabelais had experimented with telescoping scales. However, Bartram's work and letters evince an earnestness that is almost entirely devoid of the satire of these literary precedents. He vertiginously combines the miniature and the gigantic scales that Jonathan Swift had so explicitly distinguished in *Gulliver's Travels* (1726) and that Susan Stewart, drawing on Swift, holds apart in her analysis of how the small and the large generate opposed modes of conceiving the human self and body. For Stewart, the miniature precipitates a temporal alteration (she suggests it both speeds and stops time) by which a human being conceives a mimetic relation between herself and the closed world of the miniature, in so doing internalizing and closing off her subjectivity.[82] Conversely, for Stewart the gigantic distorts the human body only to map it onto the natural world, which becomes interpretable through the measure of the outsized human form and an analogue for it. Whether focused on the miniature or the gigantic, Stewart's reading suggests that from the eighteenth to the twentieth centuries literary accounts of inhuman forms and the natural world tell human beings the story of their own subjectivity.[83]

While Stewart's reading focuses on the poles of the small and the large, her suggestion that in both cases the human is the measure on which to scale the cosmos cannily echoes Kant's proposal in the third *Critique* that the human subject uses his body as the template through which to produce the measure so central to the exercise of reason.[84] Kant's point is not that the human body is the only or the best unit of measure; his incidental usage of the human body as a unit of measure is symptomatic of a late eighteenth- and early nineteenth-century philosophy that understands the human being as the measure through which the world can be mapped and compared so that judgment can be exercised. However, Bartram's play with scales does not imagine the human body as the template through which the cosmos might be measured, raising the question of how to understand the work of surveying and measuring the cosmos if the human being and body are not imagined as its apotheosis. In *American Lotus* the relative size of tropical species is unclear, as are the intervals between them. Refusing to attend to the intervals and increments necessary to take measure, whether temporal or spatial, Bartram's drawing cannot give rise to the syntheses that ground Kant's project.[85] In Bartram's work, it is impossible to conceive nonhuman bodies, forces, and environments as so many metaphors for human subjectivity.[86] Given his effacement of the human being and body and his conversion of measure and scale into a scene of suspended vertigo, it is not at all clear that Bartram believes that reason, understanding, or aesthetics might reveal the centrality of human beings and bodies, the measure of the universe, or a harmonious cosmos. Wholly outside the analogical scene in which the human body serves as the measure of the cosmos or in which measure can be calculated to produce the comparative account of planetary forces that other vitalist natural history enforces, Bartram's vision demands a thinking of imagination and relation outside of measure that almost certainly means to emphasize a divinity that is not concerned with human conceptions of measurement. Nonetheless, this account of the expression of divinity in nature shapes Bartram's understanding of how human beings should conduct themselves in relation to other life-forms.[87]

American Lotus's reflection on the relation between the life-forms that compose the cosmos opens onto two distinct interpretations. The first interpretation notes that the flytrap on the far left foreground stands with open mouths behind the crane. The crane, whose neck crosses a gigantic lotus leaf, stands open mouthed behind a fish whose presence outside of this foregrounded tableau suggests that the arrival of a consumptive event through which the foreground moves into the background to create a hallucinatory scene marked by the copresence of apparently incompatible scales. The plant and the animal are separated as distinct life-forms, but instead of mimetically reflecting each other, the flytrap might consume the animal.[88] The possibility that the plant is after the animal is dramatized by Bartram's placement of a bird, not an insect, before the plant's mouths, confirming his own as well as Humboldt's belief that plants' force could exceed that of animals. Hallock notes that this image indicates Bartram's ecological orientation.[89] Yet if Bartram's vertiginous collation of scales as well as his attention to intensified plant vitality is ecological, it pushes the ecological to a cosmopolitics attentive to the risks that emerge from the intersection of life-forms. If Bartram, like Humboldt, imagines that the cosmos consists of the unity of intersecting and transforming life-forms and environments, Bartram's *American Lotus* suggests that this unity is not achieved in advance. Rather, it is a negotiation developing across distinct but copresent scales and modes of being and in which the plant life that often exists in symbiotic relation with human beings and other animals might also destroy animal life, whether through literal consumption as this image suggests or by broadcasting its vegetable matter into the air where it enters into and disorganizes human bodies.

This same image also offers a second interpretation, this one emphasizing that any life-form, including the American lotus, has the power to withdraw from or otherwise refuse the negotiations through which bodies and media forge relations in an oikos. This interpretation again begins with the flytrap and the miniaturized crane. This time, instead of moving past the leaf that frames the foregrounded tableau, note that the leaf's edges turn inward as though it might invert itself to enclose the crane, completing the consumptive action anticipated in the first interpretation but in a quite different direction. Here, instead of passing into the background as it does in the first interpretation, the tableau offers a palindrome, a sequencing of plant-animal-plant that swallows the animal into vegetable life. This second interpretation does not simply suggest risk, skip scales to suggest the vertiginous relations through which life-forms interact, or recognize the violence of the relation between organisms. It also proposes that the violence of this scene of relation comes from the plant's capacity to assert its difference from and power over the animal. All life-forms are part of local and planetary relations, but they are not swallowed into an undifferentiated oneness; rather, they assert their singularity, which includes a capacity to opt out that would have important consequences if Bartram were to apply his natural science to the political world to suggest that a part is best understood as a singularity that can remove itself from the wholes it composes.

In suggesting that *American Lotus* opens up two interpretations, one attending to leaps of scale and risky negotiations through which life-forms and ecologies emerge, the other attending to the singularity of assemblages and ecologies, I do not intend to favor one interpretation over the other. Rather, I would hold these interpretations together to have them yield an American cosmopolitics in which the relation of matter, bodies, scales, and systems might yield symbiotic cooperation, uncomfortable mergings, or even destruction for any or several of the entities on the scene. In this cosmology, a part—whether particulate, bodily, or a complex system—might refuse to participate, as happens in the second interpretation of *American Lotus* in which the lotus leaf stands to swallow the animal, completing and also closing off relation.

This second point of my definition of this Americanist cosmopolitics emphasizes that differences among singularities remain even if analogical orderings are weakened. Bartram's lotus is formally distinct from the animal that it threatens, and it is distinct from the human animal. That Bartram recognizes the lotus's difference from himself and human beings more generally is evident in the fully opened leaf to the right of the drawing. Turning its surface from the sun to the viewer, the leaf reveals venation ramifying from its center. This leaf is not a face, the petiole's mark upon the leaf is not an eye, and its turn toward the presumably human viewer cannot be mapped onto the human gaze. Instead of a looking whereby the plant mirrors the animal back to itself, Bartram's lotus asserts its difference. Bartram's attention to the relation between distinct entities anticipates tropical botanist Francis Hallé's emphasis on the formal difference between plants, which he describes as "vast fixed surfaces," and animals, which are "small mobile volumes."[90]

Over the course of this chapter, I have argued that for late eighteenth-century nonmechanist materialists both the plant and the agential matter it produces indicate that the part is a non-self-identical singularity that cannot be dissolved into the whole. I have suggested from the outset that this account of form and system has political significance. As we have seen, vitalist materialists risked being branded political radicals in part because, even as they reasserted the power of divinity, their accounts of the autonomy of parts evinced a democratic tendency that, if this was not enough, expanded the *demos* to include nonhuman forms. The capacity of the part as singularity is perhaps nowhere more explicitly articulated than in Bartram's work. The political significance of this natural history is also particularly opaque in his work, especially his published writing. Bartram's trajectories and his writings indicate a departure from Franklin's citizen-subjectivity and, as we have seen here, a departure from the republican machine in which parts undeviatingly serve the whole; yet the strongest current of his life and his work is a recessiveness that does not lend itself to asserting a politics. Nonetheless, the vitalist materialist cosmology that lurks in Bartram's fragments, hidden-away letters, and unpublished images does verge on an alternative mode of personhood and politics. Most obviously, the mode of personhood we might glean from Bartram is not in keeping with eighteenth-century natural historians' tendency to assume the centrality of human life and the human body.[91]

Moreover, in his attention to the relations between matter, forms, and systems, Bartram offers occasion for a rethinking of the relation of the self (human or nonhuman) to the other (human or nonhuman) that subtends many twentieth- and twenty-first-century theorizations of personhood. As the previous chapter proposed, Bartram's writings about life in the tropics do not allow the transcendence of Anglo-European subjectivity. Investigating Bartram's ecological and budding cosmopolitical orientation develops further this insight by suggesting a proliferation of diverse and also entwined singularities that does not fantasize a transcendent Other while nonetheless recognizing others. If any singularity participates in milieus that proliferate with others, they are not Derrida's desired but unencounterable others, nor are they the encountered and generally benign others of Habermas's public sphere. In Bartram's germinal cosmopolitics, others are always encountered, and these others can (but do not necessarily) interact with and transform the forms and systems in which they participate. Here, microcosmos from elephants to earths engage in relations that produce the cosmos.

Bartram's writings on what he calls vegetable "tribes" take, farther than either Rush or Humboldt, the political and cosmological significance of vegetable agency. However, he also attempts to divide the natural historical from the political, in so doing turning from his cosmopolitics. This is perhaps most evident in his accounts of Native Americans. Well known to later scholars for his interest in and defense of American Indian civilizations, Bartram makes clear that the Cherokee, Muscogee (Creek), Natchez, and other American Indian peoples with whom he interacted have diverse histories and cultural practices that are distinct from and in some respects preferable to those of Anglo-Europeans. "Our youth" he proposes, would be morally improved if they would "repair to the venerable councils of the Muscogulges."[92] He insisted that Indian nations have incentive to and are justified in "defend[ing] their territory and preserv[ing] their rights" against the "invasion[s]" of Anglo-Europeans and the unjust seizure of their land.[93] In fact, in his effort to counter Anglo-European efforts to (in the words of a southeastern Indian chief he cites) "wrong the Indians out of their land," Bartram several times suggested that American Indian nations have a concept of private property.[94] Given that Bartram recognizes an American Indian idea of property in common (even as he also recognizes that specific Native Americans had moved from holding property in common since contact with Anglo-Europeans), he was clearly well aware that most Native Americans did not have the same conception of private property as Anglo-Europeans. That Bartram obscures his knowledge of the complexity of American Indian conceptions of property in order to suggest that American Indian cultures recognized private property suggests he recognized the political stakes of natural history and aimed to use his work to protect Native American rights. In his misrepresentation of American Indian notions of property, he comes close to, if he also sublimates, a cosmopolitics that would require contending among divergent valuations of commonality and property through difficult and uncertain negotiations.

However, Bartram abdicates his right to argue for the political stakes and negotiations that follow from his natural history. In *Travels*, he concedes that the rights of Native Americans are "high concerns of government" and that, as such, he is "fully convinced that such important matters are far above [his] ability."[95] As was the case with his defense of Afro-American resistance, Bartram expressly turns away from what he names as political. In dividing natural history from political life, he puts forth a conception of politics as a "high" concern that is the proper domain of a select few. To be sure, Bartram might well have produced this division to protect natural history, the politics it occasioned, and himself from the divisive and increasingly bipolarized politics of the postrevolutionary years. Nonetheless, the effect is to separate natural history from politics and to radically limit the democratic significance of his cosmopolitics. Even more problematically, even as he disavowed what he deemed to be political by separating it from the natural historical, Bartram's published work does offer an underground political claim that is contested in his unpublished work. At the close of the introduction to *Travels*, he proposed it necessary to determine whether Native Americans would be interested "to adopt the European modes of civil society" and further wondered if this assimilation "would be productive of real benefit to them, and consequently beneficial to the public."[96] His recognition that some American Indian nations might not find it in their best interests to adopt Anglo-European political and cultural forms or join their interests to those of the United States makes clear that he understands the strong likelihood of incommensurate interests. However, he concludes his inquiry by claiming that he was "satisfied . . . that they [American Indians] were desirous of becoming united with us [Anglo-America]," in so doing promising a harmony in advance that makes Native Americans' differences and resistances—in short, their agency and politics—recede even farther than those of his plant agents.[97]

II

3

On Parahumanity

Creole Stories and the Suspension of the Human

Parahuman

In April 1764, Fenelon, the governor of Martinique, wrote:

> Je suis arrivé à la Martinique avec tous les préjugés d'Europe
> contre la rigueur avec laquelle on traite les nègres et en faveur de
> l'instruction qu'on leur doit pour les principes de notre religion . . .
> Je suis parvenu à croire fermement qu'il faut mener les nègres
> comme des bêtes.[1]

> [I arrived in Martinique with all the European prejudices against
> the severity with which we treat the negroes and in favor of
> instructing them in the principles of our religion . . . I've come to
> firmly believe that it is necessary to guide the negroes like beasts.]

Despite its utter banality, Fenelon's apologia for slavery is notable as an
example of the colonial categorization of Africans in the diaspora as neither human nor animal but as what I call parahuman beings.[2] A category
opened up by colonials attempting to manage black persons, particularly
their capacity for collective resistance, the *parahuman* is distinguishable
from other bodies produced in emerging biopolitical regimes because her
body was broken in parts: an ear amputated for petit marronage, a hand
for theft, an arm pulled from the body by the sugar mill, and sometimes a
head cut from the body for resistance so total as to warrant death. If we are
to take Fenelon at his word, the parahuman body that is guided, or governed ("*mener*"), as though it were an animal body is in analogical relation
to the animals and to the human beings to which it is proximate. Under
the logic of colonialism, this analogical relation worked to produce a hierarchy of species whereby the African slave was conceived as an interstitial

form of life that could be exploited for labor power in the way animals were and that also protected Anglo-Europeans from recognizing their own animality.

In taking up the term *parahuman*, I aim to challenge the hierarchal organization of life-forms that was common to colonial anthropologies and natural histories: I put animals, parahumans, and humans in horizontal relation (that is to say, *para* or beside each other) without conflating them. In addition to describing a relation whereby one category is beside another, presumably prior category, the prefix *para-* can describe a perversion of that prior category (*paranormal, paranoia*). Taking up this double signification of the prefix *para*, I propose that tracing the figure of the parahuman in the eighteenth and nineteenth centuries reveals a perversion of the category of the human that was effected by diasporic Africans' performance of their parahumanity.

Afro-Americans' parahumanity has generally been overlooked in favor of analyses that rehabilitate Africans and Afro-Americans to the rights of man and the realm of the human (this is true of the very different analyses of James Earl, Ottobah Cuguano, Frantz Fanon, and Henry Louis Gates).[3] Instead of staying with this hierarchical arrangement that values human beings over other life-forms—a hierarchy whose structure was produced in no small part by colonialism—I aim to investigate the identificatory processes and the strategies of resistance that developed through the performances of those designated as parahuman. In order to build this analysis, I offer an archive of Creole stories through which we can trace the existence and development of the parahuman. I then offer an interpretation of this archive that shifts from prevailing understandings of Creole tales that, because they overlook parahumanity, interpret Creole tales as symptoms of colonialism instead of reroutings of colonial valuations of animality, humanity, and the relation between them. Although my interpretation of Creole tales diverges from the seminal analyses of Frantz Fanon, Maryse Condé, and Édouard Glissant, their work offers a series of clues that I follow to develop my argument that Afro-Americans drew on the brutal colonial circumstance of dismemberment and bodily disaggregation to produce models of personhood that developed from the experience of parahumanity and in relation to animal bodies. These models of personhood registered a deep skepticism about the desirability of the category of the human, in so doing indicating an enlightenment tradition that is not founded on legitimizing or expanding the modern, secular category of the human, which has been the dominant critical understanding of enlightenment, including those analyses that extend to the colonies.[4] Parahumans built modes of self and politics that were not simply critiques of the category of the human but suspended it so as to prohibit any simple return to it.

Toward a Parahuman Archive

I offer Matthew Lewis's *Journal of a West India Proprietor* (written from 1815 to 1818, and published in 1834) as a primary text in the archive of works that might be gathered under the rubric of parahuman tales.[5] The London-based novelist, playwright, and plantation owner proposes that early nineteenth-century Jamaican plantation culture was a performance that Afro-Americans understood and directed far better than he could. His slaves "acted their part so well, that they almost made me act mine to perfection." In fact, as far as the slaves on his Jamaican estates were concerned, Lewis was as much possessed by them as he possessed them.[6] One of the Obeah practitioners on his Cornwall plantation, a slave named Adam, bragged that he could control Lewis's mind; Lewis denied the charge, but it did not stop the circulation of rumors. At his slaves' request, Lewis agreed to have his portrait painted by an enslaved Afro-American artist. Although Lewis dismissed the resulting portrait as wholly to the side of British representational conventions, he reported that his slaves declared the painting and its subject were the "very same 'ting" and they concluded that it perfectly achieved their goal of producing an artifact through which they might speak with him when he was gone—either after the absentee landlord Lewis had left his Jamaica plantations to return to England or after he died.[7]

In fact, Lewis was soon gone in both senses. He left the colony not long after the completion of the portrait; when he returned and again departed from the colony, he died at sea twelve days after his ship sailed from Jamaica. His coffin was wrapped in a canvas sheet, weighted with anchors, and thrown into the ocean only to soon resurface. The canvas loosening from the coffin billowed into a sail, and a trade wind carried his body back toward Jamaica. Biographers have speculated that he died of yellow fever, which Lewis's *Journal* recorded as spreading through the island just before his departure. Some of his friends and acquaintances, however, suggested he might have been poisoned or otherwise succumbed to his slaves' machinations.[8]

The accumulating details indicating that Lewis inadvertently figured in local Obeah culture as well as the speculation surrounding his death suggest the deep polyvocality of his plantation writings. Like other Anglo-Europeans writing in and about the colonies, Lewis not only made visible the terrain he meant to call forth but also evoked traces of other terrains, entirely different inhabitations of territory that cannot simply be overlaid onto his own mappings of the plantation zone. Moreover, Lewis, increasingly at odds with elite London culture as well as Jamaican white Creole culture, felt particularly compelled toward Afro-American cultures.[9] Although this compulsion does not make his accounts of diasporic African cultures more accurate, it did make him an especially verbose commentator on Afro-Jamaican cultures, which has led anticolonial and postcolonial writers and critics to appropriate Lewis's Jamaican writings as source texts.[10]

Lewis's unusual polyvocality is linked to the fact that he spent so much of his time during his West Indian sojourns with Afro-Americans, including griots (storytellers) and sometimes Obeah practitioners. These classes of enslaved African persons had developed codes and rituals through which possession no longer simply indicated ownership of property because it also opened onto cosmologies in which one force could move through and temporarily overwhelm another, producing additions that changed the movements of bodies and histories. There is no need to interpret possession in overly mysticizing terms to acknowledge that these rituals of possession indicate that Lewis was correct when he admitted that he not only manipulated his slaves but was also manipulated by them. Although the slaves' rituals of possession worked to a variety of ends, one of their effects was that Lewis's writings became a portal through which fragments of diasporic Afro-American cultures passed into the historical record.

Consider the Ananse story Lewis transcribed in a March 1816 letter to a friend in England. The story, which he had heard told by a female slave whom he nicknamed Goosee Shoo-shoo, chronicles the plight of an Afro-American mother who lives under a cotton tree, a tree that Lewis singled out in his *Journal* as especially picturesque and that Afro-American cultures in Jamaica and elsewhere singled out for its otherworldly root structure, which served as a crossroads between the living and the dead as well as the visibly and the extravisibly perceptible.[11]

The mother who lives under a cotton tree gives birth to a son who does not have a head. She thinks to ask a bird to sit on her son's shoulder to fulfill the offices her son cannot: eating as well as talking, seeing, and hearing. However, she cannot immediately find a bird willing to help in this "very peculiar situation of affairs," and, what's more, her son has fallen in love with a princess who might find it odd if he had a bird perform all cephalatory functions. Giving up on her first plan, the mother appeals to an owl to help her determine how her son might gain a head. Supposing that no creature would believe that a human child was born without a head, the mother first tells the owl that her son's head tumbled from his body, then that he accidentally ate it. Following the owl's suggestions for what a headless being might do if determined to gain a head, the boy first puts on the head of an ass, then the head of a hog. He attempts to court the princess, but wearing the ass's head he is the butt of jokes, and wearing the hog's head he is almost eaten.[12]

Finally, on her third visit, the mother confesses to the owl that her son was born without a head, which the owl had already known; he then advises the mother to have her son present himself to the king and princess without a head, which he does. The princess, a figure of royalty akin to the kings and princes Édouard Glissant claims represent plantation owners, is horrified by her headless suitor.[13] But the king declares that he will make the boy a head: with the lash of a whip, two ears appear; with a drop of rum, his mouth appears; and, on putting a gold coin in the boy's hand, his eyes appear. Having gained a head, the boy and the princess marry and live with plentiful supplies of rum and tobacco.

Lewis understands the tale as a confirmation of and allegory for Anglo-Europeans' belief that Afro-American persons were parahuman beings whose only path to *cogito* and the organicism he associated with humanity was through the brutalities of colonial violence and racism. Still, keeping in mind that Lewis never speaks with one voice, it is possible to take up other problematics raised by this tale. Most pressingly, this tale and Lewis's *Journal* more broadly raise the question of how persons in the eighteenth- and early nineteenth-century diaspora understood the breaking of Afro-American bodies, a breaking that was both a historical fact under colonial codes that allowed dismemberment and even decapitation as punishment, and a breaking that circulated as image and story in the cultural productions of Anglo-Europeans and especially Afro-Americans. Moreover, this tale also raises the question of how Afro-Americans understood their relation to other forms of animal life to which they were often compared by Anglo-Europeans and with which they were often conjoined in diasporic folk stories.

In Jamaica, as in other colonies whether British, French, Dutch, or Spanish, plantation owners and their representatives, as well as the machinery of the plantation, would sometimes amputate black persons' bodies, sometimes also decapitating them. Both the Barbados Slave Code (1661) and the French *Code Noir* (1685) stipulated that the mutilation of slave persons, including the amputation of body parts, was an appropriate punishment for disobedience and rebellion (Figure 8).[14] The *Code Noir* legalized this punishment by dismemberment, dictating that petit marronage (defined as disappearance for a month) would be punished by cutting off a slave's ears and that longer or repeated periods of marronage would be punished by cutting the tendons at the back of the knee or even amputation of the leg from the knee.[15] In her account of colonial life in Jamaica, Maria Nugent, the wife of governor Robert Nugent, notes that hatchets were kept on hand in the sugar mills to cut off limbs caught in the machinery.[16]

This mutilation and amputation of the bodies of black persons that was sanctioned in legal codes and in economic practice became iconic in both Afro-American oral cultures and in Anglo-European literary culture. It can be seen in the proliferating legends of the Saint-Dominguan slave-turned-maroon Makandal, who was radicalized after his arm was torn from his body by the turning of a cane mill and who, after terrorizing the plantations in the northern part of the colony, was said to escape execution by transforming himself into a fly. It also can be seen in Voltaire's account of Candide who, in Surinam, encounters a slave missing his leg and his hand who explains this as the price of European sugar, and in William Blake's image of a slave being mutilated on the rack (Figure 9). Slaves were classed as property akin to animals, but that slave codes detailed how they should be punished indicated one crucial respect in which slaves were distinguished from animals—not that they should be punished as animals were certainly punished, but that their protections and acceptable punishments needed to be encoded in law. Whereas the animal body was posited as an organic body, the punishments of disfigurement and amputation made the slave body, at least in legal terms, an always potentially dismembered body.

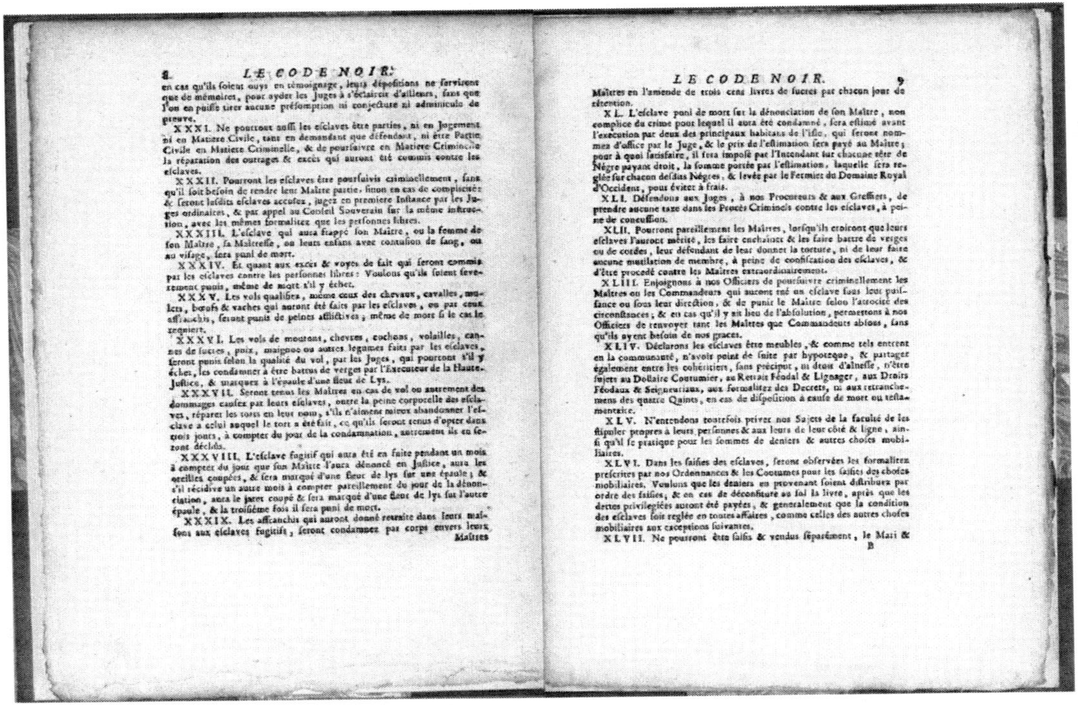

8 LE CODE NOIR.

en cas qu'ils soient ouys en témoignage, leurs dépositions ne serviront que de mémoires, pour ayder les Juges à s'éclaircir d'ailleurs, sans que l'on en puisse tirer aucune présomption ni conjecture ni adminicule de preuve.

XXXI. Ne pourront aussi les esclaves être parties, ni en Jugement ni en Matiere Civile, tant en demandant que défendant, ni être Partie Civile en Matiere Criminelle, & de poursuivre en Matiere Criminelle la réparation des outrages & excès qui auront été commis contre les esclaves.

XXXII. Pourront les esclaves être poursuivis criminellement, sans qu'il soit besoin de rendre leur Maître partie, sinon en cas de complicité: & seront lesdits esclaves accusez, jugez en premiere Instance par les Juges ordinaires, & par appel au Conseil Souverain sur la même instruction, avec les mêmes formalitez que les personnes libres.

XXXIII. L'esclave qui aura frappé son Maître, ou la femme de son Maître, sa Maîtresse, ou leurs enfans avec contusion de sang, ou au visage, sera puni de mort.

XXXIV. Et quant aux excès & voyes de fait qui seront commis par les esclaves contre les personnes libres: Voulons qu'ils soient severement punis, même de mort s'il y échet.

XXXV. Les vols qualifiez, même ceux des chevaux, cavalles, mulets, bœufs & vaches qui auront été faits par les esclaves, ou par ceux affranchis, seront punis de peines afflictives, même de mort si le cas le requiert.

XXXVI. Les vols de moutons, chevres, cochons, volailles, cannes de sucres, poix, maignoc ou autres legumes faits par les esclaves, seront punis selon la qualité du vol, par les Juges, qui pourront s'il y échet, les condamner à être battus de verges par l'Executeur de la Haute-Justice, & marquez à l'épaule d'une fleur de Lys.

XXXVII. Seront tenus les Maîtres en cas de vol ou autrement des dommages causez par leurs esclaves, outre la peine corporelle des esclaves, réparer les torts en leur nom, s'ils n'aiment mieux abandonner l'esclave à celui auquel le tort a été fait, ce qu'ils seront tenus d'opter dans trois jours, à compter du jour de la condamnation, autrement ils en seront déchûs.

XXXVIII. L'esclave fugitif qui aura été en fuite pendant un mois à compter du jour que son Maître l'aura dénoncé en Justice, aura les oreilles coupées, & sera marqué d'une fleur de lys sur une épaule; & s'il récidive un autre mois à compter pareillement du jour de la dénonciation, aura le jaret coupé & sera marqué d'une fleur de lys sur l'autre épaule, & la troisiéme fois il sera puni de mort.

XXXIX. Les affranchis qui auront donné retraite dans leurs maisons aux esclaves fugitifs, seront condamnez par corps envers leurs Maîtres

LE CODE NOIR. 9

Maîtres en l'amende de trois cens livres de sucres par chacun jour de rétention.

XL. L'esclave puni de mort sur la dénonciation de son Maître, non complice du crime pour lequel il aura été condamné, sera estimé avant l'exécution par deux des principaux habitans de l'isle, qui seront nommez d'office par le Juge, & le prix de l'estimation sera payé au Maître; pour à quoi satisfaire, il sera imposé par l'Intendant sur chacune tête de Négre payant droit, la somme portée par l'estimation, laquelle sera reglée sur chacun desdits Négres, & levée par le Fermier du Domaine Royal d'Occident, pour éviter à frais.

XLI. Défendons aux Juges, à nos Procureurs & aux Greffiers, de prendre aucune taxe dans les Procès Criminels contre les esclaves, à peine de concussion.

XLII. Pourront pareillement les Maîtres, lorsqu'ils croiront que leurs esclaves l'auront mérité, les faire enchaîner & les faire battre de verges ou de cordes, leur défendant de leur donner la torture, ni de leur faire aucune mutilation de membre, à peine de confiscation des esclaves, & d'être procedé contre les Maîtres extraordinairement.

XLIII. Enjoignons à nos Officiers de poursuivre criminellement les Maîtres ou les Commandeurs qui auront tué un esclave sous leur puissance ou sous leur direction, & de punir le Maître selon l'atrocité des circonstances; & en cas qu'il y ait lieu de l'absolution, permettons à nos Officiers de renvoyer tant les Maîtres que Commandeurs absous, sans qu'ils ayent besoin de nos graces.

XLIV. Déclarons les esclaves être meubles, & comme tels entrent en la communauté, n'avoir point de suite par hypoteque, & partager également entre les cohéritiers, sans préciput, ni droit d'aînesse, n'être sujets au Douaire Coutumier, au Retrait Féodal & Lignager, aux Droits Féodaux & Seigneuriaux, aux formalitez des Decrets, ni aux retranchemens des quatre Quints, en cas de disposition à cause de mort ou testamentaire.

XLV. N'entendons toutefois priver nos Sujets de la faculté de les stipuler propres à leurs personnes & aux leurs de leur côté & ligne, ainsi qu'il se pratique pour les sommes de deniers & autres choses mobiliaires.

XLVI. Dans les saisies des esclaves, seront observées les formalitez prescrites par nos Ordonnances & les Coutumes pour les saisies des choses mobiliaires. Voulons que les deniers en provenant soient distribuez par ordre des saisies, & en cas de déconfiture au sol la livre, après que les dettes privilegiées auront été payées, & generalement que la condition des esclaves soit reglée en toutes affaires, comme celles des autres choses mobiliaires aux exceptions suivantes.

XLVII. Ne pourront être saisis & vendus séparément, le Mari &

B

Figure 8. Excerpt of 1735 edition of Le Code Noir. *Article 38 of the* Code Noir *stipulates that slaves who escaped the plantation for a month would have their ears cut off and be branded on one shoulder with the* fleur de lys. *If a slave were to repeat the crime of marronage, his or her legs could be cut (potentially amputated) at the hamstrings, and he or she would be branded on the other shoulder with the* fleur de lys. *The punishment for a third offense was death. Courtesy of the John Carter Brown Library at Brown University.*

Céſt à ce prix que vous mangez du ſucre en Europe.

Candide Chapitre 19.

Figure 9. A slave whose arm and leg are amputated tells Candide that the breaking of the slave body is the price of consuming sugar in Europe. C'est à ce prix que vous mangez du sucre en Europe, *illustration from chapter 19 of Candide, François Voltaire (1694–1778), engraved by Pierre Charles Baquoy (1759–1829), 1787. Engraving, black and white photograph, Moreau, Jean Michel the Younger (1741–1814) [after], Bibliothèque Nationale, Paris, France / Giraudon / The Bridgeman Art Library.*

The plight of headlessness so central to Lewis's Ananse story was not a typical punishment under slavery, but it would certainly have been permitted under legal codes that stipulated that masters would not be punished for murdering their slaves and that rebellious slaves could be put to death. In fact, punishment of slaves by decapitation was probably comparatively rare in the colonies, as murder made it impossible for planters to use the slave's labor.[17] Also, before the late eighteenth century, when the guillotine was developed to make decapitation a humane and democratic form of punishment, decapitation was often (although certainly not always) a punishment allotted to nobles. Thus, in Aphra Behn's *Oroonoko* (1688), a novella haunted by the Puritans' decapitation of Charles I in 1649, it is the royal slave Oroonoko who performs the work of decapitating (he beheads his wife Imoinda to remove her from the power of the slavocracy), and the English colonists who perform the work of bodily mutilation when they burn, dismember, quarter, and then distribute the parts of his body.[18] Likewise, when the mixed race, property-owning Vincent Oge rebelled against Saint-Domingue's colonial authority in 1790, he was publicly executed by being broken on the wheel before being beheaded.

When slaves and free persons of color were decapitated, it was probably a punishment allotted to those whose rebellion was so total as to severely undermine the organization of labor and bodies required by the plantocracy. Lewis, for instance, noted that one day he "happened . . . to ask . . . to whom a skull had belonged, which I had observed fixed on a pole by the roadside, when returning last from Montego Bay," and he was told it belonged to a rebellious African who murdered and removed the ears from his master, and who in turn was executed and his head fixed on a pole "*in terrorem.*"[19] This slave's crime is telling: in cutting the ears from his master, he turned upon the plantocracy one of the punishments it exacted on slaves. This slave's replication of the sort of punishment masters routinely visited upon slaves would make the Anglo-European body as much a site of fragmentation as the slave's. However, the plantocracy's response of severing the slave's head forecloses this slave's production of an equivalence between white and black bodies. In this instance, decapitation indicated the master's absolute power to determine the shape and uses of black bodies, the slave's life or death, and the structure of the society to be produced from this conjunction of biopolitical and sovereign power.[20]

Decapitation served as a reminder of the master's absolute power over black persons, who were forbidden the right to determine the shape and movement of any body, be it their own or their masters'. However, the spectacle that Lewis recorded raises another possibility. It may have been intended to terrorize the black population, but, as Lewis's interest indicates, it also captivated the colony's white population, making them aware that the plantation system existed under the threat of slave rebellion that could destroy it. In his novella "Benito Cereno" (1855), Herman Melville would suggest that the severed head of the slave rebel was a "hive of subtlety" far more terrifying to white masters than to rebellious slaves. Melville evokes and inverts Lewis's suggestion that Afro-Americans lack cogito by cannily suggesting that what was most terrifying about such spectacles was not that black persons were cunning and thus just as intelligent and human as white persons; rather, he suggests that the fear was that their cunning was linked to Afro-American collectivizing. Collective action by slaves could swiftly move a territory from the plantation order to a slave-produced order, whether that of marronage, which was prevalent throughout the region, or that of black republicanism as achieved in Haiti. Indeed, Melville presents the severed head of the slave rebel as an icon that signaled to at least some whites that they could never be entirely sure whether they were in the social and economic form of the plantocracy or in a black-produced subversion of it.

The Ananse tales Lewis records confirm that headlessness was also linked to subversion in Afro-American orature.[21] In one story, a girl encounters a headless woman under a cotton tree who asks her what she sees. The girl replies, "Nothing," and the woman pronounces her good and promises her good things, which soon come to pass when the girl breaks open three eggs, one that bears a water jug, the next a sugar plantation, and the third a carriage.[22] The girl's stepsister travels the same route the next day, but when the headless woman under the cotton tree asks her what she sees, she replies, "Me see one old woman without him head!" This is a bad answer, perhaps because it suggests headlessness should be considered a defect but primarily because it betrays dangerous knowledge. If the woman's "circumstance" of headlessness "were to come to the ears of the buckras [white plantation owners], it might bring her into trouble" because it would betray her as an Obeah woman. When this bad girl breaks open three eggs, the first is empty, the second bears a menacing snake, and the third produces the headless woman, who berates the girl for her rudeness and lies.[23] This tale suggests that by the early nineteenth century headlessness and other forms of bodily mutilation were not only understood as an effect of colonial violence but also had been integrated into and gained significance within the Obeah practices of slaves and maroons. To be headless, in short, was not simply to suffer at the hands of colonial racism but a circumstance that Obeah cultures had revalued as engendering a certain power, although what precisely this power consisted of needed to remain unspoken among those who recognized it.

This specific tale shows how the fragmentation of Afro-American persons came to be vested with power in plantation spaces. Headlessness was not simply a trope common to the Obeah practices and the Ananse stories associated with British colonialism in Jamaica—it was also a more general trope in Afro-American cultures of the diaspora. The diffusion of this trope is evident in the folklorist William Bascom's typology of African and Afro-American tale types.[24] Of the fourteen tale types Bascom proposes, many feature the dismemberment of human or other animal bodies and three prominently feature headless protagonists. One of Bascom's most common tale types features a talking skull. Another involves a man motivated by a desire to imitate a sleeping bird, who asks his wife to cut off his head. Yet another relates the story of two animals, one who buys a dog, the other (usually a rabbit) who buys a dog's head because he does not have enough money to buy an entire dog.[25] The animals go hunting, and the dog kills a deer, but the rabbit runs to the deer, attaches his dog's head to it, and claims the deer for himself. In the Afro-American versions of this story, slavery and racism enter the plot when a master or boss appears on the scene to claim the deer as his property, at which point the rabbit claims that it was the other animal's dog that killed the deer because a dog's head cannot hunt.

As the tale type suggests, poverty and colonialism's literal disaggregation of bodies and cultures engender the capacity to swiftly negotiate alternate conceptions of agency: the rabbit's cleverness is his ability to inhabit simultaneously an Afro-American cosmology in which agency develops from the fragmentation of animal and human bodies and an Anglo-European cosmology in which agency depends on the integrity of the animal body. If the irony at play in Melville's iconography of headlessness is that the master does not know whether he inhabits a world of his own making or one made by his slaves, the Dog's Head story suggests that one of the powers developed by Obeah women and other black countercultures was the knowledge of inhabiting these worlds simultaneously as well as a capacity to move between them to produce conceptions of personhood and collectivity that were orthogonal to plantation colonialism even when they were situated within it.

Stories featuring bodily fragmentation, severed heads, and human beings in relation to animal life recur across sources as varied as Lewis's Ananse tales, Amos Tutuola's *Palm-Wine Drinkard* (which recounts the story of a "complete man" who only gains this completion by renting a series of body parts that must be returned each day to human and animal owners, leaving him a skull who lives in community of skulls), Aimé Césaire's Negritude poetry, and Patrick Chamoiseau's creole tales.[26] This catalogue of acephaly, bodily fragmentation, and animal–human relations makes clear the wide range of colonialisms across which these tales developed and circulated. Many of the tales Bascom cites as evidence were recorded in what were, at the time they were recorded, not only postslavery but also postcolonial nations (Haiti, Brazil, Columbia, Venezuela, and in some cases Cuba); others were recorded in still-colonial spaces (Jamaica until 1962, the Bahamas until 1973, and Martinique, Guadeloupe, and French Guiana, which all remain under French conservatorship).[27] This suggests the wide dispersal and persistence of the colonial problematic of disjointed bodies in decolonizing as well as supposedly postcolonial spaces.[28] In each case, the fact of headlessness, while certainly not in any simple sense positive, inaugurates a movement among competing cosmologies that testifies to the brutality of the worlds these figures negotiate and also allows the production of collectivities that, to varying degrees, stand in opposition to colonialism's market economy.

To expand this last point, consider Aimé Césaire's poem "Beau sang giclé" ("Beautiful Spurted Blood") (1960). As A. James Arnold notes and Patrick Chamoiseau makes clear in *Creole Tales* (1988), which uses Césaire's poem as its epigraph, "Beau sang giclé" atomizes a Creole story about a man, Ye, whose hungry family eats an enchanted bird only to vomit it back up, at which point the bird's disaggregated parts demand to be put back together, which the peasant family accomplishes through much labor and only by destroying their hut:[29]

> tête trophée membres lacérés
> dard assassin beau sang giclé
> ramages perdus rivages ravis

enfance enfance conte trop remué
l'aube sur sa chaîne mord féroce à naître
　　ô assassin attardé
l'oiseau aux plumes jadis plus belles que le passé
exige le compte de ses plumes dispersées.

trophy head lacerated limbs
deadly sting beautiful spurted blood
lost warblings ravished shores
childhoods childhoods a tale too stirred up
dawn on its chain ferocious snapping to be born
　　oh belated assassin
the bird with feathers once more beautiful than the past
demands an accounting for its scattered plumes.[30]

Césaire's opening invocation overlays the brutalization of parahuman bodies (*tête trophée membres lacérés*) and that of the bird whom they consume (*ramages perdus*). Neither has been reconstituted by the poem's close, which demands an accounting for the brutality and violence of colonialism, here conceived not only as the violence imposed on the colonized but also the violence performed by the colonized who contributed to the destruction of their own past and brutalized animal life.

One interpretation of Césaire's poem and parahuman tales more generally would suggest this accounting requires that parahumans become human beings characterized by completed and organic bodies closed off from other bodies. Yet it is not clear that Césaire's poem or Chamoiseau's rendition of it idealizes a move from parahumanity to humanity. In Chamoiseau's version, the body pieced together from vomited pieces cannot be the thing it was. Instead, at the story's close the fantasy of the completed body emerges as a "dream" that vests the impossibility of organicism with lyric intensity.[31] Ye and his wife effect resolution not through the consolidation of parts but through a further disaggregation: they tear apart their peasant hut, and in doing so produce a worlding of the local through which a collective of the dispossessed might be forged. This conclusion suggests an entanglement of parts (of bodies and places) and also of the past in the present, which allows the present to be expanded and reinhabited. Indeed, the predominant motion of Césaire's poem and Chamoiseau's tale is outward, not the inward movement of consolidation, integration, and systemization grounding the organicism that signals the completed body that Lewis associates with humanity.

The archive of parahumanity and the powers of parahumanity that I have assembled here allow us to move toward an interpretation of Goosee Shoo-shoo's story. The mother in Goosee Shoo-shoo's tale perceives her son's condition as an insufficiency and offers one plot line through which the story moves. Yet the figure of the owl suggests a rotation that offers another plot through which the condition of acephaly is revalued. Recognizing this second plot line requires noting that, from the start, the tale presumes the possibility of existing without a head, since the boy does in fact live without one. The body in parts does not, then, signal the nonexistence of death but rather the disaggregated and nonhuman existence that emerges in both Obeah practice and in the Dog's Head stories collected by Bascom. This second movement of plot suggests that fragmented and brutalized parahuman beings might gain adequacy not through identification with their supposed superiors or through the consolidation of the human body but by staying in parahumanity and staying in relation with other forms of animal life. The possibility of staying in parahumanity, a condition of fragmentation between the human and the animal, surfaces in the mother's idea that she might have a bird sit on her son's shoulder to bring him food and give him voice. The mother's sequence of conferences with the owl again suggests the possibility of staying in parahumanity and existing through cross-species relation.

Staying in parahumanity dissolves Fenelon's analogical relation of animals, slaves, and humans. Analogical relation is in fact no relation at all because it casts bodies as a mirrored but noncontiguous series. The movement from analogy afoot in the parahuman tales is complex and quite far ranging. The parahuman is not a closed body but an opened and dispersed series of parts. This entity does not rely on other forms of life as *analogical* support; instead, it relies on other proximate life-forms as *actual* support that allows the performance of necessary functions.

The key points here are, first, that the body is opened such that parts of this (non)body touch and participate in other forms of life and that other forms of life participate in it. This means, second, that parahumanity signals a relation grounded on the touching of life-forms, generally although not necessarily proximate life-forms. Third, the agency built through the touching of proximate life-forms does not allow a consolidation or closing of the parahuman body but a sufficiency built on the intimacies borne through incompletion. Fourth, this conjunction of parts allows sufficiencies that do not signal the merging of parts into new hybrid bodies. The intimacy of these bodies is a collation that comes together for a time but keeps open the possibility of other collations of parts (as we saw in the conclusion of the Dog's Head stories); as such, it never settles into hybridity, by which I mean the collation of life-forms to produce a new identity. This leads to the fifth significant aspect of parahumanity: it is not hybridity that offers a response to the brutal fragmentations of colonialism but the negotiation of intimacies that can endure for certain times and can also be contracted and dissolved. This last point indicates that parahumanity is distinct from postmodern theories of fragmentation and dissemination because it is not built on either fantasies of new kinds of hybrid identities or on a logic of unremitting dispersal; instead, it fantasizes the copresence of a series of negotiations that allow both construction and intimacy as well as dissolution and alienation.

Of course Goosee Shoo-shoo's story only partially and in its second plot allows this parahuman possibility. Even as the mother imagines and produces the possibility of parahumanity, she also fails to recognize the significance or the adequacy of this mode of personhood. Instead, she attempts to produce her son as a whole body. She attempts to close down a cross-species relation and to put in its place an intraspecies relation based on identification and kinship with masters. Yet even if parahumanity is not the story's main plot, its final scene makes clear the brutal consequences of identificatory strategies based on mimetic identification with white bodies. For all its circumlocutionary logic, this second movement of plot offers a quite clear didactic that is the story's primary thrust: it is forms of personhood based on analogy and mimesis that make animality and parahumanity into negative conditions. Instead of following the straight movement of plot and the straight line of desire, this second plot urges a circumlocution that would keep open the condition of parahumanity.

Disaggregating the Human

My claim that headlessness and fragmentation became part of a black countercultural response to colonialism is not the dominant way these stories have been read. In *La civilisation du bossale* (1978), Maryse Condé divides Creole tales into two types. First are those featuring animals, which she proposes date from the earliest period of colonialism and feature a speechless, dark, and closed universe governed by colonialism's absolute hierarchies and in which "tout vaut mieux qu'un nègre" (anything is better than a black person).[32] Second are those featuring human beings, which she suggests date from a later period and feature black agents who have opened the world but at the cost of interiorizing colonial stereotypes of blackness and identifying with whiteness.[33] Yet Lewis's Ananse tales as well as the tale types Bascom charts suggest a category of story that features parahuman agents in relation with both animal agents and human agents, and this indicates a third category of story.[34] In tales featuring parahumans, it is not the case that animals stand in for human beings, as Condé and other scholars have proposed is the case in animal tales.[35] Rather, only certain animals—for instance, the rabbit—possess traits associated with human beings (concepts of property, for instance) and yet are at the same time not equivalent to the human beings from whom they are distinguished. And these characters are clearly not equivalent to animal beings either.

As we have seen, parahuman tales are structured by a logic far more complex than a simple symbology in which animals in general can be understood to stand in for black persons. Nor is it the case that parahuman agents are entirely allied with unequivocally human agents such as masters, who Condé suggests are the locus of identification in the later Creole tales. In the parahuman tales, the master's cosmologies and conceptions of sufficiency are regarded with a good deal of irony, as we see in the Ananse tales Lewis records, which make clear the not precisely positive fate of the parahuman boy who gains a head and a princess or of the bad girl who believes black women must have heads.

One reason it is worth recognizing and keeping open the category of the parahuman is because colonials would have hated it. To be sure, the category of the parahuman was produced by colonial natural historical and economic practices. This production, however, took for granted that parahumanity was an absolutely negative condition. The conception of parahumanity as a negative but potentially (if never actually) surmountable condition shapes Lewis's interpretation of the Ananse tales he transcribes. For him, stories in which Afro-Americans cast themselves as headless bodies could only be read as evidence of their awareness of their insufficiency, even if he was vaguely aware that Obeah had incorporated the fact and image of the body in parts and especially of acephely as part of a strategy of resistance. The assumption that black human beings are, so to speak, headless is one of the most sustained subterranean claims of Lewis's Jamaican writings. Indeed, because Goosee Shoo-shoo lets her narrative culminate with bounties of rum and tobacco that move from the diegetic to the extradiegetic frame, at the story's close Lewis explicitly breaks into and closes off this extradiegetic scene of communal plenitude to offer a moral that he suggests brings closure to a story that would otherwise devolve into a purely appetitive performance: "people who may have the misfortune to be born without heads, may be assured that telling lies will prove the very worst cement for preserving heads of any description."

Toward the close of the *Journal,* Lewis makes explicit his belief that Afro-Americans' cognitive deficiencies make them parahuman: "Naturalists and physicians, philosophers and philanthropists, may argue and decide as they please; but certainly . . . there does seem to be a very great difference between the brain of a black person and a white one."[36] This judgment indicates the two conjoined conclusions Lewis makes about parahumans and parahuman tales. First, he takes such stories as evidence that black persons lack cogito, which he presents as a bodily incompletion that signals a distance from humanity and that at the same time renders them more impoverished than beasts, which are at least complete in their mindlessness. Second, he proposes that black persons' lack of cogito might be ameliorated by submitting to instruments of colonialism, ranging from the whip wielded by the king in Goosee Shoo-shoo's story to the rationalizing teleological arc imposed by his own narration.[37]

Of course, in order to understand the uses Lewis had for parahumans and parahuman tales it is necessary to emphasize that he was far less interested in Afro-American identificatory processes than in assuring the unequivocal humanity of Anglo-Europeans. A number of educated eighteenth- and early nineteenth-century Anglo-Europeans suspected that those beings categorized as *Homo sapiens* were unable to convincingly evince the wisdom for which this species was named. Developing this point, Giorgio Agamben has proposed that Linnaeus helped to produce a classificatory schematic that recognized the fundamental animality of human life. Linnaeus believed that at least some human beings were capable of displaying the cogito that distinguished human beings from other animals, but he also believed that not all humans were able to do this, regardless of their purported race. More precisely still, Linnaeus believed that producing one's humanity required recognizing one's animality, which is to say it required recognizing oneself as suspended between human and animal being, a suspension that is very close to parahumanity.[38]

There are two different kinds of parahumanity at play in Agamben's analysis, and everything depends on emphasizing the difference between those who do not recognize their animality—and because of this mystification are blindly suspended in their parahumanity—and those who do recognize their animality, and in this anagnorisis assert humanity as a condition borne of recognizing one's parahumanity. The two routes through which humanity verges on parahumanity suggest that human beings' parahumanity was a general eighteenth-century problematic, not one exclusively experienced by subaltern persons. However, in response to this general problematic, colonialism allowed a roundabout through which the problem could be bypassed. Neither Lewis nor Linnaeus explicitly claimed that Anglo-Europeans are complete and unquestionably human beings, but by suggesting that black persons mimic Anglo-Europeans to achieve sufficiency and humanity, both nonetheless implied that this is the case, thus moving around the fundamental incompletion that almost certainly undergirded Anglo-Europeans' own relation to their bodies, cogito, and humanity.

By focusing on Afro-Americans' and Africans' supposedly diminished cogito and their correspondingly lower form of humanity, Anglo-Europeans projected onto raced persons what they sensed (and sometimes stated) was a problem of a general human insufficiency. Then, in suggesting that these raced persons mimic Anglo-Europeans to achieve completion, they not only displaced the problem but also imagined themselves as the solution to that displaced problem. To be sure, the problem of human beings' insufficiency remained completely unresolved, but this play of projection and resolution must have been one of the psychological boons colonialism provided Anglo-Europeans. By shifting their focus from a more general parahumanity onto black agents' parahumanity, Lewis and other racial typologists cast black persons as paradigmatically parahuman beings. If Lewis believed that these parahuman beings should aspire toward the integration of body and mind he associated with Anglo-Europeans, this aspiration, however successfully realized, could only yield a pseudo-organicism accomplished by the superaddition of a prosthetic cogito. Thus, this sufficiency testifies to a prior and ongoing insufficiency that recalls black persons' nonorganicism and failed identificatory processes and that deflects attention from colonials' own parahumanity and fragmented identities. So if Agamben's analysis would suggest that the subaltern's parahumanity indexes a more general condition of parahumanity, Lewis's colonial narrative sublimates this general condition by producing a relation, at once teleological and hierarchical, between the categories animal, parahuman, human. Thus, while the human and humanism have often been offered as liberatory categories, Lewis's *Journal* suggests that the production of the human is often achieved through the racialization of parahumanity.[39]

Black abolitionist critiques of the racism of colonial apologists such as Lewis often extended to Anglo-Europeans the parahumanity that colonials attempted to reduce to racial blackness. Ottobah Cuguano's *Thoughts and Sentiments on the Evil of Slavery and Commerce of the Human Species* (1787) argues that Anglo-Europeans who participated in the slave trade were as insufficiently human as the Africans dislocated by the trade: the former lacked proper sentiment, the latter lacked education, and both lacked salvation.[40] Yet if Cuguano emphasizes that Africans were not unique in being insufficiently human, he nonetheless stays with Lewis's and other colonial apologists' argument that the parahuman is hierarchically below the human and should discipline herself through education and evangelicalism so as to become human. Thus, the hierarchy, mimesis, and telos that are central to Lewis's response to black parahumanity are equally central to Cuguano's rerouting of this colonial problematic. What's more, his concerted focus on the potential of Africans, Afro-Britons, and Afro-Americans to be improved through the superaddition of Anglo-European culture—particularly Christianity—does not challenge Lewis's diagnosis that organicism was a central property of human persons, and that black persons did not evince it.[41]

Frantz Fanon's famous claim that decolonization requires the substitution of one "species of men by another species of men" offers a way to keep open parahumanity as a category through which an alternative to colonialism could emerge. Indeed, the fragmentation of the body so central to parahumanity seems to be at play in Fanon's early theorizations of subaltern identity. In *Black Skin, White Masks* (1952), Fanon offers a brilliant alternative to Jacques Lacan's argument that a human being is distinguished from other animal beings by experiences of fragmentation, fantasized organicism, and alienation that first occur in what he calls the mirror stage.[42] For Lacan, the baby playing in the mirror comes to prefer the image of her whole body over her experience of her awkward and fragmented body. This identification with the mirror image is motivated by a desire to repress her sense of her disaggregated body, and the ego that results from this identification is not unified but divided as it depends on her preference of what is imaginary and outside herself over her actual body and experiences. This account of the entity that Lacan called the *subject* emerges through experiences of fragmentation and a resulting desire for an idealized organicism that is never attainable. The unattainability of this desired organicism, far from a reservoir of sheer negativity as it would have been for Lewis and even for Linnaeus, is constructive and pleasurable because it motivates the cultural production that is the mark of humanity.

Although Lacan's mirror stage is not primarily concerned with the distinction between animals and humans or with the soma as such and is wholly unconcerned with the effects of racism on subjectivity, it is the image of the organic if never actually attainable human body that grounds Lacan's dialectic of lack, desire, and cultural production, and it is precisely this image of the body that was so compromised for diasporic Africans in colonial plantation spaces. If it seems unlikely that slave and maroon children routinely played in front of mirrors (Lacan's mirror stage is not simply a metaphor, after all, but also a developmental stage that assumes the literalness of the scenario it poses), it also seems quite likely that even if a slave or maroon child were to pass through this stage this same child would have to contend with images of bodies like her own that were literally broken into pieces.

Colonized persons' historically distinct experience of fragmentation requires a retheorization of fragmentation, the body, and identity. In *Black Skin, White Masks*' engagement with Lacan, Fanon takes up this work of constructing a theory of personhood that accounts for the fact that the colonized's fragmented body meant that she could never have the fantasy of her body as an organic whole, which Lacan imagined necessary to the dialectic of subjectivity. In a digressive footnote, Fanon turns from Lacan's mirror to propose a sociological scene of reflection in which the "real Other for the white man is and will continue to be the black man. And conversely. Only for the white man The Other is perceived on the level of the body image, absolutely as the not-self."[43] Although this would seem to be a straightforward dialectic in which the black man and white man each serve as the imago for the other, Fanon believed the Antillean black man so identifies with whiteness that his imago is, like the white man's, black.[44]

As Françoise Vergès put it in her interpretation of Fanon's mirror stage, "although the hallucination should be the white for the Antillean, it is another black who serves this function."[45] In the midst of the colonial drama of animalization and identification with whiteness, there emerges another possibility not reducible to either: a mode of personhood based on the experience of fragmentation, an experience and imago half-recognized by black persons and repressed by Anglo-Europeans.

Fanon's response to Lacan's mirror stage turns on the image of the fragmented Afro-American body, making clear that it is precisely a historical difference of the body that is ultimately at stake in slipping the Lacanian scene. In the place of Lacan's infantile gestalt of the child, the mirror, and the image of the organic body, Fanon offered a series of colonial gestalts in which black and white persons encounter images of disaggregated, disorganized, and disappearing bodies. The anxious European who imagines "the Negro in the guise of a Satyr." The "theme of the Negro in certain deliriums" that "ranks with . . . zooscopy," which is to say the hallucination of animal bodies. The man who suffers from what Fanon calls heautophany, or the disaggregation of experiencing one's internal organs on the outside of the body. Antillean children who imagine Africans as beings who "cut off heads and collect human ears." A man so black that he can make himself disappear into the night.[46]

This series of images returns the parahuman's disaggregated body and its capacity to disorder colonial economic and environmental productions. Indeed, Fanon's account of the disordered and disordering black body is the imago for all persons in the colonies, suggesting a Creole mode of personhood that would overturn both the Lacanian and the colonial modes of identity which, for all their differences, are both dialectics of fragmentation and organicism through which human identity coheres over and against animal being. Fanon's series of colonial gestalts suggests that in the American colonies subject formation could not result from a dialectic in which an imago of the organic body served as the productive counterpoint to primary feelings of disaggregation. Rather, fragmentation, present from the start, could only be echoed, amplified, and redirected by the image of the fragmented body. Bodies in parts, in animal combinations, disappearing into atmospheres flash through Fanon's footnote and in his writing more broadly, suggesting that attending to American colonialisms should require a detour from a psychoanalytics of subject formation that depends on images of organicism and the closed, interiorized loop of psyche-body that could be put in distinction to the opened, unminded animal body. In its place, Fanon's work opens the possibility of a colonial form of personality not modeled on Anglo-European forms, and that takes as its starting ground parahumanity.

Yet Fanon, whose focus turned increasingly from the Antilles to northern African decolonization, does not fully draw out this logic. The form of personality that would emerge from the category of the parahuman almost entirely recedes in the main line of Fanon's work, which theorizes a Manichaean colonial scene marked by the absolute division of the humanity accorded whiteness from the animalization performed on blackness. By this analysis, any agency the colonized possessed comes from his rejection of animalization and the animal: when the colonizer "turns [the colonized] into an animal," the colonized "laughs to himself" as "he knows that he is not an animal; and it is precisely at the moment he realizes his humanity that he begins to sharpen the weapons with which he will secure its victory." According to Fanon's later analysis, a genuine postcolonialism closes down parahumanity and its fragmentations, rejects animality, and culminates in the attainment of a humanity characterized by organicism. Fanon argues that anticolonialism requires that anticolonial forces "develop" the "brains" of the people, "fill them with ideas, change them and make them into human beings."[47]

Fanon's evasion of the American scene and his eventual development of identificatory models that recoil from animality are no doubt one of the reasons that he describes Creole tales as well as botanical-religious practices like Obeah and Vodou as cultural formations that only have value for those with no other options (that is, no option of what he would regard as genuine—which is to say total—freedom). Dismissing both Creole and African valuations of parahumanity, Fanon proposes that when the colonized asserts his freedom "he will have no more call for his fancies. After centuries of unreality, after having wallowed in the most outlandish phantoms . . . the [decolonized subject] . . . does not hesitate to pour scorn upon the zombies of his ancestors, the horses with two heads, the dead who rise again, and the djinns who rush into your body while you yawn."[48] This refutation of the tales and implicit rejection of the concepts of the body, the parahuman, and the relation with the animal adumbrated therein remains the strongest tendency in critical interpretations of the tales, which understand parahumans as equivalent to animal characters. Thus A. James Arnold argues that diasporic Africans' tales testify to slaves' problematic "interiorization of the image their masters had of them. . . . Through their own folktales, the slaves had incorporated and expressed others' stereotypes of them."[49] By this reading, tales like Goosee Shoo-shoo's or the Dog's Head can only be interpreted as fundamentally tragic symptoms of the psychology of slavery that indicate a false consciousness that failed to address the systematic exploitations through which colonial capitalism developed.

The personhood that emerges from parahumans, which Fanon develops only to leave behind, is developed further by Glissant's concept of diversion. *Diversion* describes diasporic Africans' strategic redirection of colonial power dynamics through circumlocutionary styles of speech, story, and action. This circumlocution was partly an effort to avoid confronting colonizers in unwinnable head-on conflicts, but it had the effect of showing that experiences of fragmentation of the body could give rise to a cross-cultural style grounded on expansion and assembly that avoided the holocentrism, the teleological drive, and the hierarchies that structured colonial as well as many anticolonial social and political formations. In *Caribbean Discourse*, Glissant's primary example of this practice of diversion is the extreme simplification of Creole or black American speech. Although apparently childishly simple and straightforward, this speech proliferates ambiguity and misdirection, allowing movements to open up to the sides of its supposedly simple articulation.

Creole tales, including the parahuman tales, were another practice of diversion. Clearly these tales were acceptable to colonials like Lewis because they showed slaves performing the category of the parahuman that colonialism opened to them. Yet as Glissant's analysis suggests, the Creole tales were also modes of circumlocution that revealed the limits of the colonial world and then used the very performance of parahumanity to transgress these limits and produce cultural forms whose understandings of the body, the person, and resistance were officially forbidden, such as the headless Obeah woman's knowledge of the power of bodies and persons that had been broken into parts.[50] The Creole tale, Glissant has proposed, proceeds through flat, fragmented, and wholly unpsychologized characters who offer no "exemplary 'solutions.'" These flat, unpsychologized tales undermine chronologies that assume the linear movement of time or the consecration of ritual, and thus depart from the subjective as well as the spatial and temporal organizations of the Anglo-European nationalisms long associated with the emergence of modernity. If the largely print-based cultures of modern nationalism were grounded on the psychology of the subject, the linear movement of history, and the integrity of the community formed through myth and ritual, the largely oral cultures of creole resistance were not built on this ground. Although the tale always indicates the "place" of its telling, Glissant emphasizes that it offers no sense of either the "joy [or] pleasure of landscape" because "the landscape of the folktale is not meant to be inhabited." Continuing to press metaphors that emphasize Creole tales' departure from the topoi of habitation and the psychological and cultural formations that come from it, Glissant proposes the tale as a "place you pass through, [that] is not yet a country."[51]

That the Creole tale effects a passage that is "not yet" an arrival might seem to indicate its insufficiency, at least if it is imagined that passage must be understood as a transitive process that promises the attainment of place. However, the movement of diversion is not toward an arrival and emplacedness but an expansion that produces reversions and entanglements that relentlessly spatialize telos and in so doing produce a history structured by return, repetition, and pluralized genealogies.[52] Here, passage is not a completed movement through time, nor is it a completed movement from one point to the next. Instead, it involves a proliferation of movements across overlapping temporalities and spaces as well as a combination of fragments that form assemblages. To be sure, parahuman tales certainly do indicate some desire for transitive passage and organicisms of the body and the person. However, the tales' engagements with colonial histories reroute this desire and affect so as to (as Glissant's translator Betsy Wing puts it) produce a "real change of direction" that allows the "act of taking another path, or forcing evolution to grow in a different course."[53]

Glissant attended to the forms of culture and personhood that emerge from the fragmentations that subtend the American scene, but he remained almost entirely silent on parahumanisms, the relation of humans and parahumans to animals, and the fragmentations of the black body.[54] This silence is striking, given that Glissant's later work would elaborate on Deleuze and Guattari's philosophy, which proposed "becoming animal" as a performance that loosens subjective identifications with either human or animal forms of being to thereby open up lines of flight from the normative and mimetic subjectifications of modern capitalism. Glissant might well have shown diasporic Africans' experiences of bodily fragmentation and parahumanity as a central historical example of the emergence and potentials of a personhood modeled on neither humanity nor animality and that did not develop through the dialectics of subjectivity—a dialectics in which the production of the (human) subject requires the retrojection of that which is produced as not-human. But in Glissant's philosophy, parahumans do not exist, animals can only "mark the way," and it is mornes, seas, and swamps that evince agencies that traverse plantation capitalism.[55] This almost total silence might be striking, but it is not especially puzzling. The colonial infrastructures that produced the category of the parahuman produced effects so pernicious that even in twenty-first-century American and postcolonial studies it has not yet been possible to approach animals, animality, and parahumanity. Even as nonhumanisms have become increasingly common to other areas of cultural study, the animal and the parahuman remain at best dangerous categories for postcolonial and anticolonial movements and at worst intellectual and political dead ends.

Nonetheless, it is necessary to take up these dangerous intellectually and politically suspect categories. Looking to subalterns' inhabitation and resignification of parahumanity indicates that Afro-American cultural forms slipped the Manichaean colonial scene that was governed by two mimetic possibilities—that of imitating animals (the process of being guided like animals, which Fenelon demands) and that of imitating humans (the process of being guided like humans, which Lewis's colonial morality demands). Subaltern agents' inhabitation of parahumanity suggests a mode of personality that is not modeled on either of these categories, even as it responds to both. What's more, Fanon's recognition that the parahuman body functions as the imago of all persons in American plantation spaces anticipates a more far-ranging account of an American personality, one that recognizes the centrality of colonialism and racism to its production.

Parahuman tales recognize the historical power of the category of the human being and the related category of human rights that were ascendant in the eighteenth century. Yet they also recognize and forge a departure from the colonial economic and cultural engine through which the modern categories of the human and rights emerged. These tales suggest that claiming one's humanity was rather like writing in English in that it implicated the claimee inside the logic of colonialism. It is not so much that parahuman tales fantasize positions outside of colonial history but that they indicate modes of inhabiting the colonies and colonial histories that depart from the logic of colonialism and the modes of redress possible within it. Thus, parahumanity is not simply a critique of humanism or an ironic, even parodic, inhabitation of categories whose value was largely determined by colonialism. Either of these would be important moves, to be sure, in the ways that Afro-American practices of cakewalking or reperforming blackface minstrelsy aim to claim and restructure configurations of humanity and nationality grounded on racist fantasies of blackness.[56] The position of the parahuman offers a possibility a great deal more far-reaching than an irony culminating in a (postcolonial) humanism that emerges from and recalls its colonial history and that is at least partly purged of it. Recalling the etymology of the term *parahuman* makes clear that it cannot be prior to the human. Rather, it is a category that is parasitic on and thus after and also beside the human.

This means that what is most important about parahumanity as it was performed by black actors in the colonies is not that it leads the way to humanity, whether a humanity ironically or sincerely professed. What is most important is that it is an identificatory category that recalls yet is also beside and after the human and human rights. If colonials racialized the parahuman to produce the human as an exceptional and paradigmatically Anglo-European identity, the parahuman counters this normative humanism and the vision of the political it grounds. The category of the parahuman recalls and keeps open the category of the human and at the same time makes it a nonexceptional category, by which I mean configures it as a not entirely anthropic category. In so doing, it suggests an alternative to Agamben's analyses of states of exception that, whether they attend to anthropocentrism or structures of sovereignty, depend on a reification of the identity and category of the human that stops short of accounting for colonialism or ecology.[57]

Parasitic on and yet distinct from the human, the parahuman recognizes the horizontal relation and mutual dependence of life-forms, as we see in the second movement of plot in Goosee Shoo-shoo's story. The parahuman's nonexceptionality anticipates a mode of personality that inhabits and keeps open a number of antithetical modes of existence that might be inhabited, including that of the bird, the commodity, the human being, the specter, the monster, and even an atmospheric nonbeing (the possibility we see in Fanon's account of the black man who disappears into the night). The expression of one of these forms of existence does not signal the end of these other possible forms of existence. For instance, when in the conclusion of the Dog's Head story the rabbit expresses the colonial vision of the body in claiming that everyone knows dog's heads cannot hunt, I do not think we are to believe that at this moment the rabbit claims for himself the colonial's position or his vision of the body. Rather, the parahuman protagonist expresses the humanist position while keeping in play the parahuman vision of the agency of nonhuman forms and of bodies in parts. As this implies, this mode of personhood is not simply and primarily performative (although it is also that) because it is a negotiation of a number of identificatory possibilities that are kept open even after one possibility is expressed. Parahumanity is not, then, a suspension of the category of the human that involves not-choosing. It is a parasitism and a paradox in which choosing keeps the nonchosen in play as a potentiality.

Lest it seem that parahumanity is a speculative mode of personality that only occasionally and weakly flashed forth from the American colonies, I close with two examples that offer a genealogy of this mode of personhood in the colonies. First, the explicitly political example of the 1805 Haitian Constitution that was produced by a number of mostly nonliterate ex-slaves and persons of color and transcribed by secretaries. As a number of critics have recently shown, the Constitution challenges the colonialism and racism that formed the bedrock of other modern nationalisms.[58] Yet one of the most stunning moves of the Constitution is its departure from the rights of the human and of man that were the basis of other eighteenth-century nationalisms. Thomas Jefferson opened the U.S. Declaration of Independence within the course of "human events" and the National Assembly of France, in addition to more radical theorists (Robespierre, de Gouges), insisted on the rights of man or woman. However, this first Haitian Constitution opens by claiming the authority of "l'Etre-Suprême, devant qui les mortels sont égaux, et qui n'a répandu tant d'espèces de créatures différentes sur la surface du globe, qu'aux fins de manifester sa gloire . . . par la diversité de ses œuvres" ("the Supreme Being, before whom all mortals are equal, and who has scattered so many species of beings over the surface of the earth, with the sole goal of manifesting his glory . . . through the diversity of his works").[59] This is, then, not a claim for humans or for man in the modern secular sense of those terms but an articulation of equality in diversity on a species level that opens the terrain of the political to nonhumans.

Figure 10. Wifredo Lam, La jungla, 1943. Lam's painting of the cane field at night emphasizes the disaggregation of the parahuman body, its entwinement with vegetable forces, and the power that comes from this composition. Copyright Museum of Modern Art, New York / Art Resource.

That the preamble of this first Haitian Constitution detours from the enlightenment humanism of other early nationalisms indicates the possibility of a politics that is aware of the colonial legacy on which human rights depend and opens parahumanity not simply as a personal and identificatory possibility but also as a political possibility. This minoritarian politics and aesthetics that intermittently flashes up from the colonial and postcolonial archive crystallizes in the work of the Cuban painter Wifredo Lam. Descended from a Chinese father and an Afro-Cuban mother, Lam's maternal great-grandfather was a free black man who, when he tried to claim property, was punished by having his hand cut from his body and was known afterward as Mano Cortada.[60] This history of disaggregation that Lam drew from family history, from his godmother who practiced Santeria, and from observing the continuation of colonial racism in postindependence Cuba, indicates the experience of the body in parts was not simply the experience of slaves but also of free blacks and their Afro-Chinese descendants. The breaking of the body and the concomitant emergence of a series of copresent possibilities and cosmologies structures Lam's most famous painting, *La jungla* (Figure 10). Set in the light of cane fields at night, opened scissors in the far right corner indicate the drama of cutting that the painting responds to and spectacularizes. Indexing colonialism's breaking of bodies into parts such that it is impossible to categorically distinguish between human, animal, and vegetable bodies, the painting does not suggest that redressing the history of colonial brutality requires consolidating the parahuman so that it leads back or forward to the human body and human subjectivity. Arms extend into vegetable life that culminates in almost vibrating human feet. All this without forming any body with determinate contours. Instead, Lam offers an assemblage that proliferates heads, which are at once human, feline, divine, and profane, recalling the possibility expressed in both Obeah stories and in Melville's "Benito Cereno" that heads separated from bodies anticipate more-than-human collectivities. This more-than-human collectivity presaged by Lam's painting is not a collectivity that allows an entity to be everything at once. Rather, it iconicizes the body in parts as a dense and nearly oppressive opening through which distinct forms of life are also conjoined and copresent, producing a mode of personhood and politics not grounded on human exceptionalism.

4

Persons without Objects

Afro-American Materialisms from Fetishes to Personhood

Persons and Objects

Phillis Wheatley, much remarked-upon during her own life and later as the first African American poet, is particularly notable for the disappearances performed by her poetry. Her elegies never mourn the end of life on earth, as life on earth is scarcely described and best left behind. And she hardly bothers spinning fancies about the spring, as the seasons pass swiftly into meditations on failure ("Imagination," "A Hymn to Morning") or, in her more optimistic poems, the spiritual union of persons with God ("To a Lady on the Death of her Husband," "A Funeral Poem on the Death of C.E."). When her poems acknowledge the colonial natural world—the hurricanes of the tropics, the plants tossed by these hurricanes, New England's cold, or Jamaica's rocks and "fervid shores"—it is as bare locative facts that quickly give way to spiritual or metaphysical abstractions ("To a LADY on her remarkable Preservation in an Hurricane in *North-Carolina*," "On Imagination," "To a LADY on her coming to North-America with her Son, for the Recovery of her Health").

Her life also reads as a series of removes. In the letters that survive, Wheatley reveals little about herself. In the only known portrait, a profile, she looks up and out of the frame. And after bearing three children who died soon after their births, she died herself at 31, buried in an unmarked grave, the poems that were to make a second volume of her poetry almost all lost. Her first biographer, Margaretta Matilda Odell, relates that Wheatley had poor recollective powers: although she was probably seven when she was kidnapped from Africa and brought first to the West Indies and then to Boston, she claimed to remember little about her African childhood other than her mother pouring water before the sun at its rising. She required pen and paper to recall the fancy of one moment in a later one.

Odell proposes that the problem was not that Wheatley was completely without memory since otherwise she could not have mastered English, Latin, and after that poetic form. Rather she suggests that Wheatley's peculiarly blank memory resulted either from her unusual mental acuity or from her "lack of early discipline," presumably in Africa where one childish fancy was allowed to pass absurdly into the next without being organized by associative chains of reason or recollection.[1]

A receding biographical subject, Wheatley sometimes seems to remain only as an echo of the colonial economic and aesthetic forms that so brutally shaped her life. This echoic quality reverberates through her only published collection, *Poems on Various Subjects* (1773),[2] which hews so closely to the themes and forms of Milton and Pope that critics have judged it derivative or, at best, an example of how the mimicry of the dispossessed can ironize colonial forms. But even this latter reading is not quite apt as she does not return to colonialism its history and forms entire. If Wheatley's poems frequently but fleetingly evoke colonial natural history and political events, early national pageantry, and accounts of mercantilistic exchange, all of which were common to the neoclassical traditions in which she participated (for instance, consider Milton's "Lycidas," Thompson's "Four Seasons," Pope's "Rape of the Lock," or Barlow's "Columbiad"), they also strive toward a spiritualized refinement that rarefies the heft of this world. Repeatedly, her poems juxtapose darkness and light, the low and the high, earthly pleasures and divine illumination, not only giving precedence to the latter terms but imagining poems as vehicles through which this refinement might be achieved ("On Being Transported from Africa to America").[3]

My claim that Wheatley's poems systematically attempt to convert the material into the ethereal and echoic might seem counterintuitive, particularly in light of recent criticism that has positioned Wheatley in relation to an African material history and diasporic politics. For instance, one of her best readers, John C. Shields, argues that Wheatley's primary poetic image is the sun, an image he proposes fuses an African culture of sun worship to classical themes.[4] Yet if Wheatley is keenly interested in the sun, it is not as a corpuscular force or as a way of referencing African or any other classical tradition but as the vehicle through which she arrives at her most favored abstraction, "Light," which she conceives as an absolute etherealization most generally available not in poetry but in death, which she represents as the complete elimination of all things earthly ("Thoughts on . . . Providence," "To a Lady on the Death of her Husband," and "On the Death of a Young Lady of Five Years of Age").[5] Sublimating the worldly, Wheatley's poems fantasize an ethereal realm in which the division of spirit and matter and subjects and objects that structured reigning seventeenth- and eighteenth-century philosophy, aesthetics, and economics had been somehow resolved in favor of the immaterial.[6]

If Wheatley's interest in rarefaction is most obviously evident in her persistent theme of etherealization, a small body of her poems performs another, linked sort of rarefaction: contracting and stalling the poetic forms they evoke. "On Imagination," for instance, recalls Milton's epic ambitions only to announce it will not (or cannot) attempt an epic ambit. This habit of rarefying classical and neoclassical forms is evident in her revision of Ovid's and then Pope's Niobe, the tale of a pagan queen who believes her mortal body as well as her possessions are divine but is punished for this belief when Apollo (sometimes in conjunction with Artemis) kills all fourteen of her children and then turns Niobe into a stone whose only human attribute is that it weeps. The final moment of this drama conveys the crucial irony in which the woman who refuses to esteem the divine over the human is punished by being transformed into seemingly brute matter. While this theme as well this closing irony would seem to be entirely amenable to Wheatley's interest in an ideality that must be divided from any materiality, Wheatley stops her rendition before the moment Niobe turns to stone, staying with her grief.[7] That Wheatley stops just short of the climactic moment that completes virtually all narrative accounts of Niobe is no doubt partly because her poem means to reference Richard Wilson's painting of Niobe,[8] which like other neoclassical renditions of this scene (for instance, Jacques-Louis David's), depicts Niobe surrounded by her dead and dying children.

Wheatley's ekphrasis partly explains her stalling of Niobe's narrative arc, but this suspension that closes down her favorite theme of rarefaction also closes down the conceit that gives shape to Ovid's verse and that also sustained commodity production and exchange in the eighteenth-century colonial world: a person could become a thing. This possibility that persons might become things had a good deal of significance in the colonial moment in which she writes, particularly for Africans and African Americans who were routinely valued as objects. Because this conversion of persons into things was so central to the colonial world in and about which she wrote, her avoidance of this theme invites close attention to the relation presumed to bind persons to things in the late eighteenth-century Atlantic.[9]

To be sure, a contemplation of the relations between persons and things is not at all the project that motivates Wheatley's rarefactions. In producing a poetry that converts the substantial into the ethereal and Caliban into Ariel, Wheatley distinguishes herself as a spiritual agent who removes herself from the materialism that eighteenth-century New Englanders often condemned as endemic to colonial cultures and that eighteenth-century Anglo-Europeans more generally saw as a particular liability for persons of African descent, who were not only objects themselves but were charged with the improper valuation of material objects. Yet if Wheatley "sets roots only in the sacred of the air and evanescence," as Édouard Glissant argued about another of the denizens of the black Atlantic,[10] we can follow her pattern of rarefaction to arrive at a question that turns her rarefactions back toward the materialisms that are their ultimate source: what were the cosmologies of spirit and matter circulating in the black Atlantic, and how might accounting for these mythologies and the practices that derived from them change how we understand political possibility not simply for denizens of the black Atlantic but also for Anglo-Europeans also moving through and producing it?

In posing and pursuing this question, I mean to suggest that in addition to being interpreted as an avatar of an Afro-American evangelicalism that moves in rough parallel to or is part of Anglo-European evangelical traditions, Wheatley might be conceived as a portal through which we might pass to retheorize the relation between persons and objects in the Atlantic world. My suggestion is that Wheatley's turn from materiality returns us again to materiality and allows a reconsideration of the status of materiality, objects, and objectivity in early Afro-American culture. By staying with this rather counterintuitive interpretation of Wheatley and a series of other early black evangelical writers, including John Marrant, John Jea, and Mary Prince, whom I join with eighteenth-century Anglo-European travel writers and later theorists of Afro-American culture, I bring to light a submerged tradition of Afro-American spiritualism that shows how we might trace an Afro-American personhood that emerges in relation to, and not against, the materiality of objects, particularly the most maligned objected of the diaspora: the Afro-American fetish.

Diasporic Africans' production of fetishes recognized that objects, far from being wordless or mute, could be conceived as dense interiorities or constellations of force that could store, process, and actualize information and that were also crucial to the production of the collectivities, or assemblages, through which personhood was articulated. In using the term *assemblage* to describe diasporic African production and personhood, I draw on the philosophy of Gilles Deleuze and Manuel de Landa, which departs from the assumption that persons or politics can be understood as arising from the dyadic exchanges of subjects and objects. Instead, they propose that both subjects and objects might be derived from the exchanges of bodies (not simply human), actions, and passions as well as the effects of bodies interacting, which together compose entities (including persons) that are "characterized by *relations of exteriority.*"[11] This theory of the assemblage elucidates a central characteristic of the diasporic African personhood I take as my theme in this chapter: namely, that a person is not an insular being distinct from entities and forces outside of herself but an entity whose component parts are always pulled into other exchanges. Here, subjects and objects are recalibrated as assemblages that are animate and entangling. It then follows that personhood is neither an a priori category nor a mode of being oppositional to objects, but a composition produced through the relation of (para)humans, artifacts, and ecological forces.[12]

The Fetish in the Eighteenth Century

Analyzing the emergence of this mode of diasporic personhood requires an investigation of the fetish, a term and concept that was used by Anglo-European colonials to discount African and Afro-American practices and artifacts. During the early years of the eighteenth century, the term *fetish* passed from Portuguese merchants into Dutch, English, and French parlance via the writings of colonial factors, especially Willem Bosman's *New and Accurate Description of the Coast of Guinea* (1704), as well as the narratives and letters of slavers and explorers including John Adams, John Newton, and William Smith.[13] Over the course of the century, the term passed from mercantilistic and colonial contexts and into philosophical ones such as Charles de Brosses's *Du culte des dieux fetiches* (1760) and Kant's *Observations on the Feeling of the Beautiful and Sublime* (1764). By the end of the century, the terms *fetish* and *fetishism* were explicitly pejorative and exclusively associated with Africans in and out of the Americas. However, as William Pietz's analysis of the colonial etymology of the term *fetish* and the practices associated with it make clear, it must be understood as a colonial term that signifies the deeply personalized (or cathected) techne produced by Africans *and* Anglo-Europeans in the Atlantic world.[14]

Drawing on Pietz's argument that the term *fetish* was born of and testified to cross-cultural interactions, Srinivas Aravamudan argues that in Olaudah Equiano's *Interesting Narrative of the Life of Olaudah Equiano, or Gustavus Vassa, the African* (1789) the term and practice of fetishism do not exclusively signify African technologies. By his telling, Equiano was born an Eboe and kidnapped into slavery as a child; after years spent laboring on ships in the Atlantic world, he eventually purchased his freedom and would go on to produce the abolitionist autobiography *Interesting Narrative*. Positioning himself between African and Anglo cultures, Equiano suggests that fetishes include the "implements" used by African magicians who were also doctors as well as Anglo-European technologies, particularly that of the book.[15] Given that Pietz proposes fetishes as material constructions that forge "an identity . . . between certain otherwise heterogeneous things" that are then incorporated into personhood,[16] it follows that an African priest's techne and an Anglo-European book are both fetishes. After all, they are both material constructions that bring together heterogeneous entities—gourds, herbs, soil, lyric, nails, paper, glue, narrative, print—and that, after their production, become quasi-autonomous entities that nonetheless continue to impact the persons who produce and come into contact with them.

Books, clocks, medicinal packets, and memory jars might all equally be fetishes. However, as Aravamudan proposes, the "part of fetishism that was compatible with economics was eventually absorbed by global trade, and those African practices that were . . . not end-oriented and commercial . . . were deemed . . . 'fetishistic' in a pejorative sense."[17] By this analysis, the term *fetish* designates relations between persons and things that are part of and absorbed into capitalist exchange (a designation that borders on the Marxist notion of the fetish that is more familiar to scholars) and at the same time it designates "non end-oriented" relations between persons and things that cannot be incorporated into capitalism and that were identified with Africans. In recovering this second designation of the fetish, Pietz proposes that fetishes, especially when associated with Africans in the diaspora (which is to say, that part of exchange not entirely incorporated into capitalism), indicate a deviant materialism that precedes

and exceeds capitalist exchange.[18] The potential of this deviant materialism to counter the concepts of persons, objects, and exchange on which
colonial capitalism depended was half recognized by eighteenth- and early
nineteenth-century Anglo-Europeans, which is part of the reason they so
consistently and unequivocally denounced African fetishism as evidence
of African irrationalism.

In documenting the cross-cultural significance of fetishes, both Pietz's
and Aravamudan's readings refuse the use of *fetish* as a pejorative term, in
the process bringing to the foreground a complex, nondialectically structured Atlantic world in which books cannot be interpreted as signs of
Anglo-European rationalism and magic cannot be interpreted as signs
of African and Afro-American primitivism. Drawing on their expansion
of the meaning and practice of fetishism in the eighteenth century, I turn to
fetishes that were not books but were, instead, widely recognized by
Anglo-Europeans as fetishes in the eighteenth and nineteenth centuries:
diasporic African artifacts. In turning to these artifacts, I hope, most simply, to add to the complexity of critical understandings of the Atlantic
world. I also hope this shift from the book to the black-produced artifact
helps to elaborate those aspects of fetishism that exceed and pass out of
Atlantic exchange, in the process indicating modes of personhood distinct
from those predicated on the consumption and manipulation of techne
through which the material was systematically divided from the spiritual.

Accounting for these artifacts is a complex enterprise. Historians agree
that fetishes ranging from amulets to larger vessels were used by Africans
in the diaspora, but their knowledge of these fetishes is based largely on
texts written by Anglo-Europeans.[19] These are the same texts that not only
wholly covered over the Anglo-European fetishism that Pietz and Aravamudan document but that also posited Africans' use of fetishes as one of
the reasons they could be excluded from the category of the human and
valued as products akin to objects and animals. The French naval officer
Dralsé de Grandpierre, for instance, proposed that African fetishism was a
process of turning "ridiculous objects into gods" that "give[s] us the right
to consider them less as men than as animals."[20] The Martinique-born
natural historian Moreau de Saint-Méry proposes that fetishism made
Saint-Domingue's black population unfit for "analyzing religious ideas intellectually" because they "turn all their belief to external manifestations."[21]

In response to Anglo-Europeans' consolidating position that fetishism
was distinctly African, primitive, and evidence of a failure to rationally

distinguish between the interiority of spiritual life and the exteriority of material life, eighteenth-century black writing is almost entirely silent. Like Wheatley's poems, this body of writing stops short before the object world. Indeed, Aravamudan would have difficulty getting any other eighteenth-century black-authored text to yield a reading of the fetish as the product of cross-cultural exchange because Equiano's *Interesting Narrative* is perhaps the only one to attend to the range of fetishes—from African religious artifacts, to clocks, to books, to commodities—that circulated in eighteenth-century Atlantic cultures. From Wheatley's poems through John Jea's and John Marrant's spiritual autobiographies to Ottobah Cugoano's manifesto for human rights, eighteenth-century black writing says almost nothing about fetishes and fetishism, although the narrative arc common to this body of work—an arc that moves away from materialism and the natural world and toward spiritualized and dematerialized systems—implicitly disavows fetishism. The prevalence of this narrative arc no doubt informs Henry Louis Gates's reading of eighteenth-century black writing through the trope of the talking book.[22] In deploying this trope, eighteenth-century black writers emphasize the distance between a former state in which they believed that books could talk and a present state in which they recognize books as belonging to the category of Anglo-European technological objects that mediate between brute nature and spirit. Gates suggests that black authors who traverse this distance mark their passage from the world of objects to enter into a print-mediated subjectivity through which they critique the colonial expectation that black persons could be objects, and at the same time they reinscribe the dialectic between objects and subjects.[23]

Gates's argument performed the tremendously important work of making black writing part of an eighteenth-century Enlightenment tradition. However, it is now necessary to trace a different mode of personhood from that documented by Gates. Instead of channeling black writing's silence on fetishism into a progressive narrative as Gates did, it is possible to argue that this silence suspends and even departs from transformational narratives.[24] Instead of disavowing fetishes and other material objects, eighteenth- and early nineteenth-century black-produced texts refract the material world into biblical history, in the process transforming both materiality and biblical history as well as the linear notion of history and influence Gates presumes.

For instance, John Jea begins his *Life, History and Unparalleled Sufferings* (1811) with a scene of cultivation that, instead of detailing the specificity of the New York plantation on which he lives, moves quickly to an account of three plagues—worms, then caterpillars and locusts, and finally a storm—that destroy his master's crops. If the particularities of the colonial natural world are encoded into the cycling of biblical history, Jea also suggests that evangelical Africans are particularly able readers of the typologies thereby produced. Noting that his master "remained ignorant of the hand of God being in these judgements," Jea indicates that cycles of profit and loss and the effects of insects and storms are judgments.[25] While these events are incorrectly relegated to secular history by his Anglo-European master, Jea suggests they are correctly interpreted by Afro-Americans tasked with working his master's plantations. In her *History* (1831), Mary Prince also posits a typological natural world, suggesting that a flood that destroys houses and terrain on Turk's Island is divine retribution for the "wickedness" of the "Buckra men" who twice pulled down a religious alcove that the slaves had built from "boughs and leaves."[26]

Four decades before Prince, John Marrant also passed colonial spaces into biblical typologies when he described his travels though South Carolina and Georgia in terms of the Book of Daniel, figuring himself in the position of Nebuchadnezzar, the king, idolator, madman, and visionary. Like Nebuchadnezzar, Marrant ate grass like a horse, and afterward he was "directed to a puddle of water very muddy, which some wild pigs had just left." Seeing this, he "kneeled down, and asked the Lord to bless it to me, so I drank both mud and water mixed together, and being satisfied I . . . went on my way rejoicing."[27] Marrant's encoding of the landscapes of the American plantation zone through biblical history seems conventionally typological, but in figuring himself not as the Jewish Daniel but as the pagan Nebuchadnezzar he evokes a past of fetishism that is both biblical (insofar as Nebuchadnezzar was an idol maker whom eighteenth-century readers might well have recognized as a fetishist)[28] and extrabiblical (insofar as fetishism evoked a non-Christian cosmology that had particular significance in the late eighteenth century, even if this significance was generally occluded in Afro-Americans' writing and dismissed in Anglo-Europeans' writing). Thus, while Marrant's typological description of American plantation spaces joins Wheatley's poetry in covering over the natural world and fetishistic practice, it at the same time joins biblical history with fetishistic practice.

When Marrant adopts the perspective of Nebuchadnezzar, an adoption that also occurs in Jea's narrative, he complicates the rectilinear Enlightenment narrative that persists into the present. Fetishism, which is latent in the choice of Nebuchadnezzar's perspective, remains neither past nor present but potential. It glimmers in the strangeness that is a notable undercurrent in early African American writing.[29] This strangeness is evident when Jea narrates that his Native American wife suffocated their child because of his "being so religious," as though Afro-American and Native American religious beliefs routinely gave rise to scenes of brutal excess so entirely ordinary as to warrant only the flattest narration.[30] This strangeness is also evident in Marrant's claim that during his travels across southern lowlands he dressed in the "skins of wild beasts . . . a long pendant down my back, a sash round my middle without breeches, and a tomahawk by my side"; and it is evident in his suggestion that the practice of New England Evangelicalism might be a bloody, bodily remaking.[31]

The typological natural world that these early black prose writers present divagates from the meticulously detailed natural histories that Anglo-Europeans produced of these same places. Marrant's, Jea's, and Prince's Americas are not the dazzlingly fecund and splendorous landscapes that covered over the brutality of life in plantation spaces. Rather, this black-produced literary tradition depicts a stark natural world in which a biblical temporality of cataclysm and apocalypse returns. This tradition crosses into the Anglo-European one when Thomas Jefferson slid from natural history to a divine history of retribution in Query 18 of *Notes on Virginia* (1785) and, even more spectacularly, years later when Jefferson's fellow Virginian Thomas Gray produced a fabulously typological account of Nat Turner (an account that supposedly transcribes Turner's "confession" directly, although, as numerous scholars have noted, this is not the case).[32] Turner, having seen drops of blood on the corn, learned to read on the "leaves in the woods hieroglyphic characters, and numbers, with the forms of men in different attitudes, portrayed in blood."[33] Gray, following Turner, figured corn and leaves not as commodities but as media through which divine retribution is prefigured and then effected.

Marrant, Jea, Prince, and Turner all suggested that retribution for slavery would be effected in and through the natural world, a natural world in which they encoded and reinscribed the fetish in an Evangelical form that it also exceeds. These writers suggested that this retribution would be divine, but they also obliquely suggested that alcoves built of tree boughs as well as the capacity to read leaves engendered a resistance to colonialism that is immanent and not transcendent, an immanence clear in Gray's ventriloquization of Nat Turner's declaration that he had taken up Christ's yoke in order to make God's time into the present.[34] Eighteenth- and early nineteenth-century black writers' oblique references to fetishism and the relation to the natural world through which resistance to the plantation form was waged make visible a threshold that might be passed to instantiate a natural world that was neither that of biblical typology (with its dissolution of the present into the past and the future) nor that of natural history (with its splendorous collection of commodities and sublimities) but radiant with the combinatory power discussed in preceding chapters.

Many Afro-Americans crossed this threshold: black healers and poisoners and fetish-makers whose practices are often noted, if only briefly, in eighteenth-century Anglo-Europeans' natural histories. Now, I push my own analysis across the threshold adumbrated by early black Atlantic writing by turning to the Anglo-European naturalists who, if they generally intended their discourse on fetishism to justify the enslavement of Africans, also inadvertently contributed to the process of producing genealogies of diasporic African practice and resistance. Moreau de Saint-Méry complains that Africans in the colony combine "herbs, animal hair, bits of horn, and other things just as disgusting" into packets that they believed to function as *gardes corps*.[35] Moreau de Saint-Méry's qualification that these packets are "disgusting" makes clear his contribution to an Anglo-European tradition that diminished the significance of diasporic Africans' cosmologies and that ignored Anglo-European fetishisms. Still, his suggestion that Africans thought of fetishes as body guards, or as extensions of their bodies that existed outside of their bodies, elucidates three points central to African and Afro-American conception of fetishes. First, (para)human bodies exist in charged relation to fetish objects. Second, fetishes are not objects in the sense becoming increasingly common to Anglo-Europeans because they are animate forces with power over (para)human bodies. Third, fetishism emphasizes that power develops from the relation of disparate bodies and substances: the fetish is, above all, a combination of things—those things that are integrated into the fetish itself and those things and forces in which the fetish participates in the world beyond itself. Moreau de Saint-Méry inadvertently recognizes that diasporic African fetishes propose an intense relation of persons to the natural world whereby the (para)human body and person, instead of being delimited by

the skin-envelope, extends into the natural world, and whereby consciousness, instead of being a power that remains fundamentally distinct from
materiality, emerges from extensions in space through which one body is
brought into relation with other bodies and forces.[36]

Anglo-European writers attending to the American tropics were continually running up against the possibility that diasporic Africans' fetishes
evinced an alternate way of conceiving personhood. The British writer
William Earle Jr.'s novel *Obi, or The History of Three-Fingered Jack* (1800),
which he intended as an argument for the abolition of slavery and the inclusion of Africans within a relatively radical version of the rights of man,
inadvertently became an account of the fetishism it names in its title. *Obi*
(Obeah) was the name for the syncretic botanical and religious practice of
slaves and maroons in English-speaking American colonies, especially Jamaica. In its nominative sense, *Obi* can also be a word designating a fetish
as well as an oath binding together diasporic Africans.[37] Earle's novel fic-
tionalizes the 1780 rebellion of a Jamaican slave who, along with at least
fifty-eight other slaves in Jamaica's St. Thomas Parish, self-emancipated
and established a maroon community in the Blue Mountains. The novel
develops through two often-mirrored protagonists: the slave-become-
maroon Three-Fingered Jack and the British traveler George, who, in letters to a correspondent in England, recounts the tense situation in colonial Jamaica. George attempts to make African fetishism into an
ethnographic detail, documenting the practices of an Obeah practitioner
named Bashra as well as describing Jack's guardian fetish, which Earle,
cribbing the account of the British doctor Benjamin Mosley, details as a
"goat's horn, filled with a compound of grave dirt, ashes, the blood of a
black cat, and human fat; all mixed into a kind of paste."[38]

Earle's description of Jack's "obi" strives for dispassionate observation:
the fetish is nothing but a "horn" that is "filled with a 'compound.'" However, his moderate ethnographic and political project is derailed by his
concern with fetishes and fetishism. The novel opens with George's confession that Jack's presence on the island draws him into reveries in which
he fears that "there is not a *thing* called Jack whether a smoke-jack, a boot-
jack, or any other jack, but acts as a spell upon my senses and sets me on
the fret at the bare mention of it."[39] Imagining that Jack diffuses his rebellious intent into the material world, George fears the emergence of what
he sees as an Afrocentric colonial terrain in which things-become-animate-
matter will destroy the plantation system. This fantasy indicates an anx-

ious colonial recognition that diasporic African artifactual and botanical practices impacted white men who felt their own bodies existed in relation to charged "things."

Obi's opening scene registers the intersection of diasporic African and Anglo-European deviant materialisms that understood agency and anima as dispersed and not consolidated in the human body. Later in the novel, when George elaborates on the practice of Obeah, the text verges on a position that more aptly describes diasporic Africans' relation to the nonhuman world. Describing the relation of the Obeah-man, Bashra, to the terrain that surrounds him and that he draws on in the making of fetishes, George shows Bashra to be so infolded in the tropics' weaving of trees, animals, and smells that he is not in this ecology but fully of it: "Closely hid from the most penetrating eye, by the thick foliage of interwoven trees, stood the small sequestered hut of the Obiah-practitioner, Bashra, wrinkled and deformed. Snails drew their slimy train upon his shriveled feet, and lizards and vipers filled the air of his hut with foul uncleanliness."[40] Although Earle almost certainly intends this description as a discomfiting ethnographic detail, it also presents the terrain as continuous with an intensely materialized black body that holds other natural bodies within its folds. The novel's opening account of fetishism proceeds as though Jack could project his anima from his body and into other material forms; this later scene records a possibility that is simpler and gets at one of the characteristics of fetishism: the interaction between (para)human and other bodies in an ecology is constitutive of personhood.[41]

A partial knowledge of Afro-American fetish use circulates in Earle's account of Obeah in Jamaica. Most obviously, he recognizes the entanglements binding together plantation materialities. Moreover, he recognizes the power of diasporic African fetishes, which are the portion of Atlantic exchange that exceeds economic exchange and that inaugurates a recalibration of a the relations among (para)humans and other sorts of bodies. In short, Anglo-European writings on African fetishism—which Moreau de Saint-Méry conceives as a (para)human body and mind under the sway of external bodies and which Earle conceives as an imbrication of (para)human bodies in the natural world that possesses them—conceive fetishism as a practice through which persons were made part of and produced through plantation ecologies. If this concept of personhood were to apply to all persons in plantation spaces, it would undermine Anglo-Europeans' sense of themselves as autonomous agents disconnected from other animate forces. The attention Anglo-Europeans paid to the practice of fetishism is evident in the sheer volume of names they used to describe fetishes: their works documented obi, kaperlatas, makandals (after the St. Dominguan maroon and poisoner Makandal), gris-gris, and charms.[42] These names each postulate a practice or historical personage as an object, as though the practice of nominalizing might crystallize persons and objects as distinct categories, denying the necessary and constitutive exchange between them. Yet the sheer volume of these names for fetishes also suggests a colonial anxiety that Anglo-European conventions of personhood and objecthood were both impossible for all who passed through plantation ecologies.

Fetishism in the Diaspora

In order to counter colonial Anglo-Europeans' efforts to turn assemblages into inanimate objects and to account for African and Afro-American conceptions of black-produced fetishes, I turn now to the African and Afro-American accounts of fetishism that were written and recorded later in the nineteenth century and in the twentieth century. This move from one historical moment to the next is necessary in constructing early Afro-American intellectual histories, which, although they are refracted in the writings of Wheatley, Marrant, Jea, and Prince, were not solely or even primarily recorded in print cultures but rather in oral cultures. This move to later accounts of fetish production that often draw on oral cultures may be a historical leap, but Richard Price's work on maroon historiography and Annette Gordon-Reed's work on Jefferson's black descendents have made clear that oral histories offer deeply relevant and often quite accurate accounts of events and beliefs articulated in earlier moments.[43] As early Americanist scholars are increasingly recognizing, reading print sources for traces of orality and attending to oral stories that were recorded later—often on aural technologies such as the Magnetophon or the phonograph—is necessary to address questions, including those of Afro-American agency, that are occluded or only glancingly addressed when we rely too exclusively on historically specific print sources.

At the request of a Dutch missionary, in 1915 the Kongolese writer Nsemi Isaki offered an account of African fetish use in which he emphasized the fetish as a pharmacon. *Nkisi* (the Kongolese word for fetish) is always a composite fabrication that includes "medicines" that work to preserve life.[44] Anthropologist Wyatt MacGaffey explains that a fetish is a combination of medicines and materials notable for its "sheer intricacy of texture and detail."[45] Although museums often display fetishes that are representational (figures of men or dogs), MacGaffey stresses that these objects, "whether in the form of wooden figures, snail shells, raffia bags, or clay pots, are containers for 'medicines' that empower them. Without medicines the thing is just a statue or a pot, as the case may be."[46] In addition to functioning as a medicinal assemblage, Isaki explained that "the composition of nkisi," which includes both "ingredients and songs," "must follow the original model."[47] In this account, the construction of fetish is a process that includes a pharmacological element (ingredients) and a lyric one (song) and follows a specific protocol, a specific order of combination that references (indeed, repeats) an original moment of combination.[48]

These African accounts, like the eighteenth-century Anglo-European ones, suggest black-produced fetishes as nonrepresentational and pharmacological artifacts that are intensely personalized and whose production responds to the environments in which they are made. To move further into this account of the fetish, attending particularly to its relation to personhood and resistance, I turn to one of the first extended black-authored accounts of fetishes.[49] In the serialized novel *Blake; or, The Huts of America* (1859–62) Martin Delany describes a fetish used by one of Nat Turner's followers who had become a denizen of Virginia's Dismal Swamp. Delany's account of this fetish is decidedly ambivalent.[50]

> He took from a gourd of antiquated appearance which hung against the wall in his hut, many articles of a mysterious character, some resembling bits of woolen yarn, onionskins, oystershells, finger and toenails, eggshells, and scales which he declared to be from very dangerous serpents, but which *closely resembled, and were believed to be* those of innocent and harmless fish, with broken iron nails. These he turned over and over again in his hands, closely inspecting them through a fragment of green bottle glass, which he claimed to be a mysterious and precious "blue stone" got at a peculiar and unknown spot in the Swamp, whither by a special faith he was led—and ever after unable to find the same spot—putting them again into the gourd, the end of the neck being cut off so as to form a bottle, he rattled the "goombah," as he termed it, as if endeavoring to frighten his guest.[51]

Introducing this fetish through a narrator who makes clear that his under-standing of this artifact is distinct from that of the conjure man, Delany allows black fetishism to be interpreted as a superstitious, which is to say lamentable, mode of belief. In early American print cultures, African reli-gious practices that were not Christianity were typically dismissed as delu-sional. Although Delany begins by narrating fetishistic practice as evinc-ing a certain (misguided) belief that allows, perhaps even invites, his readers to negatively judge and dissociate themselves from Afro-American fetishes, he quickly abandons this skepticism to detail the fetish and the practices associated with it. In this turn, Delany moves from a concept of the fetish as evidence of a mode of (misguided) belief to a recognition of the fetish as an artifact that enables a mode of practice that produces cer-tain effects that are positive, even politically transformative. Immediately after this description of the fetish, Delany details the history and collectiv-ity that emerge from it. The narrator reveals that conjurers like the man who holds the goombah, along with famous black rebels like Gabriel Prosser and Denmark Vessey, had fought in the U.S. Revolutionary War.

Because Delany's novel is not particularly interested in the historical legacy of the U.S. revolution, his point here is not to include black combat-ants or even black-produced fetishes in a story of the U.S. revolution but instead to draw the eighteenth-century revolutionary moment into a transnational circuit that builds from the botanical, (para)human, and ar-tifactual networks produced in and expanding from the Dismal Swamp and across the tropics and subtropics. For instance, he notes that conjure men took Mocasa, a plant that grew inside the swamp, and transplanted it outside the swamp with the expectation that this plant, perhaps because of its pharmacological qualities in or outside of fetishes, might contribute to the process of radicalization that Delany advocated.[52] Conjure men and fetish makers were "ambassadors from the swamp" who moved them-selves and the plants they cultivated into plantation spaces to "create new conjurers" who had "fourteen year appointments."[53] Delany's description, then, charts a move from skepticism regarding fetishes and other black botanical practices to recognition of fetish and conjure as part of an ex-plicitly political project that allowed the production of community and resistance.[54]

Delany's account indicates the link between fetishes and diasporic re-sistance. To further develop this point, I will now elaborate the relation between fetishes and diasporic African modes of personhood that result-

ed from such resistance. To this end, I turn to an Afro-Cuban artisan's account of his construction of a fetish.[55] He begins with a kettle in which he
draws a cross:

> One places over this sign five Spanish silver reales, one at the
> center, the others at each end of the cross . . . one places to the
> side a piece of sugarcane filled with sea water, sand and mercury,
> stoppered with wax, so that the *nkisi* [fetish] will always have life,
> like the flow of quicksilver, so that it will be swift and moving, like
> the waters of the ocean, so that the spirit in the charm can merge
> with the sea and travel far away.
>   The body of a black male dog may be included to grant the
> charm the sharp sense of smell associated with that animal . . . on
> top of these objects is poured earth from an ant-heap and small
> pieces of wood. Sticks [from some twenty-seven species of trees]
> are placed around and leaves and herbs also added . . . After
> completion of this level, one throws over it chili, pepper, garlic,
> ginger, white onion, cinnamon, a piece of rue, pine seed. The
> work is completed by the addition of the skull of a woodpecker
> or buzzard.[56]

Robert Farris Thompson describes this work as a miniature; in fact, this
Cuban fetish, Delany's goombah, or Isaki's combinations of medicines and
words might be counted as miniatures in that they are artifacts into which
pieces of the ecologies in which they are made are brought together—which
is to say, they miniaturize ecologies. Yet calling these artifacts miniatures
departs from conventional conceptions of the miniature. After all, these
are not miniatures in the sense that they offer a scaled-down version of
physically existing structures or bodies. The Afro-Cuban fetish maker
suggests that the seawater and mercury included in the fetish will give the
properties of sea and quicksilver to the artifact and to the person who
bears it; yet his fetish is not a model or replica of the place(s) and entities
that it references and samples. Only certain elements of the Cuban ecology are included in the fetish, which makes clear that its effort is not to
reproduce the place of its production. Moreover, the ingredients brought
together in this fetish do not preserve the scale of the ecology that they
reference: whole *reales* are used; the sea that evokes the Middle Passage is
sheathed inside a cane stalk; a dog may be entire; sticks will do for trees,

for it is the diversity of trees (twenty-seven species are collected) and the arrangement of ingredients that seems to matter, not their scale.

Susan Stewart has theorized the miniature as a meditation on the relation of the small scale to the full scale through which the small is imagined as equivalent to and thus capable of enclosing the large. As Stewart wonderfully puts it, the miniature offers a "center within center, within within within," and she goes on to suggest that the intense interiority of miniatures produced in the eighteenth and nineteenth centuries serves as a metaphor for human interiority as a private space.[57] Yet the miniature of the fetish does not work according to the logic Stewart proposes because it does not offer a relation of the small scale to the full scale in order to replicate, enclose, and interiorize. Nor is it a metaphor for human consciousness as a private space, conceived as a containment whereby interiority amounts to a retractive process of infinite regression that verges on (but does not dissolve into) invisibility. Instead, diasporic African fetishes effect a relation of ingredients that produce a pharmacological effect, which in turn aims to create a change in the present. That is, these fetishes do not preserve some supposedly real exterior entity through a process of containment but rather attempt to produce an effect that has yet to arrive.

If the fetish allows a containment and if this containment is linked to the work of personification (that is to say, the production of a person who emerges through her relations to other animate forces in an ecology), it is not a containment that suggests regression toward the infinitely small but rather a containment that understands bodies, persons, and their agency as linked to combination and that allows this combinatory work to take place. To the extent that the fetish is a miniature, it is a miniature that arranges and combines parts whose effectiveness is signaled by making a new relation of forces in the present. As should be clear, it is not the case that the fetish does not allow for interiority (more on this to come), but it is not an interiority that fantasizes the infinite regression through which a person arrives at a nearly sacred hiddenness or privacy. Rather, it is a contraction effected by a collation of forces (some bearing historical significance and some pharmacological) through which an effect is produced in the present.

As interfaces between places, artifices, and (para)human beings, diasporic African fetishes articulate a mode of personhood that divagates from Stewart's account of an emphatically human personhood achieved through retraction from a natural world conceived as fundamentally outside of the

Figure 11. A nkisi Nkubulu. *The* nkisi Nkubulu's *knotting of packets and medicines makes clear that fetishes are combinatory technes, not representational art forms. Courtesy of Wyatt MacGaffey.*

subject, even if its likeness is smuggled within the subject's private recesses. It is not that fetish use indicates a wholesale renunciation of interiority; rather, it insists on the relation between interiorities and exteriorities such that the inside cannot serve as a metaphor for an unworldly, private, and wholly human personhood. After all, fetishes are arrangements in which insides pass on to outsides and back again.

That African and African American fetishes propose interiority as a sort of containment is clear in the importance of vessels in their production. The Afro-Cuban fetish maker assembles and arranges his ingredients in a kettle. Delany's goombah is a gourd. The *nkisi Nkubulu* (Figure 11) of the Kongo documented by MacGaffey is a collection of knotted bags and bottles. These are vessels that allow the collection and containment of ingredients whose effectiveness depends on the circulation between insides and outsides. This point is particularly evident in MacGaffey's photograph of the *nkisi Nkubulu.* Its elaborately knotted bags suggest enclosure and secrecy, but its mass of textures—the coarseness of raffia, the tight weave of burlap, the smoothness of stone (or perhaps wood)—indicates that the fetish's visual and pharmacological effect comes not through isolating medicines in bags but through a knotting that is never simply a means of producing insides but also a way of connecting singular elements into a larger effect. The *nkisi Nkubulu's* large central knot—looped but not pulled shut—emphasizes its suspension of another packet, and this looping eventually vanishes into the fetish's textures. Although the packets that comprise *nkisi Nkubulu* are tied (except for the stone, which cannot be), the folds of packets and skeins as well as the elaborate knottings at their necks make tight enclosure impossible, suggesting that this fetish is less invested in the production of a retractive interiority than in a mode of containment that also allows slidings out. Or to put it differently, the fetish is a contraction (not of essence but of ingredients) that produces an effect that might be conceived as an expansion. Through this contraction and expansion, both insides and outsides are remade, and while the distinction between them need not be altogether eliminated, it is also not enforced. Interiors linked to exteriors that loop back into interiors, fetishes affect the relation between insides and outsides and between parts and assemblages through which persons are made.

So far, I've left open the possibility of interpreting the fetish as a metaphor for diasporic African modes of production and personhood. However, my point is not that we should interpret fetishes as metaphors. I conceive fetishes as technologies that allow a collection that mediates the relations between insides and out, (para)humans and nonhumans, and through which personhood is constituted.[58] Personhood so conceived is not an essence that is produced or preserved through a retraction from the world. In fact, this mode of personhood depends on collection and combination of forces in and outside of the body. In this sense, this personhood depends on a relation to what is often called the object, although the object here is reconceived as a constituent part of the person, indeed as a technology that produces the (para)human as a person. That diasporic African personhood is nonretractive, based on collection and combination, and reconceives the object as a techne that allows the production of persons is evident in another diasporic African practice that is linked although not equivalent to fetish use: the use of *pots têtes,* as they are called in Haiti, or *govis,* as they are also called both in Haiti and in other American plantation spaces. In Haiti, a *pot tête* is used in Vodou initiation: the initiate places into a receptacle pieces of her physical body (hair or nails), objects and foods associated with a particular god of the Vodou pantheon, and her *gros bon anj,* which Colin Dayan defines as the "shadow cast by the body on the mind."[59] The expression of personality into a *pot tête* or *govi* can also occur outside a ritual situation when a person lodges some part of herself in a vessel, which serves as a hiding place. In such practices, personhood is produced and preserved through collecting component parts that allow the recollection of a singularity that emerges through relations with other forces in this world.

The way fetishes and *pots têtes* recalibrate the relation between persons and objects resonates with Fred Moten's analysis of the artist and philosopher Adrian Piper's desire to produce herself as "a silent, secret, passive object."[60] Piper's performance of herself as an object engenders a mode of personhood that comes from a sustained attention to the object, in fact a sort of becoming object through which the object is recognized as possessing an "interiority and internal space."[61] This is not, for Piper, a complete passing into the object, as she emphasizes that this performance of herself as object is a choice through which her "objecthood became . . . subjecthood."[62] The process that Piper and Moten describe, like the production of *pots têtes*, suggests that many of those made into objects by Atlantic slavery as well as artists who work in their wake have remade the relation of subjects to objects, making possible a personhood that proceeds through collaborations with nonhuman entities and that recalibrates the subject and the object.

Atlantic Relations

Putting fetishistic assemblages front and center allows a concept of the *person* as an entity that develops from rituals, at once rhetorical (that is, achieved through practices of oration) and artisanal (that is, achieved through practices of arrangement) that conjoins (para)humans with nonhuman entities, whether animals, plants, things, or elemental forces such as seas and atmospheres. The diasporic personhood I have proposed suggests a distinct Atlantic cosmology that recalibrates the object as a density and also an interiority that participates in the production of personhood. If fetish use presumes that a person and her interiority necessarily extend outside of her body proper, it also complicates the idea that a person is a contained and emphatically human entity distinct from nonhuman forces. The intense and explicit relation a fetishistic assemblage forges between (para)humans and the nonhuman world suggests a mode of personhood that elaborates on Moten's argument that the history of blackness in the Americas "pressures the assumption of the equivalence of personhood and subjectivity."[63] Moten uses the term *person* to suggest a mode of being distinct from subjectivity, even if the personhood he describes continues to be linked to and described as the effect of the plays of *subjects* and *objects, subjection* and *objection.*[64]

In order to emphasize the difference of this mode of personhood that emerges in the American tropics, I advocate not simply a movement away from the term *subject* (an argument I make in the introduction and chapter 1 as well as here, where I put *persons* in distinction to *subjects*) but also a movement away from the often attendant term *object* and the colonial dynamic between subjects and objects. Relying on dyadic understandings of subjects and objects risks overlooking the fact that, instead of simply reproducing colonial commodity culture's valuations of objects, a number of Afro-American cultural forms reconstitute objects as something other than blank and brute quantities of colonial exchange.

Fetishistic assemblages resist plantation slavery's (de)valuation of objects and things as commodities. To confirm my claim that Afro-American understandings of nonhuman things and forces often departed from those of Anglo-European colonials, we need only recall Dralsé de Grandpierre's complaint that Africans confuse objects (matter) and gods (spirit) and Moreau de Saint-Méry's belief that Afro-Americans' mentation was compromised by a tendency to materialize beliefs in things. Diasporic African fetishes valued "objects" as techne that enable the production of a mode of personhood that contributes to anticolonial resistance. This revaluation of objects registers in colonial stories in which diasporic Africans are said to have powers to exert their will and attention beyond the span of the physical body. Consider, for instance, *Obi*'s suggestion that Three-Fingered Jack's power extends into other commodities, in so doing transforming them from commodities to agents of anticolonialism.

To further elaborate how personhood as assemblage dissolves the antinomian relation between subjects and objects, it is helpful to consider the understandings of spirit and matter that frequently inform diasporic African cosmologies.[65] Afro-Cuban Santeria proposes *aché* as "a dynamic principle, an energy, a force assumed to be immanent in humans, in all of nature, . . . in wild animals, and/or plant life; it is also in all fluids."[66] In Vodou cosmologies, all bodies, including those usually designated as objects, are made of and resonant with *namm*, which the anthropologist Alfred Métraux translates as an "energy" or "effluvium" that moves all things and which the Haitian American poet and physician Reginald Crosley describes as a "force" that can be "actualized as space-time events—persons, objects, and physical matter such as urns, rocks, trees, or rivers."[67] In conceiving namn as "energy" and "force," both Métraux's and Crosley's definitions seem to suggest *namn* as a spiritual property exterior to matter. However, Crosely's clarification that *namn* is "actualized" in bodies makes clear that *namn* is not an immaterial property but a force that is inherent in, although not necessarily equivalent to, matter. Here, *namn* constitutes matter as an always-moving force that is constellated into bodies that interact with other bodies in a process that can either expand or diminish its own power and pleasure.[68] Other bodies, also made of and moved by *namn*, can negatively impact, divide, or overcome any given body. Although this clearly indicates concepts of the negative and of finitude (that is, any body is impacted by other bodies and eventually dissolved), neither negativity nor finitude is equivalent to death as conventionally conceived. Rather, these negativities and finitudes precipitate the body's entry into new systems of relations, an entry that, if it is not precisely negative, also cannot be seen as unequivocally positive.[69]

My argument that diasporic Africans forged a mode of personhood that emerges from the production and dissolution of assemblages that reject both the antinomianism of spirit and matter and that of subjects and objects poses certain hazards. Most pressingly, in positing personhood as a process that depends on the fetish's collation of material forces, I propose that personhood is emergent, contingent, and not based on the division of human beings from nonhuman entities. Given that this mode of personhood developed in plantation spaces in which black agents' humanity was brutally refused so that they could be converted into parahumans, it might seem not nearly strong enough to constitute an always potentially soluble and nonexclusively human personhood instead of sticking with the subject, which despite its problems allows a politically expedient fiction of the human as a permanent, irreducible identity that bears fundamental rights.

Moreover, although (para)humans' investments of themselves into assemblages evinces a resistant cosmology that allows for both power and pleasure, in this process of joining assemblages, sometimes (para)human beings' rhythms and desires are subordinated to those of the assembly. As Pietz and the eighteenth-century natural historians noted, the production and use of fetishes requires that persons allow their individual power to become tied to apparently external bodies, which nonetheless act as controlling organs. In attaching, even sometimes subordinating (para)human bodies to nonhuman bodies and forces, the use of fetishes might seem to mark the moment at which (para)humanity passes into nonhumanity, thereby revealing the impossibility of ever fully inhabiting the category of the human that abolitionists so vehemently argued must be opened to—or rather for—persons of African descent. As if the subaltern's final move was not not speaking, not the production of aporias that reveal the impossibility of either subjects or objects,[70] but a becoming object through which she passed out of the juridical and political categories of subjectivity and humanity in which power has traditionally accrued, in the process remaking the object as an assemblage. A remarkable move to be sure, but also a problematic one in global systems governed by these juridical and political categories.[71]

If this account of diasporic personhood as assemblage, like the parahumanity I discussed in the previous chapter, comes close to repeating the losses occasioned by colonialism, I think this is a risk worth taking. Approaching the formerly taboo topic of Afro-Americans' proximities to nonhuman life-forms and supposedly animistic conceptions of matter makes visible a mode of personhood in which dispossessed persons are not fixed in the position of loss in which the only possible response seems to be orbiting or integrating themselves into existing forms of political identity. Veering from trajectories of loss and integration, this form of personhood and its recalibration of objects ameliorates but does not eliminate the losses that accumulated in the Atlantic world.

This ameliorative personhood is evident in the diasporic African phenomenon of possession, which is common to fetish-using Afro-American cultures, most prominently Haitian Vodou but also Santeria and to some extent Obeah.[72] Possession occurs when a body is seized by a god. The inhabiting of a body by an external force might seem to replicate the colonial Anglo-European belief that black persons were weak or half-formed humans, or perhaps exchangeable objects, who could be moved by the will of masters. However, although the phenomenon of possession might seem to confirm the idea that black persons are empty ciphers who could be claimed by superior forces, it instead shows precisely the opposite: it emphasizes that a person is not an emptiness but an assemblage. The rhythms that constitute and designate a particular body are not vanished in her possession by a god: rather, they are supplemented and become resonant with the rhythms and movements of the god. On this point, the polyrhythmic style of Vodou drumming is significant: possession is linked to a musical form that allows the copresence of overlaid rhythms.[73]

Vodou gods are often imaginatively rendered as a specific anthropomorphic or zoomorphic entity. Damballah, imagined as a snake, is manifest in a pattern of drumming particular to the region and family with which he is associated. This rhythm generally precedes Damballah's joining with a (para)human body; in fact, Métraux claims that "a talented drummer can induce or terminate possessions" through his production of rhythm.[74] Damballah is also associated with the arching of rainbows and with eggs, which are often present at ceremonies where Damballah possesses a body. *Veves* (flour or chalk drawings, usually on the ground) for Damballah are more representational than most because his physical manifestation as a snake is usually clear; however, these *veves* push the representational toward the figural as the snake becomes part of a vertical pattern of arching that often, particularly at the base of the *veve*, moves into compete circles. Drumbeats, eggs, bougainvillea trees, and rainbows all contribute to possession by Damballah, a possession that does not signal the entry of the god into the blank space of the body but a collation of material forces, each resonant with the rhythmic and figural shape of an undulation that is extended into and expressed by the possessed body, which retains a memory of that rhythm even after the possession ends. If, as Dayan suggests, the corporeal logic of possession recalls a seventeenth- and eighteenth-century Anglo-European belief that the black body could be a thing possessed, its conceptualization of the body as an inherently rhythmic, motile force in relation to and even transformed by other rhythmic forces joins the fetish in refusing the expectation that a body is an empty vessel whose animation is secondary and effected through the exterior and dematerialized force of spirit. In possession, the body in relation to physical and historical forces becomes a rhythmic plenitude that syncopates with other rhythms.[75]

If personhood depends on fetishistic assemblages that join (para)humans with nonhuman entities, each force gathered in the assemblage is not simply a medium that transmits a certain content but also an agency that contributes to the working of an assemblage. If Glissant proposes that Atlantic slavery engenders a "*we* rhizomed into fragile connection to a place," the conceptualization of persons and fetishes offered here suggests that this "we" includes nonhuman forces.[76] This "we" produced by fetishistic assemblies exists without subjects or objects and does not feed itself on dead natures. Against a number of recent theorizations of the Atlantic world that propose that the dizzying losses occasioned by colonialism require a melancholic ethics,[77] I suggest that diasporic Africans' fetish production anticipates agencies and assemblages in which loss becomes like the syncope—the loss of consciousness, words, a beat—a lapse and an abyss that ghosts and births the new beat, thus entering into and expanding the arrangement. And here it is possible to return to Wheatley's Niobe, and the suspension with which Wheatley ends her version of this story. If we are after persons without objects, Wheatley's suspension freezes subjects and objects in the moment before their ossification, in so doing producing the opening that allows for the genealogy of the Afro-American materialism she attempted to sublate.

III

5

Involving the Universe in Ruins

Sansay's Haitian Anabiography

Counterfactuals

In the opening scenes of Leonora Sansay's travelogue *Secret History* (1808) as well as the novel sometimes attributed to her, *Zelica* (1820), the Haitian revolutionary general Henri Christophe sets Saint-Domingue's capital city Cap François on fire.[1] In *Zelica,* some of the white creole women fleeing the fire sit "in mute anguish" on the mountains that rise behind the city "and contemplate the city, which appeared from the [mountain] heights that crowned it to float on the sea—that sea was calm as a mirror, reflecting in one broad blaze the golden light of the sun."[2] If this vision of the city is typical of the hallucinatory splendor that often burnished colonial accounts of tropical locales, that this appearance gains luster through the reflected light of sun and fire makes clear that such rhapsodic visions of colonial landscape are chimerical. The colony of Saint-Domingue had been embroiled in a colonial war since a massive slave uprising in 1791, and the mountains from which these white women would contemplate the scene were themselves part of this war zone. The hills and low mountains enclosing Cap François figure centrally in both *Secret History* and *Zelica,* the plot of the latter text tracing white women's passages into and out of Haitian mountains "tee[ming] with danger" but where their persons and their sense of their agency was transformed.[3]

Sansay often refers to these mountains and to other geographical features by proper names—Plaisance, for instance.[4] Mansuy's 1793 plan of Cap François also notes the mountainous terrain, and among other promontories, he indicates a peak called "Morne Lory" and, across town, a street skirting the hills is designated as "Rue du Morne." In fact, *Morne* was not a proper name, nor was it a nominalization of the French adjective for gloominess (Figure 12). *Morne* and *mornes* are creole words, nouns that designate the mountains and hills that rise behind Caribbean beaches and coastlines, which Betsy Wing describes as the "savage and life-preserving land" where maroons "took refuge" and also waged war against the American colonies' plantation economies.[5] *Les mornes*, then, designate spaces at the borders of plantations and plantation metropoles where Afro-Americans and their allies drew on the particularities of the terrain to resist and even incapacitate the order of the colonial plantation zone.

It might seem as though the resistance to the plantation form that emerged in *les mornes* was simply that of human beings who used nature

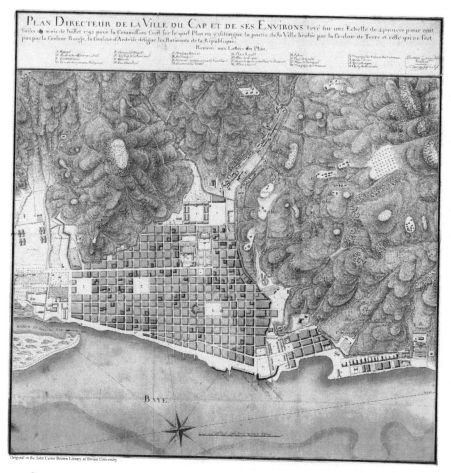

Figure 12. Mansuy's Plan of Cap François, 1793. Courtesy of the John Carter Brown Library at Brown University.

to achieve exclusively human political ends, but Glissant's as well as Derek Walcott's figuration of the agency of the mornes suggests that the Afro-American aesthetic and political traditions that grew from this resistance do not presume agency as a purely human phenomenon. Moreover, *Zelica*'s opening makes clear that at least some of the time eighteenth- and nineteenth-century colonial writers also recognized that *les mornes* testified to the enmeshment of (para)human and nonhuman agencies. Immediately after presenting the mountain as a promontory from which colonial landscapes might be contemplated, organized, and appreciated, Sansay's narrator dissolves this vision. In fact, she suggests that it is impossible to view this scene at all, as the Haitian general Henri Christophe ordered the detonation of a powder magazine causing the "mountain . . . suddenly to open," upon which "thick clouds of smoke darkened the atmosphere, and changed the brilliant light of the sun to the obscurity of midnight; whilst a noise . . . roaring at its base, was re-echoed through the caverns, resembling the last effort of expiring nature involving the universe in ruin."[6]

Sansay's representation of a Haitian general and the Haitian landscape as producing a lot of nothing is consistent with critical accounts that focus on the unthinkability of a disavowed Haitian Revolution, but this description also encodes the transformation of Cap François and its environment that was set into motion on February 4, 1802, by Christophe, a bit player in *Secret History* who emerges as a quasi-romantic hero in *Zelica*. Christophe was born a slave in Grenada and later was part of a French battalion that fought in Georgia on behalf of the colonists during the U.S. Revolutionary War. He was commanding Toussaint Louverture's troops in Cap François when Napoleon's brother-in-law General Charles Le Clerc and 30,000 French troops arrived on the island with the goal of reinstating slavery. Christophe refused to allow Le Clerc to land his troops. However, realizing that Le Clerc would simply land adjacent to the city, Christophe ordered the city's inhabitants to evacuate. He then set Cap François on fire, starting with his own home. He took particular care to destroy munitions that the French might claim.[7] The detail of the 1793 plan of Cap François (Figure 13) shows that the French military headquarters, including the powder magazine, were at the foot of *les mornes* into which Christophe had ordered the city's inhabitants to flee. When the powder magazine caught fire and exploded, it took with it the side of the mountain, converting granite into missiles that Sansay claims struck, killed, and dismembered some of

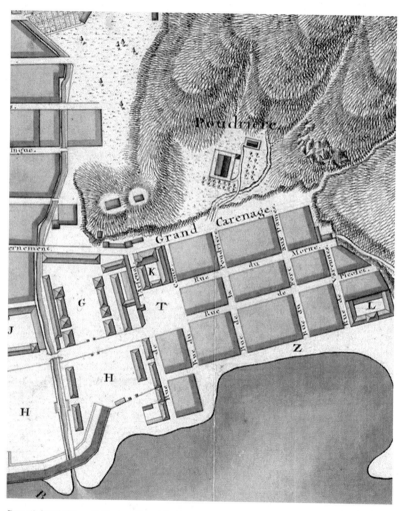

Figure 13. Detail of Figure 12, Mansuy's Plan of Cap François, 1793. This detail shows the poudrière (powder magazine) that the rebels blew up, which in Sansay's accounts causes the mountain behind it to explode. The close up also shows the Rue du Morne, a name that designates the hills that rise steeply behind Caribbean beaches and ports and that Glissant describes as "savage and life-preserving land in which the Maroons took refuge" (Poetics of Relation, iii). Courtesy of the John Carter Brown Library at Brown University.

those fleeing the city. Sansay particularly emphasizes the exploding mountain's mutilation of white women's bodies. These female "creatures . . . on whom the sun had never shone" were, if they survived this event, left stranded in mountains "strewed with severed limbs, blackened bodies, and disfigured heads—the survivors had not the last mournful satisfaction of weeping over the remains of the objects most dear to them, for their remains were not distinguishable."[8]

This scene that opens both *Zelica* and *Secret History* constellates the themes I have developed in preceding chapters. For one, both Anglo-Europeans and Afro-Americans proposing radical antislavery (whether through armed resistance or marronage) link Afro-American agency to a remaking and reinhabitation of mountainous or swampy terrains at the limits of plantations and plantation metropoles. Second, Afro-American resistance is linked to an alternate valuation of objects and property, which I have discussed in preceding chapters and will discuss in more detail presently, but is even here subtly evident in the story of Christophe's setting fire to his own home first as he incinerated the colony's most prosperous city. Third, radical antislavery is linked with the disaggregation of the body and personhood, a disaggregation that Sansay suggests is a particular anxiety of white women, even if it was clearly a more general predicament of life in the plantation zone, especially for Afro-Americans. In this chapter, I pose Sansay's Haitian writings as a case study through which to consider how Afro-American cultural forms and modes of agency such as fetish use, Vodou, and stories of bodies in parts impacted the ways Anglo-American women moving through the American tropics came to imagine their own personhood. By closing this book with an account of Anglo-American women's personhood I do not mean to privilege white women; rather, I hope this analysis will make clear that the ecologically inflected mode of personhood I have traced in the previous two chapters impacted and moved into the Anglo-European cultural forms that have traditionally been the focus of early American studies. This means that this mode of personhood cannot be conceived along racial lines. Moreover, it means that these modes of personhood passed into and circulated in the writings that literary critics have traditionally read only for their commentary on U.S. politics (whether for or against them) and their conventional performances of personhood.

So as to develop a reading adequate to Sansay's simultaneous disavowal and avowal of Afro-American political and cultural forms, I propose that her Haitian writings are structured by the work of surrogation, a term I take from Joseph Roach. Focusing on Afro-Americans who perform as Mardi Gras Indians, on white women who mimic mulatto courtesans' styles of dress and gestural language, and a series of other examples, Roach defines surrogation as a process of substitution in which one person repeats a performance previously enacted by another.[9] Although I am entirely in agreement with Roach's reading of Atlantic cultures of surrogation and draw on the theory of history it presumes, in my analysis of Sansay's writing I further elaborate on the subtleties of surrogatory performances in the eighteenth- and nineteenth-century American tropics.

Roach associates surrogation with the plasticity of identity, which in his study consists of a series of performances, none of which refer back to an essential or unitary identity or history. Yet if surrogatory performances might well imply the dissolution of the subject as a locus of a discrete essence, they might also be used to reconstitute the subject as an identity founded on a discrete essence. Because this point seems paradoxical, it is worth clarifying. On the one hand, surrogation might testify to a conception of the person as a series of masks that does not point back to any origin or forward to any coming identity. On the other hand, the identity of the performer and that which is performed might be imagined as primary and essential essences that precede the performance and remain intact at its conclusion. Here, the performer does not repeat another person's performance or an event, thereby changing both herself and the event that is repeated; she mimics another person or an event, which (as mimicry implies) remains distinct from herself. In this case, surrogation might well be understood as a performance in which an actor maintains and reinforces her distinction from that which is performed. To put this in terms of the Deleuzian philosophy I bring to bear on Roach's analysis, surrogation might suggest difference and repetition, in which case identity is secondary; but it might also suggest identity and representation, in which case identity is primary.

In the first part of this chapter, I will argue that it is this second, identitarian mode of surrogation that Sansay attempts to produce in her Haitian writings, particularly the earlier *Secret History,* which focuses on white women who gain autonomy by repeating Afro-American performances of politics and personhood while insisting that their own racial distinction separates them from Afro-Americans. This form of surrogation attempts to convert Caribbean relations, admixtures, and cross-pollinations into a field of discrete and fixed identities that even, as they come into contact, remain fundamentally distinct and (insofar as they are in relations of mimicry and not of cross-pollination) uncreolized.

This identitarian impulse is in part an effort to maintain racial differences. What these identities based on racial differences work to keep at bay are the aspects of radical antislavery that would most directly challenge colonial valuations of property and objects. Yet even if in *Secret History* Sansay deploys surrogation as a process through which white women take the place of but maintain a distinction from Afro-American persons and politics, in the second part of this chapter I read Sansay's text against its own desires. I show that the Afro-American modes of personhood and resistance that Sansay's white women surrogate produce a series of additions that are particularly in evidence in *Zelica* and through which Afro-American valuations of objects, persons, and place pass into Anglo-American personhood.

If Deleuze's theorizations shape my reading of surrogation and identity, they also shape the method of historicization I propose in this chapter. This method presumes that the revolutionary moment Sansay chronicles contains within it potentialities ("virtualities") that are materially present but not equivalent to what is actually realized in that moment.[10] This means that ideas and potentialities that might not have been possible within a given historical moment nonetheless had a material presence. Attending to these potentialities allows a reading of this past that recognizes that which was potential, not simply that which was possible in fact.[11] Although this might seem a historical enterprise devoted to the counterfactual (that which is not "actual"), this is not precisely the case, as all of the potentialities I trace in this chapter moved through the Haitian revolutionary moment in which Sansay wrote and might well interrupt its workings. These potentialities, in short, evince a material residue and power that existed in a given moment, even if it never became fully realized.[12]

The counterfactual, or that which was potential but not actual, might seem a strange line to follow in a field that has traditionally been resolutely historical, but it is also true that early American literature itself was often interested in tracing out counterfactuals and potential outcomes and histories (Charles Brockden Brown's oeuvre, for instance). In fact, Sansay's work often unfolds in the domain of the counterfactual.[13] That Sansay's Haitian works offer so many counterfactuals does not mean that her Haitian works are nothing but a series of fantasies, as Sibylle Fischer's reading of white Creole writings about the Haitian revolution might suggest.[14] To the contrary, I propose that Sansay's Haitian writings, instead of rendering or failing to render a given historical terrain, work to trace out the diffuse potentialities through which this terrain might be decomposed and recomposed. This method is not against history but against history conceived as the litany of the actual, which minimizes the accretion of potentialities that sustain and might dissolve it.

Anabiography

Leonora Sansay was born in 1773 in Philadelphia, and her father died when she was young; when her mother remarried the tavern owner William Hassel, she and her family lived in his tavern across the street from the State House, which was the de facto capitol of the United States at the time. The proximity of Sansay's childhood home to the capitol of the emerging U.S. nation, while a simple matter of chance, shaped her writings, which offer a counterpoint to the concepts of state, nation, affiliation, domesticity, and happiness then circulating in the public and private writings of the Founding Fathers, whose politics have come to dominate early American studies. By the final years of the eighteenth century, Sansay was Aaron Burr's lover, and around 1799, probably at Burr's suggestion, she married Louis Sansay, a French creole from Saint-Domingue, who in 1796 had sold his coffee plantation to Toussaint Louverture and fled the ongoing Haitian Revolution.

In 1802, Louis and Leonora Sansay sailed to Saint-Domingue, hoping that Le Clerc would succeed in reinstating the slave-powered plantation economy. After they had spent a year and a half in Cap François—during which time the French seized and deposed Louverture, and Haiti's eventual first president and emperor Jean-Jacques Dessalines rose to power—it was becoming clear that Afro-American revolutionaries would defeat the French. So Sansay traveled to Cuba and then to Jamaica, before returning to Philadelphia without her husband, with whom she almost certainly never reconciled.[15] Soon after her return to the United States, she traveled to New Orleans, where she acted as an emissary for Aaron Burr's clandestine operations at the boundaries of the newly acquired Louisiana Territory, the operations for which Burr was later tried for treason before the Supreme Court and found not guilty on a technicality.[16]

I have just offered something like a biography of Sansay, and while the widely traveled, fiercely idiosyncratic, possibly conspiratorial Sansay makes for a fascinating biographical study, her life adds up to something more like anabiography, by which I mean a series of discontinuous episodes. These exceed Sansay's own narrative compulsion to crystallize the identities of her white U.S. women protagonists and also exceed biographical criticism's drive to crystallize an identity or a personality. Sansay passed under at least five names.[17] She moved frequently, often outside of or at the borders of the U.S. nation-state and colonial metropoles like Cap François and Santiago de Cuba. She had an affinity for a wide variety of print genres, from novels to dramas to political tracts to chemistry books, and she read and wrote in French and perhaps German as well as in English. She enters the historical record fleetingly across a series of locations and archives, only to pass from it again. The opacity and discontinuity that Sansay's life poses to critical recuperations might well be attributed to the fact that she was middle-class, a woman, and so unconventional that there was no possibility she would be included in official histories and mythologies. Nonetheless, this series of facts also points to a life that unfolded at the limits of and even passed from her time's understandings of affiliation, affect, and personality. Perhaps inadvertently, Sansay's life suggests multiplying and entangled locations, performances, and vitalities that suggest the dynamism characteristic of the revolutionary Atlantic and also verge on what Jane Bennett calls "a life," by which Bennett, following Deleuze and Bergson, means a more-than-human force that "tears the fabric of the actual without ever coming fully 'out' in a person, place or thing."[18] I draw on Bennett's term and will return to it later to describe the expansion of the scenes and modes of agency that flash inchoate across Sansay's trajectories.

Secret History, originally published by the Philadelphia publishers Bradford & Inskeep and printed by R. Carr, offers a fictionalized, epistolary travelogue based on Sansay's sojourn through the revolutionary Caribbean.[19] In 1820, London-based publisher William Fearman issued *Zelica,* which was printed by William Clowes and appeared in three volumes, the entire novel totaling almost 800 pages. Like *Secret History, Zelica* was published anonymously, the author identified only as "An American." The latter text draws directly on *Secret History,* borrowing its characters, anecdotes, and themes. The Library Company of Philadelphia has attributed their copy of *Zelica* to Sansay, yet literary scholars have been slow to agree with that assessment, mainly because of changes of narrative structure and plot that I will outline in a moment.[20] However, the evidence strongly suggests that Sansay did in fact write *Zelica*. Most pointedly, *Zelica* often recycles the precise language and phrasings of *Secret History*, including Sansay's idiosyncratic formulations such as her tendency to refer to the United States (and not Europe) as "the Continent."[21] Historical evidence supports the textual evidence: a literary report published in the periodical *The Atheneum* in May 1821 lists a newly published novel called *Zelica* written by "Madam de Sansée," one of the many variant spellings Sansay used of her name.[22]

Although in many ways *Secret History* and *Zelica* tell the same story of U.S.-born white women negotiating the final stages of the Haitian Revolution, Sansay makes several significant changes across the works. First, *Secret History* chronicles three Caribbean locations—Saint-Domingue, Cuba, and Jamaica—while *Zelica* is set entirely in Haiti. Both works feature a beautiful protagonist named Clara who many critics believe is a stand-in for Sansay and who elicits erotic investments from most men and some women who come into her orbit. In *Secret History*, Clara ultimately leaves her violently abusive husband and, along with her confidante and "sister" Mary, returns to Philadelphia. In *Zelica*, Clara stays with her husband despite his numerous infidelities and occasional abuse, and in the concluding scene she dies when she is accidentally stabbed by a white French partisan of the revolution, thus never leaving Haiti. *Secret History* is an epistolary work in which most letters are written by Clara's sister Mary to Aaron Burr, although several of the concluding letters are exchanged between Mary and Clara. This narrative structure changes dramatically in *Zelica*, which relates its plot through third person omniscient narration. Although the novel still focuses on two female protagonists, the character of Mary is replaced by Zelica, who is the child of an Afro-American courtesan and a white, French creole father who supports and fights in the Haitian Revolution, sometimes in blackface.[23] In the latter work, then, one of the main protagonists is of mixed race; other forms of racial crossing emerge as an explicit theme in the novel, most obviously in one of its main plot lines, which features the epidermally white Zelica and Clara's courtship by Haitian generals: Zelica by Christophe and Clara by the fictionalized character Glaude, who bears some resemblance to Dessalines (he is African-born and described as motivated by an implacable desire to take revenge against white creoles and Frenchmen).[24]

Both *Secret History* and *Zelica* give sustained attention to the limited options available to women—especially but not exclusively white women—in postrevolutionary states. *Zelica* lambastes Zelica's father, who, while he helps to "[break] the chains that bound a people," nonetheless "despotically disposes of [Zelica's] hand; he is an enthusiast for liberty, yet leaves his . . . daughter no choice between the most abhorred slavery, mental bondage—and death."[25] *Zelica,* in particular, depicts the Age of Revolution as a predominantly masculine enterprise in which women are bartered between Anglo-European and Afro-American masters. This attention to the limited options available to women is less a reflection of Sansay's own position on the place and potentialities women might claim (her own trajectories make clear she recognized other options) than it is a representation that offers a critique of the official politics developed by the postrevolutionary states that emerged in the United States, France, and Haiti.[26] If Sansay's account of gender is mainly in the line of critique, in *Zelica* she opens up two other threads. First, she keeps her women protagonists in postrevolutionary Haiti as if to explore the possibility that this postrevolutionary state offered women greater options than did others—this despite the supposedly oppressive desire of black men for white and white-looking women. Second, she explores the possibility that women should choose death instead of participating in postrevolutionary states where women's autonomy was so severely constrained: women might circumvent patriarchal desires, *Zelica* proposes, by "immolating" themselves.[27] Between these two potentialities, *Zelica* traces the submerged emergence of a third, which I will develop: a becoming Haitian, in which women's autonomy was not predicated on their relations to men and was not in any simple way equivalent to death.

Surrogation

Michael Drexler's influential analysis of *Secret History* focuses on the two histories of violence charted by the book.[28] First, the brutal slave revolution that is the background for much of the work. Second, the brutality of the white French creole St. Louis toward his white American-born wife Clara that constitutes the foreground. The increasingly paranoid St. Louis begins to keep his wife under lock and key, and he eventually threatens to rub acid on her face so that no other man can or will possess her. Drexler shows that Sansay's collation of these two histories of violence emphasizes the parallels between rebelling Afro-Americans and Anglo-American women, both of whom are treated as objects and property by white creole men.[29] Pushing this point further, Drexler suggests that Clara's eventual flight and achievement of independence from her brutal husband are inspired by her observation of Afro-American revolution. As Drexler first makes clear, the place where Clara flees when she leaves her husband is the mountainous village of El Cobre, Cuba, which in the eighteenth century was constituted as an independent pueblo composed of royal slaves and free people of color and whose surrounding mountains were a stronghold of marronage.[30] Both the pueblo and the surrounding maroons "entailed . . . reformulations of the meaning of slavery" such that slavery and freedom, instead of congealing as absolute and opposed terms, were recognized as existing in a continuum.[31]

Although Clara does not closely document the racial composition of the communities to which she flees, the continuity between slavery and freedom is a central theme in both *Secret History* and *Zelica*. Moreover, that El Cobre and the surrounding mountains where she eventually retreats were predominantly Afro-American communities inflects Clara's account, which chronicles her retreat to "an obscure village, whose inhabitants are regarded as little better than a horde of banditti," where she stays in a hut furnished only with a hammock.[32] Free Afro-Americans, maroons, and revolutionaries were often described as brigands and bandits, and this spare furnishing was typical of maroon and pueblo communities. As Drexler makes clear, Sansay's white women gain liberation through a sort of paralleling and replication of the movements of black revolutionaries and maroons. In fact, his analysis suggests Clara's flight into the mountains and hills where she achieves liberation from her husband might be understood as a form of marronage. Here, the potentiality of marronage first considered in Bartram's *Travels* returns, not as an exclusively Afro-American mode of resistance and personhood that remains closed off from Anglo-Europeans who, at least in Bartram's imagining, must choose between citizen-subjectivity and melancholia, but as an expression of agency that might be claimed by U.S.-born white women.

The fact that Sansay's white women recognize and have been influenced by the Haitian Revolution and marronage has led literary scholars working on *Secret History,* including Drexler, to regard it as offering, even advocating, what Elizabeth Maddock Dillon calls "cross-racial alliance."[33] However, although *Secret History*'s protagonists are certainly influenced by the free blacks, maroons, and Afro-American revolutionaries with whom they are in close proximity, particularly Clara when she flees to El Cobre, in this section I read Sansay's texts with the grain of its own desires, and I argue that especially in *Secret History* she is not interested in tracing cross-racial alliances as the basis of a utopian communitarianism.

To be sure, as Drexler and Dillon point out, one of *Secret History*'s effects is to reveal cross-racial relations; however, in order to work through the complex racial dynamics of Sansay's oeuvre, it is important to first read Sansay's text with and not against her own desires.[34] In doing so, it is evident that *Secret History* attempts to deploy surrogatory operations that ossify racial divisions, closing down the potentiality for cross-raciality and dissolutions of identity that continually resurface in her Haitian writings. Here, I mean surrogation in the narrow identitarian sense as a process through which *Secret History*'s white women mime and put themselves in the place of Afro-American revolutionaries while at the same time working to forget or otherwise disavow this relation. That *Secret History*'s surrogatory operations attempt to avoid cross-racial sociality is evident in its structure: the plight of Anglo-American women is foregrounded, that of Afro-American revolutionaries is backgrounded, and foreground and background are kept in contrapuntal relation. To be sure, Clara's flight to El Cobre does indicate a moment when the foreground and background converge (which I will return to presently), but Clara so obliquely renders this as a place of black alternative social formations that it evinces her larger investment in maintaining a separation.

Sansay's effort to maintain a distinction between her white women protagonists and the black revolutionaries whose example they mimic as they strike for independence is particularly evident in one of the anecdotes about life in postrevolutionary Haiti that she offers in both *Secret History* and *Zelica*. Before the anecdote, a bit of background: Jean-Jacques Dessalines, who led the final stages of the revolution, ordered the slaughter of many of the French and French creoles who stayed on in the new state after his declaration of Haitian independence in 1804. Although this massacre has been taken as evidence of Dessalines's unequivocal hatred of all whites, by the time the first Haitian Constitution was issued in January 1805, Dessalines along with other Haitian leaders had developed and institutionalized a fully wrought and quite subtle position on race in the new republic, which made clear that he did not ultimately advocate a unilateral racial politics. First, the Constitution stipulated that no white men could claim citizenship or property in Haiti. It then exempted German and Polish soldiers as well as white women and their children from this stipulation. And then, in the final clause dealing with race, it designated that all Haitians, which would necessarily include the Germans, Poles, and white women referenced in the earlier clause, would henceforth be known by the general term *black*.[35] To stay in postrevolutionary Haiti was, in short, to become black, although here blackness is unhitched from its epidermal signification and given a national and cultural one.

This generalization of blackness would prove a problem in Sansay's construction of surrogatory relations that reinstate racial distinctions. Thus, *Secret History* rejects this revaluation of blackness by implying it is equivalent to and only representable as cross-racial sexual violence, a representation that structures the anecdote Sansay offers in both works. Sansay dated this anecdote as occurring during Dessaliness's massacre of the whites and thus before his universalization of blackness (probably in the spring of 1804). She relates that Madame G—, a white French creole woman who had fled the island during the earlier stages of the revolution, returned to revolutionary Saint-Domingue when the French forces arrived because she imagined that a French victory would allow her daughters to claim their "parental inheritance." After the collapse of the French forces, she followed the counsel of "one of the black chiefs" and stayed in postrevolutionary Haiti in hopes that, rather that a life of exile, she and her three daughters might make a life for themselves in the new state.[36] Sansay recounted that a black general told Madame G— that he would protect her family by marrying her eldest daughter Adelaide; in response to this proposal, Madame G— announced that "death [would] be preferable to such protection," and Adelaide fainted.[37] The general took Madame G— up on her declaration that she would prefer death to a cross-racial alliance, and she and her two younger daughters were hanged at the gallows. Adelaide, who continued to refuse the alliance, was "hung ... by the throat on an iron hook in the market place, where the lovely, innocent, unfortunate victim slowly expired."[38]

Although Sansay dates this incident as having occurred in 1804, the anecdote's anxieties about miscegenation and the decomposition of whiteness suggest that she interpreted the event with an eye to the recodification of race that was accomplished by the 1805 Constitution. Here, Dessaliness's resignification and generalization of blackness is compressed into the threat of white women's sexual penetration by black men. The anecdote indicates Sansay's refusal of Dessalines's generalization of blackness, but it does not simply evince her refusal—it also assays a surrogation, as is evident in the anecdote's conclusion. The white woman Adelaide is presented in terms reminiscent of those of antislavery abolition: she is innocent, a victim, and perhaps most tellingly, her dying body is put into the posture of the dying Afro-American slave iconicized by Blake's engraving for Stedman of a "Negro hung alive by the ribs" (Figure 14).

Clearly this anecdote's effort to shore up the property of whiteness is an effort to forget that the Haitian Revolution did evince cross-raciality and that, at least some of the time, white French creole and U.S.-born women understood that they stood to gain from this situation. Other less obvious genealogies were also being forgotten when white women were figured as the inheritors of the liberation achieved by Afro-Americans' radical antislavery. It was not simply the property of whiteness but the status of property more generally that was at stake in the Haitian Revolution and in other articulations of radical antislavery. After all, at the start of the revolution, slave property articulated its vitality, resistance, and autonomy. The implication of this line of radical antislavery was that property could not simply be conceived of as passive units of exchange or inheritance and this implication did not always and exclusively apply to the particular object called slave property. As I argued in chapter 4, Afro-American cultural forms like fetish production and Vodou, both of which were visible in colonial Saint-Domingue and postcolonial Haiti, complicated conceptions of property, object-status, and commodification by suggesting that organic and inorganic forms cannot simply be counted as passive units to be meted out by human agents.

One of the undergirding if not generally fully articulated possibilities that subtends this line of antislavery was a dissolution of the colonial conceptualization of the object, which would force a large-scale revaluation of property that could in turn challenge the bourgeois models of sociality and personality that historians have argued resulted from the Age of Revolution. Indeed, this different valuation of property and exchange emerged as a real contest in postrevolutionary Haiti. Unlike Louverture, who tried to keep the plantation system's organization of property in place although this time fueled by free instead of slave laborers, Dessalines attempted a more radical reorganization of property: he claimed the land of the class of propertied free mulattoes and, although it is not certain if he planned to distribute it in small packets to every citizen or keep it under state control,

A Negro hung alive by the Ribs to a Gallows.

London, Published Dec.r 1.st 1792, by J. Johnson, S.t Pauls Church Yard.
II

Figure 14. Negro Hung by the Ribs, *engraving by William Blake, 1794. Sansay's narration of Adelaide's death mimics the iconographic posture of Blake's slave. Courtesy of the John Carter Brown Library at Brown University.*

he proposed that all Haitians had a claim to the land. Dessalines's assassination and dismemberment in 1806 was in part the result of his effort to democratize property.[39] This decidedly unbourgeois revaluation of property, objects, and place is also forgotten by *Secret History* although, as we shall see, it does not disappear.

Secret History's effort to cover over the more radical implications of the antislavery from which its white women protagonists draw inspiration structures its conclusion when the primary letter writer, Mary, articulates the ideal toward which eighteenth-century white women should strive: bourgeois, companionate marriage, which is a rather extraordinary conclusion given the work's account of marriage as a scene of domestic violence.[40] Yet even as Mary idealizes this model of bourgeois female personhood, she recognizes that for Clara companionate marriage and the linked phenomenon of tightly enclosed desire and affect were impossible. "When a woman, like Clara," she writes "can fascinate, intoxicate, transport, and whilst unhappy is surrounded by seductive objects, she will become entangled, and be borne away by the rapidity of her own sensations, happy if she can stop short on the brink of destruction."[41] Sansay's concluding attention to the distance between Mary's idealization of domestic felicity and Clara's entangling desire for "destructive objects" recalls the book's opening division of idealism and destruction, but here the destructive potential Mary first ascribes to Afro-Americans returns in an Anglo-American woman on her way to Philadelphia. That Clara recalls and carries with her not just the positively valued liberation associated with Afro-Americans but also exoergic desires and object relations that need only some event to call forth their destructive potential suggests that Sansay's surrogatory operation has failed.

Possession

That *Secret History*'s effort to use surrogation to divide black from white cultural forms falls apart at its conclusion calls for a further investigation of how surrogation plays out in the American tropics. If surrogation always involves one performance recalling and taking the place of another, it is not simply a process of recollection and displacement but also one of addition. A performance through which a person posturally, stylistically, and imaginatively puts herself in the place of another person, being, or event also opens that person to the addition of others through which she becomes, quite literally, more than herself.[42] In the case of white women surrogating radical antislavery, the addition at the scene of surrogation is not unitary. After all, Sansay's white women draw on a history and style of resistance that gave rise to practices of personhood departing from the constellation of affect, desire, and embodiment that eighteenth- and nineteenth-century Anglo-Europeans more usually advocated as the grounds of personality.

Benjamin Franklin famously argued that through force of habit a person could perform himself as his ideal version of himself, thus emerging as a stable, coherent, socially and economically successful personality. However, Sansay's protagonists' performances do not arrive at any such stability or coherence. Nor are they underwritten by an idealist identity that precedes all performance. Although her protagonists are entirely as performative as Franklin's representative man, what is added to these white woman who mimic Afro-American styles of resistance is not a movement toward an ideal that underwrites the performance (the Franklinian mode), nor is it the addition of a single other who is brought onto the scene through surrogation. The latter is the tendency of the American gothic, which speculates that a being or moment that seems to be outside the containment of a particular human body could be reconstituted on its inside (as in Poe's "Ligeia" when the Lady Ligeia returns in the body of the Lady Rowena, and in "The Fall of the House of Usher" when the atmosphere and matter of the house possess both Usher and Madeleine) or, vice versa, to speculate that the insides of a particular individual could be reconstituted on the outside (as in Brockden Brown's works, particularly *Wieland* when Carwin's person is projected onto and structures social arrangements outside of his person proper). Instead, Sansay's texts reveal this addition as a constellation of different performances that compromises surrogatory efforts. Sansay's surrogation is meant to be a controlled process by which properties associated with one body and its performance are enacted by another, a transfer that presumes the enclosure of the surrogate body, which in turn presumes the containment of the person in and by the body and the stability of the identity associated with this body. However, Anglo-American women's surrogation of modes of personhood that conceive the human body as an always open collation of more than human forces gives rise to a surrogation characterized by a surfeit of additions that can exceed and open up the surrogatory body.

To clarify this point, it is worth briefly recalling how fetish production and Vodou shape the conceptualization and performance of the Afro-American personhood that Sansay's protagonists surrogate. Fetish use conceives the (para)human body as exceeding the skin envelope. It also attends to a (para)human body's relation to and transformation by organic and inorganic materialities that are not conceived as dead stuff but as potentially animate matter. Vodou similarly conceives the human being not as a closed interiority but as a structure that can be inhabited and supplemented by gods and other materialities. In fact, Vodou performances reverse racial surrogation's propensity for forgetting that which is performed by emphasizing the amassing presence of other persons, times, and timbres that accrue in the structuration of personality.[43] Taking these cultural forms into account as part of what is surrogated by Sansay's white women allows us to return to Bennett's concept of "a life" and to push it into a register that attends to the particularities of the American tropics. Surrogation in revolutionary Saint-Domingue and postrevolutionary Haiti is, at least potentially, a practice through which a person holds within herself not a previous person or her history but a collation of organic and inorganic forms. This collation can give rise to the disruptive potentiality that Bennett designates "a life" and that Afro-American fetish makers and Vodou adepts conceive as the total agency of the material world, an agency capable of tearing open the actual and giving rise to unexpected combinations of animate forces.

That Sansay's surrogatory operation holds within itself the seeds of a change in personhood that moves beyond a simple choice of a more or less bourgeois subjectivity is evident in her repeated invocations of the breaking of white women's bodies. Recall that the scene of the mountain exploding that opens both *Secret History* and *Zelica* testifies not simply to Afro-Americans' destruction of nature but also to their destruction of the integrity of human bodies. This introductory invocation of the body in parts returns with force in both works' accounts of the slaughter of the French men, women, and children who remained in postrevolutionary Haiti in 1804. In *Zelica*, Clara, walking on the streets of Cap François after the massacre, literally stumbles over the "arm of [her friend]."[44] Quivering and indistinguishable pieces of bodies lie heaped on the streets. Napoleon's propagandist Jean-Louis Dubroca's 1804 pamphlet *La Vie de J. J. Dessalines* similarly describes postrevolutionary Haiti as occasioning white women's bodily disaggregation. In an engraving by Mexican illustrator Manuel Lopez that accompanied the 1806 Spanish-language edition (Figure 15), lines of trees (probably coffee trees) in the background recall the plantation economy's organization of terrain while a black man behind a rock presents a grotesque new terrain dominated by an outsized white woman whose body is cut into pieces, a baby attempting to latch onto her stiffening breast ("*el pecho yerto*").

That this body cannot be pieced together again is evident not only because of its simple deadness but also because of the artist's rendering that proleptically (if accidentally) presents body pieces that cannot be recomposed: the wound to the base of the woman's head and the wound to her neck do not align and the calf pulled from her body looms larger than the leg that remains attached to it. The potentiality running through Sansay's, Dubroca's, and Lopez's images is not simply an echo of counterrevolutionary responses to the French Revolution, which often focused on the cutting of heads from bodies not simply as historical fact but as a symptom of the supposed unreason of revolution, although certainly this discourse is present, particularly in Dubroca's and Lopez's works (Figure 16). The more critical potentiality running through this iconography in which Afro-American resistance renders the body in parts is that what Aravamudan calls *tropicopolitans* would break open the then dominant Anglo-European conceptualization of the human body as an integral, discrete, and self-sufficient unit, thus forcing a movement away from a political tradition in which this body functioned as the main unit and for which it provided a central metaphor. That these counterrevolutionary responses to Afro-American resistance so often turn to the destruction and violation of white women's bodies suggests that what was at stake was not only a shifting political symbolics but a destruction of the modes of genealogy and family associated with and founded on the careful management of (white) women's bodies.

Sansay's as well as Lopez's turn to narrative and visual rhetorics of overwhelming, almost farcical brutality suggests that for many Anglo-European colonizers and creoles alike life in postrevolutionary Haiti was thinkable only as brutality, death, and the arrival of nothingness. But, as is always the case in Sansay's Haitian writings, this nothing also evinces something. For one, this iconography appropriates and reverses colonial accounts of the black body in parts. This is more than a simple reversal; it is evidence of an anxiety that a reconceptualization of the body and personhood in

Manuel (poes) Lopez, div.º y Grave flesc.º

Fue muerta y destrozada en el campo esta infeliz pᵃ.
haver resistido a los deseos brutales de los Negros
y el niño perezio de hambre asulado buscando el pecho
yerto de su Madre

Figure 15. Manuel Lopez, Fue muerta y destrozada, *1806. This engraving for the Spanish-language version of* The Life of J. J. Dessalines, *a fiercely anti-Haitian work written by one of Napoleon's propagandists, references Dessalines's 1804 massacre of the remaining French and French creole whites to suggest that the disaggregation of the body was a general condition of black revolution. Courtesy of the John Carter Brown Library at Brown University.*

DESALINES.

Figure 16. Manuel Lopez, Desalines [sic], 1806. Another engraving from the Spanish-language edition of The Life of J. J. Dessalines that links Dessalines to the disaggregation of white female bodies. Courtesy of the John Carter Brown Library at Brown University.

conditions of maximal uncertainty was no longer simply the predicament of Africans in the diaspora but a general fact of life in the American tropics. Although such iconography would seem to present postrevolutionary Haiti as a space of pure negativity, in *Zelica* Sansay keeps Clara in the postrevolutionary state as if to consider what, besides disaggregation, becomes of Anglo-American women who stay on. This interest in keeping Clara in postrevolutionary Haiti evinces a glimmering sense that the bodily disaggregation and relation to *oikos* that occurred in the tropics—not only because of the forces of climate and encroaching plant and animal life but also because of the plantation form that built itself upon these regional particularities—might be experienced as the basis of a reconceptualization of the person and political life as an entanglement and a divagation along the lines emerging in the Afro-American fetishes and animal stories discussed earlier.

Sean Goudie's reading of *Secret History* offers a way to trace how Sansay's Haitian writings register a change in personhood. Goudie picks up Drexler's observation that Clara flees her husband to a space of marronage and pushes it farther, arguing that in El Cobre Clara comes into contact with Afro-Caribbean religious traditions and becomes a devotee of the Vodou goddess Erzuli. Goudie, who supposes that Sansay offers no explicit evidence that Clara was exposed to Vodou, bases this argument primarily on Clara's marked admiration of a local feast devoted to the Virgin Mary. Goudie, noting that diasporic Africans in the Caribbean often used Catholicism's Marian iconography and feasts to invoke and celebrate the Vodou goddess Erzulie, suggests that these traces of Vodun passed into creole cultures more broadly. Thus, even if Clara cannot quite name what she finds so pleasingly excessive about the festival to Mary, this celebration that occurs in a space of marronage was almost certainly, at least for some celebrants, linked to Vodou and suggests that Sansay subtly and perhaps inadvertently inserts Clara into a (Haitian) creole tradition that would countermand surrogations that attempt to segregate and sediment identities.

It is certainly possible that Sansay would have had some knowledge of the Vodou goddess Erzuli, even if this knowledge is not directly referenced in *Secret History*. What's more, in detailing Clara's captivation with the Virgin at El Cobre, Sansay enters Clara into a diasporic nexus that extends beyond those of the French and Haitian Antilles that Goudie proposes. Hispanophone critics have long noted that the Virgin of El Cobre marks the intersection of at least three converging traditions that colonialism brought into contact and merged into the symbol of the virgin. Antonio Benítez-Rojo explains that the worship and myths of the Virgin at El Cobre bring together "three sources of meaning: one of aboriginal origin (the Taino deity Atabey or Atabex), another native to Europe (the Virgin of *Illescas*), and finally, another from Africa (the Yoruba *orisha* Oshun)."[45] Drawing on these three sources, to which Goudie's reading of Clara's relation to Haitian Vodou suggests a fourth, suggests that *Secret History*, like the Virgin itself, might be interpreted as a "meta-archipelagic text, a . . . confluence of marine flowings that connects the Niger with the Mississippi, the China Sea with the Orinoco, the Parthenon with . . . an alley in Paramibo."[46] This episode, set in the mountainous, heavily black and mulatto Cuban backcountry at the borders of the pueblo and the maroon, indicates the intercolonial and cross-spatial relationality from which Clara achieves personal agency. After all, this is not only the moment Clara flees her abusive husband but also, as Goudie points out, the moment that Clara first contributes her own letters to the travelogue.

By Goudie's reading, the intercolonial and cross-spatial relations through which Clara gains a creole identity remain under the surface of the travelogue, as though part of the oceanic undertow that courses through the work from Mary's opening fantasy of foundering at sea to the final voyage in which the creolized Clara sails to postrevolutionary Philadelphia. Yet if *Secret History* gives scant evidence that Sansay was thinking that Clara's creolization was affected by Haitian Vodou or Afro-American fetish use and its revaluation of objects and property, this is not the case in *Zelica*. Like other early accounts of what is now called Vodou, *Zelica* makes several references to what it designates as Afro-Americans' superstitious customs, which Zelica suggests is "the most official power in the country."[47] In the final book of *Zelica*, an Afro-American Vodou priestess named Madelaine joins Zelica and Clara as one of the novel's chief protagonists. Madelaine builds a fetish in the novel's climactic scene. At the start of the fetish ritual, Madelaine "gathered dry sticks . . . and raised with great symmetry a pile in the form of an altar, on which having placed a small caldron . . . she put into it . . . a large quantity of bees'-wax [and] . . . black sealing-wax." This "was the commencement of the most potent charm directed by African magicians, and "beneath" Madelaine's "plastic hands it assumed every moment a nearer approach to the human form."[48]

Sansay's description of fetish production is quite unreliable. That this fetish is representational and in the shape of a human being runs against

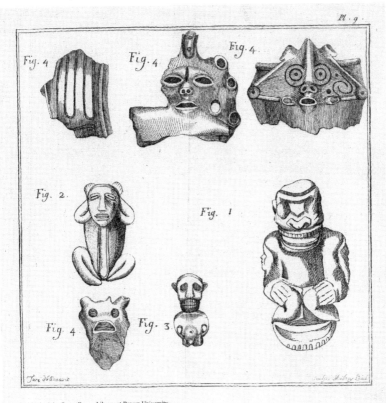

Original in the John Carter Brown Library at Brown University

Figure 17. Père Nicholson, Haitian Stone and Pottery Artifacts, 1776. Nicholson pays very little attention to Afro-American cultural forms and suggests that all of these idols are relics of the Arawak, who had been exterminated at the time he was writing. Even if these idols are all Native and not Afro-American, Afro-American slaves and maroons, like Anglo-European natural historians, collected Native American artifacts, often incorporating them into their own cultural forms. Courtesy of the John Carter Brown Library at Brown University.

more reliable contemporaneous accounts as well as later art historians' and anthropologists' work that emphasizes that fetishes were nonrepresentational and not generally anthropomorphic. Indeed, Sansay's account does not accord with Père Nicholson's narrative and visual account of what he calls idols in *Essai sur l'histoire naturelle de St. Domingue* (1776) (Figure 17). Nicholson catalogues all these fetishes in a chapter dealing with the then virtually extinct Arawak Indians, an organization that structurally closes down the possibility that some of these idols might have been Afro-American productions. Nor does he comment on the fact that

Afro-Americans in Saint-Domingue appropriated American Indian practices and artifacts.[49] However, Nicholson's account, which Sansay might well have accessed because it was probably available in Philadelphia and in Cap François as well, makes clear that "idols" do not replicate the form of the human body as it was generally represented in eighteenth- and nineteenth-century Anglo-European aesthetic conventions.[50]

Although Sansay's account of fetish production is unreliable even among generally unreliable and obscuring eighteenth- and nineteenth-century Anglo-European accounts, her description of the fetish ceremony does get at some key aspects of Afro-American fetish construction. For one, her description of Madelaine's collection of materials recognizes that a fetish is a recipe that draws together pieces of a series of local ingredients to change the organization of life in the present. She is also incipiently aware that fetish-production assumes the plasticity of the material world, even if she gives this attribute to Madelaine's hands and not to the artifact she crafts or the events that follow from its production.

The aim of Madelaine's fetish is ostensibly to protect Clara from her black suitor Glaude so that she can flee postrevolutionary Haiti and avoid becoming black as well as the disaggregation of the body associated with it. However, that Clara is to be protected from becoming black, from the disaggregation of the integral body, and from the nothingness of Haiti via the agency of an Afro-American fetish indicates a fundamental ambiguity in the office the fetish is to perform.[51] If the office of the fetish is to protect Clara from blackness and its imagined correlations so as to maintain the closed integrity of her body, it clearly does not and cannot fulfill its office. At precisely the narrative juncture when Madelaine completes the fetish and brings it to Clara, Clara is pierced by a dagger and dies in Glaude's arms. Yet it is not at all clear that the fetish has not fulfilled its office: Sansay's paradoxical suggestion that protection from blackness and disaggregation requires the intervention of an Afro-American cultural form notable precisely for its aesthetics of fragmentation suggests a desire for that which is supposedly being foreclosed. Moreover, the precision of the narrative's sequencing of the fetish's arrival and Clara's penetration and death suggests the fetish's work is not to hold off blackness and disaggregation of the body but to catalyze a movement toward them.

Given that Afro-American cultural forms are consistently associated with destruction in Sansay's writing, it is not surprising that Clara's becoming Haitian is figured as equivalent to her death. Yet Sansay's allusions and narrative framing suggest an addition and a passage, which if it is only graspable as death, is also more than that.[52] Writing that Madelaine "adorns [Zelica] like a bride . . . not like a victim destined to the grave," Sansay raises the possibility that the opening initiated by the arrival of the fetish might be conceived as a transformation that is not simply a death.[53] Clara's body, twined in jasmine and encased in what Sansay describes as "an envelope" made of palm leaves and held together by flexible twigs, is raised onto an eminence overlooking the sea before it is finally buried, her grave faithfully tended by Madelaine. This description not only nostalgically renders Madelaine as though she were not a Vodou priestess but a devoted slave, it also suggests that Clara, instead of surrogating radical antislavery and black revolution, is so entirely suffused by the additions that come with her surrogatory load that she opens into and stays in the place of Afro-American revolution. She does not return to herself, and she does not become epidermally or in a narrowly identitarian sense black, as Sansay's writing anxiously imagines might happen to white women in post-revolutionary Haiti. In this concluding tableau, Clara, twined with *oikos,* verges on an ontological revaluation in which, through the agency of the fetish, she is changing from a closed to an opened body, from a racially determined "white" identity that nonetheless mimics Afro-American practices to a creole and Haitian person.

Madelaine's ritualistic arrangements of the body suggest Clara's becoming place. This conversion of a person into a locality recalls the fate of Dessalines, who was pulled to pieces by his murderers, whose pieces were then gathered and buried, and who was then apotheosized as the place of Haiti.[54] This conversion is not simply that of a man into a god but also of terrain, which takes on the attributes of the despised and redeemed hero. The terrain's incorporation of Dessalines makes his and other Afro-Americans' belief that objects and land were animate matter central to the mythology of postcolonial Haiti. This and other mythologies of Dessalines's revaluation of place and of objects were beginning to develop in Haiti at precisely the time Sansay was writing *Zelica.* Timoléon Brutus's biography of Dessalines records a song he was taught in 1901 by an old man who claimed it was sung after the 1803 Battle of Vertiers that ended the Haitian Revolution.[55] In this song, Dessalines is celebrated for bringing the people a *ounga nouveau* or a new fetish. Dessalines's use of fetishes and his own reputed participation in Vodou implicated him in Afro-American cosmologies that presumed the decentralization of the body and that further stipulated that any body, artifact, or force could become animate through ritual oration or arrangement. This expansive understanding of animacy might well have provided the ideological ground that gave rise to his interest in converting the property of mulatto elites into a commons shared by all Haitians. By the second decade of the nineteenth century, Dessalines, his fetishes, and his interest in property in common would have evoked the possibility of a postrevolutionary political organization that contrasted sharply with that developed by Christophe, who after Dessalines's death crowned himself King of Haiti and put into place a feudal labor system in which property, spirit, land, and persons were all centered in the monarch.[56]

Clara's concluding conversion into place evokes mythologies of Dessalines that presume that the production of a genuinely postcolonial state requires a reconceptualization of animacy and place that substantively departs from the conceptualizations of each that were common to colonial and then national regimes. However, the novel's concluding scene turns from the far-ranging implications of this ritual to offer a banal quasi-romantic interest in the melancholic relation between persons and places (Madelaine predicts that Clara's husband will return to the world while "my poor mistress lies cold and forgotten on the mountain").[57] Nonetheless, the trajectories Sansay follows in her Haitian writings as well as those she gives Clara make clear that then-regnant models of human agency and sociality were not adequate to at least some Anglo-American women. The companionate marriage through which Wollstonecraft imagined women might articulate their agency is out of the question. Moreover, Clara's trajectory does not suppose an adequate form of personhood was a simple matter of expanding existing bourgeois republican nationalism so that the ladies might be remembered, as Abigail Adams advocates. Nor does she stay with the coquette's strategy of constant choosing that amounts to a not-choosing. Instead, the portents of destructivity, ruination, fragmentation, and death that she so persistently accumulates in her works make clear a desire for a destructive difference that breaks the conventions of life and personhood then dominant in postrevolutionary Philadelphia. This is not evidence of a death drive or masochism, but rather is the only way possible to stage her desire for a dramatic shift from existing models of agency and social life. For all its negativity, Sansay's work strives to instantiate a productivity. The surrogation through which Sansay attempts to negotiate this shift is, however racially problematic, an operation that allows an opening to the movements of counternormative desires, agencies, and socialities. And this surrogation itself ultimately gives way to a possession by place that anticipates the coming of a personhood not scriptable for Sansay. Yet even if Sansay's productivity remains only a trajectory, it opens the critical project of following the curve of her involution to defamiliarize and pluralize our understandings of agency in the period so that they attend to the impact and dissemination of Afro-American modes of personhood and resistance.

In fact, there is evidence that Sansay herself may have followed the trajectories her work gives only as potentialities. She spent the summer of 1809 immersed in chemistry books and chemical experiments that she studied to glean knowledge that would help her to make artificial flowers. Her fledgling artificial flower business proved a success, and by the spring of 1810 she had opened a manufactory that employed ten people, most of them women.[58] (Might some of these employees have been Afro-American or mulatto, and might this be one of the reasons that by 1820 she was less interested in the relation between white women than in that between white women and women of color?) She was still in business in 1814 when she sold and displayed her flowers at the Philadelphia Exposition of Fine Arts. If one of the questions scholars have put to Sansay's oeuvre is how it is that between *Secret History* and *Zelica* she became so much more interested in Afro-American actors and agency, perhaps part of the answer can be found here. In working with chemistry (which, as noted in chapter 2, was one of the sciences most associated with vitalist materialism) and in producing flowers, perhaps employing Afro-American as well as white women, she was at the interstices of both eighteenth- and early nineteenth-century vitalist materialism and Afro-American fetishism.

Vitalist materialism—from its incarnations in chemistry, to the botanists' interest in the spontaneous life of tropical vegetation, to mesmerism's interest in the superfine fluid coursing through organic and inorganic bodies—gave rise to the belief that power and animacy were diffuse forces that exceeded the body and that linked humans to animal and nonhuman agents. Fetishism, the production of artifacts through which the body could be opened to its outsides, including nonhuman forces, further decomposed Anglo-European concepts of the body as a discrete and bounded form. In fact, Sansay's artificial flowers themselves might be thought as quasi fetishes in that they were artifacts that, once produced, had power through their circulation to change Sansay's agency and personhood, a transformation evident in the decreasing attention to domestic happiness in her fiction and in her decreasing attention to Burr and to male sponsorship more generally in her personal correspondence. In the second decade of the nineteenth century, Sansay devoted herself to the aesthetic and communal life developing in her manufactory. Perhaps it was through this work of producing artificial flowers that she became ever more interested in staying in the place of Haiti to imagine the reconfigurations of body, personhood, and place available there.

Afterlives of Ariel's Ecology

In the opening chapter of Edgar Allan Poe's *Narrative of Arthur Gordon Pym of Nantucket* (1838), Poe's protagonist, Pym, is swept from the brig *Ariel* when it is run down by the whaler *Penguin*. Pinned to the keel of the *Penguin*, Pym rides the Atlantic, facing downward to the sea's depths and drowning. *Pym*'s opening sequencing of storms, shipwreck, and the delivery of the Anglo-European Pym to the sea by the agency of an Ariel, this time a ship rather than a spirit, recalls Shakespeare's play, which is one of *Pym*'s several literary precedents. Like the other literary precedents circulating in *Pym* (Defoe's *Robinson Crusoe*, Coleridge's "The Rime of the Ancient Mariner"), *The Tempest* is referenced in order to be mutated. Instead of the structures of subjection and social and political order that emerge from these precedents, Poe casts Pym in an erratic trajectory that dissolves autobiography (evident in Pym's lack of a sense of either history or guilt), sedimented social organizations (evident in Pym's cannibalization of a shipboard companion), and known cartographies (evident in the work's concluding drive off the edges of any known mapping of space or terrain). In the work's penultimate sequence, when Pym, along with the half-Crow, half-Canadian Dirk Peters, finds himself stranded on the tropico-polar island Tsalal, he declares, "We alone had escaped from the tempest of that overwhelming destruction. We were the only living white men upon the island."[1] This declaration of whiteness is so deeply shot through with irony as to announce precisely its inverse. Most obviously, Peters is not white. More pressingly, Pym himself has been increasingly coded as savage in the several chapters preceding this declaration. Pym's erratic trajectory involves him in a process of creolization that began in the opening sequence when the *Penguin*'s wayward bolt passed into his neck and out just below his ear, impaling him on the ship's bottom. Pym's declaration indicates that this "tempest," which by this point references subaltern resistance as well as elemental and ecological processes, has become a planetary phenomenon.

If Pym hoped to find a new personal or political configuration in his zigzagging trajectory across the Atlantic, down from the tip of South American where the Atlantic joins the Pacific, and then beyond all known territories, he instead discovers that there is no escape from colonialization and ensuing processes of creolization.

That Pym recasts The Tempest as a colonial contest unfolding on a planetary scale indicates the expanding geopolitical frame on which tropical unrest and agency were conceived by the midcentury moment in which Poe wrote. What's more, Pym's attention to planetary creolization indicates how the themes I have followed in this book verge toward and then veer away from the canonical archive of American literature in which Pym has been included since the publication of Leslie Fiedler's Love and Death in the American Novel (1960).[2] In verging on this canonical archive, I do not mean to infuse the archive and the questions I have pursued into the American canon so as to expand it with new readings in minor keys. Rather, I mean this verging as the occasion for a line of interrogation that reclaims Poe's Pym as a minoritarian work, by which I mean a work and genealogy that develops within a majority tradition and that offers a port through which character or critic might move to produce alternate forms of personhood and sociality. As Deleuze and Guattari propose, minority languages and literatures might be understood as "that which a minority constructs within a major language" and that effects the "deterritorialization of languages, the connection of the individual to a political immediacy, and the collective assemblage of enunciation."[3] By their account, minor literatures forge "the revolutionary conditions for every literature within the heart of what is called great (or established) literatures."[4] If this definition of the minoritarian suggests that the minoritarian depends on a majoritarian language and literature from which it emerges and that it cannibalizes and revolutionizes, the reading of Pym I offer here indicates that minoritarian works, far from being in opposition to and thus dependent on the crushing presence of canonical traditions, decompose canonical traditions from within, in their place producing a new field, by which I mean a new organization of space, self, and sociality that has the power to pass the majoritarian tradition into minoritarian lines.

The canonical organization of space, self, and sociality and the minoritarian flight from it are tensely juxtaposed in Pym. In the opening sequences, the Ariel moves horizontally across the sea's surface. Although it is a sailboat and not a cargo vessel, the Ariel, like the whaling ship Penguin that will destroy it, follows the usual horizontal trajectory of the Atlantic ships that moved commodities, specimens, and persons between state forms. Yet when the two vessels collide Pym is cast beneath the ship. Although his body continues to move more or less horizontally (more or less because the ship's violent rolling from this horizontal course is what makes Pym visible to the crew of the *Penguin*), Pym's gaze is to the sea's depths. He has lost consciousness and gives no record of what he sees; however, the ensuing creolization that makes him unable to determine whiteness from blackness allows us to speculate that his gaze, or perhaps more aptly his orientation, is toward lost ships, cargos, and persons, including the Afro-Americans dumped into the sea and those who jumped into it to escape colonialism's system of horizontal exchanges, hoping to access another Africa, this one not located in existing geopolitical space but below the sea. The important point here is that *Pym*'s opening sequence offers two distinct orientations. First, the sea journey is a sojourn between land and landings that, even if it evades the dictates of territorial orders, leaves territorial orders in place. Second, the underwater journey is a site of loss that engenders a creolization that fantasizes and in some cases effects a movement beyond territorial orders. This second orientation is *Pym*'s minoritarian line, and it is this second line that the work follows to its limit, as is evident when at its close Pym vanishes from the face of every map. The reader is assured that Pym's disappearance from maps did not cause his death, as is evident from the fact that Pym has narrated the story after the completion of his sea journey. If Pym's disappearance from maps is not equivalent to his death, when the story shifts from Pym's narration to that of an unnamed narrator it makes clear that Poe was not able to conceive further Pym's downward trajectory.

If Poe leaves Pym caught between the majoritarian order and its structuration of self, sociality, and geopolitics and a minoritarian line that would dissolve each of these structurations, I want to push beyond this stalemate to testify to the presence and effects of this minoritarian line that moves through the book. That *Pym* might be read as a variation on the minoritarian line I have been following for the course of this book is evident in its attention to the disaggregation of the body, a disaggregation that becomes more pronounced as Pym's locations become more tropicalized when he moves ever southward. The disaggregating body—which is a shadow theme of Bartram's botanical writings, is a central focus of parahuman tales and Afro-American fetishism, and becomes increasingly foregrounded in Sansay's anabiography—is everywhere evident in *Pym*. The theme of bodily penetration first emerges in the opening pages when Pym's neck is bisected by the *Penguin*'s bolt. Increasingly *Pym* intensifies the theme of the penetration of the human body to focus on dismemberment, organs on the outside of bodies, and the wholesale dissolution of bodies. Consider the apparent bisection of Peters on the brig *Grampus* where a "thick line" is "pulled so forcibly around his loins as to give him the appearance of being cut nearly in two."[5] One chapter later, Pym, Peters, and two other sailors stranded on the *Grampus* encounter a ghost ship from which a man summons them. When the ship tacks, the man is revealed to be a corpse animated by a seagull: its head, embedded in the man's back, moves his body in gestures that approximate those of human life. On being witnessed by Pym, the gull detaches itself from the man's body and, with a human liver in its beak, spirals slowly above the *Grampus* before dropping its cargo on deck, which motivates Pym's first impulse toward cannibalization.

In the preceding pages we have explored Afro-American fetishes that presume the opening of the human body and the relocation of organs to the outside. In *Pym*, this opening up of the body and movement of organs to its outsides is linked to a process of becoming savage (that is also, for Pym, a process of becoming African), which is enacted in the work's next sequence when Pym, Peters, and their two companions decide that the only way to avoid starvation is to cannibalize one of their party. The Anglo-European sailor Parker is then killed and cut into pieces; his hands, feet, and head are discarded into the sea, and the remaining meat and blood are "devoured."[6]

From the point of Pym's cannibalism forward, bodies of all sorts go to pieces. Pym's friend Augustus's leg falls casually from his body at his death. In Tsalal, Pym recounts events in which Anglo-European Atlantic explorers' encounters with natives are bizarrely crossed with Afro-American marronage and slave rebellion. The native Tsalalians are something of a composite of the Arawaks Columbus encountered in the West Indies (at first encounter they seem perfectly innocent and are astounded by Anglo-European technology—particularly mirrors) and Africans in what Poe seems to imagine as their natural state (they are entirely black, entirely brutal, and quite capable of destroying the Anglo-European civilization that would instrumentalize them and their territory). The Tsalalians come to resent their Anglo-European visitors' colonial ambitions, at which point they "absolutely" tear them "to pieces in an instant."[7] Pushing this fixation with dismemberment to a spectacular conclusion, Pym, observing the scene at a distance, records that the natives then accidentally perform a mass electrocution that galvanizes him and converts the natives and the Anglo-Europeans they had killed into "a chaos of wood and metal and human limbs" that, before it can fall to the ground, is exploded again to yield a "dense shower of the minutest fragments" that moves "in every direction around us."[8]

Sharon Cameron has argued that one of the great themes of the American literary tradition is the relation of the body to its outsides, a theme she suggests is linked to questions of what constitutes an identity and what constitutes the proper relation of parts to wholes.[9] She includes *Pym* in this American archive. And yet, as we have seen, *Pym*'s exploration of the theme of the body to its outsides does not simply participate in the majoritarian tradition that Cameron so brilliantly traces because it also passes *Pym* back toward the minoritarian line we have been following. *Pym*'s relentless investigation of the disaggregation of the human body, like the Afro-American parahuman tales and fetishes that I put in relation to it, is less focused on questions of identity as such than it is on the project of recreating the terms through which identity and bodies are conceived. And, instead of focusing on the relation of parts to wholes, the motivating impulse of this archive and of *Pym*'s shower of bodies in parts is to render bodies as parts that must be thought as outside of or only in deeply equivocal relation to any wholes. Parts do not compose wholes, then. They can also be cast outside of wholes, even if they may participate in some gathering at another time. Reading *Pym* in this minoritarian line, it becomes clear that everything must not converge. This momentum of *Pym*'s minoritarian line allows for a centrifugal movement that countermands the centripetal tendencies of the Americas' majoritarian tradition.

Pym's proliferation of parts outside wholes, whether that of the body, the nation-state, or even the planet, might seem a sort of chaos that inaugurates an anarchic condition in which no form or order is possible. Certainly this would seem the most probable interpretation of the spectacular double explosion of bodies in *Pym*, which is not described as a positive or desired event and would probably not have been seen as positive by Poe. As Colin Dayan shows, Poe's criticism of Longfellow's "The Slave in the Dismal Swamp" (1842), which idealized Afro-American revolutionizing in the southern lowlands, echoed the proslavery forces' response to Nat

Turner's rebellion, indicating Poe's tolerance for such positions.[10] While Poe almost certainly meant this spectacular explosion of bodies to strike readers as a horrifying climax that they must turn from, this climax is anticipated by another, more positively coded meditation on the theme of the proliferation of parts. In the account of Tsalal's natural history that precedes this explosive conclusion, Poe suggests that the theme of proliferating parts need not be thought as pure disorder. Like Bartram before him, Poe will play out his most radical possibilities by converting recognizably political concerns into natural historical and materialist ones. The Tsalalians are apparently animists, which is to say, a culture that understands nonorganic matter to possess, or be moved by, spirit. Because the preponderance of eighteenth- and early nineteenth-century Anglo-European writings imagine it is a short skip from animism to fetishism, it is no surprise that Pym claims that they are also idolaters. Like most Anglo-European colonial writers, Pym is, on the face of it, deeply critical of animism and fetishism, which is, he suggests, one of the reasons that the Tsalalians are beyond the pale of civilization and consequently why their raw materials can be exploited without reservation.

It is likely that Poe's opinion of African and Afro-American apparent animism was as disparaging as Pym's of the Tsalalians, but it is important to note that Poe is consistently fascinated with animism, which he explores with some frequency in Anglo-European contexts. Consider, for instance, "The Fall of the House of Usher" (1839), where matter possesses the power of volition, or "The Colloquy of Monos and Una" (1841), where bodies and matter express volition and movement even after the organization of life in the body is over, or even "A Tale of the Ragged Mountains" (1844), in which mesmerism can make human bodies and minds into passive matter that can be manipulated by the mesmerist. The point at issue across these stories of Anglo-European animism is the possibility of a monism in which Poe suggests there would be no difference at all between subject and object and an imaginary act and an empirical fact, a collapse of difference that Poe sometimes seems to desire but also finds horrifying.[11] If the fantasy and horror at play in Poe's Anglo-European animism is that all difference collapses, Poe locates a quite different possibility in the Tsalalians and the becoming savage that is the compulsion of *Pym*'s minoritarian line: an animism in which forms and identities do not collapse but become further diversified.

This diversifying materialism is most clear in Pym's account of the peculiar properties of the water indigenous to the island. This water "was not colourless, nor was it of any one uniform colour—presenting to the eye, as it flowed, every possible shade of purple; like the hues of a changeable silk. . . . Upon collecting a basinful . . . we perceived that the whole mass of liquid was made up of a number of distinct veins, each of a distinct hue; that these veins did not commingle."[12] When this water is cut across horizontally, whether by a knife or by any other foreign body, traces of this cut vanish, and the water closes over this foreign body. When a blade is passed through the water vertically, the veins separate and do not immediately if ever come back together. These two cuttings of water seem to suggest two different things: cut horizontally, the water maintains the integrity of its existing structuration; cut vertically, it divides. Yet the division effected by this second cut does not cause the water to lose its status as water but rather indicates a more various expression of its fluidity, as there are now more parts that make up the mass and at the same time remain distinct from it. In this key passage of Pym's Tsalalian sojourn, the general impulse is toward differentiation within plurality. It is the capacity to preserve distinction that is in each point emphasized: this water can maintain its integrity against the cut of blade or body while not in any sense being opposite to them. At the same time, this water can also be further divided such that a given stream of particles can become distinct from the general flow that it also composes.

Pym's narration makes clear the centrality of this Tsalalian water to his natural history of the island and to the colonial history that derives from this natural history. The water of Tsalal, he proposes, was a miracle as extraordinary to him as mirrors were to the Tsalalians. The contrapuntal relation of native water and Anglo-European technologies implies that immersion in native ecologies might produce an equally profound effect on Anglo-Europeans as Western technologies do on native persons. In contemplating the island's natural history, Pym verges on recognizing that the proliferation of parts that he associates with savages and savage bodies and that is also evident in native ecologies testifies to a diversification that is not equivalent to chaos. I dwell on this point in order to suggest that although the countergenealogy of the body, parts, and matter that circulates in the works I treat in *Ariel's Ecology* emphasizes parts that are not, and cannot be, integrated into wholes, this is not equivalent to pure disorder, fragmentation, or total loss. Rather, it is a theme and practice of dividing and differentiating that fantasizes diversity as the originary American event.

In following *Pym*'s minoritarian line to emphasize the diversification of bodies and cultures as well as the linked theme of anticolonialism and new ecologies, I join my analysis of Poe to Wilson Harris's production of a countermythology of the Americas.[13] Harris proposes that *Pym* demonstrates how imperial fantasies succumb to a pan-American mythos of cross-cultural contact whose primary tropes are fantasies of drowning and rituals of cannibalism. Experiences of foundering, cannibalism, and the closely related experience of the body in parts recall the "suppressed dialogue *between partial* orders."[14] One of the accomplishments of Harris's hallucinatorily dense account of this cross-cultural poetics is its emphasis on the prepositional work of determining the relation between things and actions, a prepositional work that is of primary importance, as it is the necessary if nearly imperceptible means through which he moves from subjects, objects, and actions to effect his vertiginously gorgeous cross-cultural poetics. This prepositional emphasis is evident in his attention to experiences of going under, moving between, and passing over. Harris's interest is not, ultimately, an interest in movement or action as such. After all, prepositions are not actions but the means through which to imagine the relation and orientation of parts. Thus, when Harris emphasizes that every order is partial, he means not simply that it is incomplete but more precisely that it is composed of parts that can be put into varying arrangements by prepositional inflection. In shifting from one arrangement to another, from a horizontal line to subaqueous depths, for instance, the field changes in its entirety: its subjects, objects, and actions, its persons, sociabilities, and spaces recompose.

Harris's account of the Americas as a relation among parts is the condition of possibility for the continuation of the creolization and diversification that I have theorized across the archive assembled here. My hope is that the minoritarian line I have tried to follow in this book might contribute to Harris's effort to produce a geopolitics, a history, and an aesthetics that dissolves majoritarian cultures into a cross-cultural poetics. This passage from the majoritarian to the minoritarian has as its trope the dissolution of land into sea, which was always not simply a theme sounded by Bartram, Sansay, and the Afro-American writers and storytellers I have assembled here, but a conceit and an intuition I followed to pass from territorial and canon-bound understandings of the Americas. The rotation of vision that I have proposed for the entirety of this book is necessary to produce a creolized American studies that not only critiques or avoids the imperial United States and its cultural power but attempts a methodology, an aesthetics, and a mythos that has the power to deliver us to other Americas.

Acknowledgments

I am happy to have this opportunity to acknowledge the persons and institutions that helped me to write this book. I am grateful to those readers and audiences who at various stages in the work's progress offered criticisms and suggestions that made my work harder but also helped make the book better. On this count, I am particularly grateful to the anonymous readers for the University of Minnesota Press and to Richard Morrison, all of whom offered advice that was instrumental. Thanks to Natania Meeker for inviting me to present an early version of chapter 2 to the Department of French and Italian at the University of Southern California, where I benefited from the tremendously generous and incisive questions. Thanks to John Williams and the Americanist Colloquium at Yale University for an invitation to present an early draft of chapter 4, where I received a number of excellent challenges and suggestions that changed the shape of the finished project. Thanks to Susan Scott Parrish for reading a version of chapter 4, for sharing her own work in progress, and for her enthusiasm for the project. Thanks to Thomas Hallock for sharing his unpublished work on Bartram with me. Thanks are due Erika Stevens, who read various portions of the manuscript and whose editorial assistance was invaluable in the manuscript's final stages, and also to my production editor, Barbara Goodhouse, and to my excellent copy editor, Vickie West, for their extraordinary work.

I am grateful to the institutions and especially the people who supported me with their belief in my work and this project. I would like to thank Brook Thomas, who first got me thinking about American mythologies when I was an undergraduate at University of California–Irvine. Thanks are also due Chris Newfield, who was my advisor during my master's work at the University of California–Santa Barbara and whose example inspires my own effort to elucidate the larger stakes and passions driving intellectual work. My greatest debt is to Priscilla Wald, whose scholarship led the way for my own, who was a stellar advisor, and whose commitment to addressing the problems and possibilities of American literary studies remains a motivating inspiration. I am grateful to the other members of my committee, Cathy Davidson, Jan Radway, and Houston Baker. Their forthright criticisms, sound advice, support, and the bravery of their own work helped me to produce this book, which turned my earlier work inside out and left most of it on the wayside.

I gained immensely from seminars and discussions with professors and students who were at Duke University during my time there, including Srinivas Aravamudan, Ian Baucom, Matt Cohen, Joe Donahue, Tom Ferraro, Sibylle Fischer, Michael Hardt, Barbara Herrnstein-Smith, Jenny Hubbard, Jaya Kasibhatla, Julie Kim, Rob Mitchell, Vin Nardizzi, Eden Osucha, Thomas Pfau, Jimmy Richardson, Maurice Wallace, and Jini Watson. During my final year at Duke, I was awarded a McNeil Center fellowship, which allowed me to access Philadelphia archives and where I benefited from conversations with a number of excellent Americanists working there at that time. Particular thanks to Chris Iannini for his intellectual generosity. I was very fortunate to have a fellowship at the Cornell Society for the Humanities. My thanks to the extraordinary staff—Mary Ahl, Megan Dirks, and Celeste Pietrusza—and to all of the members of the 2008–2009 seminar. Particular thanks to Sam Baker, Christine Marran, Tim Murray, Marcus Rediker, and Aaron Sachs.

In the fall of 2010, I was lucky to have had a research fellowship at the John Carter Brown Library, and I thank all the staff there, particularly Allison Rich, Val Andrews, and Ted Widmer. Thanks to the English Department and College at Emory University for allowing me to take research leaves. Special thanks to my colleagues Jonathan Goldberg, Rick Rambuss, Ben Reiss, Deborah Elise White, and especially Michael Elliott. I could not imagine a better first job, and I could not have written this book without the support of these colleagues as well as that of the members of my writing group at Emory: Andrea White, Michele Schreiber, and Dierdra Reber. I also benefited from the excellent contributions of the graduate students in my 2010 seminar "Elements Atlanticisms Ecologies." Thanks, finally, to Jennifer Heil, Ania Kowalik, and Elliott Zink for their work as research assistants. Over the years I have presented my work at a number of conferences and am grateful to all of the Americanist colleagues who invited me to speak on panels and who helped the project with their questions and comments.

I am grateful to my parents, my brothers, and all of my aunts, uncles, and cousins (especially Jennifer Sigafoos and Joe Colburn, my close-in-age-mates whose intelligence and interest in ideas nourished my thinking for as long as I can remember). Particular thanks to my neighbor Lavonne Johnson (whose extraordinary range of interests made me aware that there are always other worlds), my aunt Kathleen Foley Sigafoos (who showed me how exciting thinking can be), and especially my mother Susan Foley Allewaert (whose support was crucial and whose grace is inspiring). Finally I would like to thank those close friends whose generosity, wit, and liveliness sustained the intellectual project and also sustained me by taking me out of it some of the time: big thanks and appreciation to Lauren Coats, Alex Cook, Nihad Farooq, Joe Fitzpatrick, John Inouye, Jennifer Jones, Jacques Khalip, Krista Lindgren, Frédéric Neyrat, Martha Elena Rojas, and Ben Strong. I dedicate this book to the memory of my grandfather Tom Foley, whose generosity and good humor benefited me so immensely.

Notes

Introduction

William Shakespeare, *The Tempest,* ed. Peter Hulme and William H. Sherman (New York: W. W. Norton, 2004), 1.2.395–400.

1. While *The Tempest* collates Mediterranean and Atlantic histories, I focus on the mythology that can be gleaned from its Atlantic history. Peter Hulme, *Colonial Encounters: Europe and the Native Caribbean* (New York: Routledge, 1992), offers the seminal account of the play's engagement with Atlantic as well as Mediterranean histories. On the play's Atlantic genealogies, see also Jonathan Goldberg, *Tempest in the Carribbean* (Minneapolis: University of Minnesota Press, 2003), another work important to my own and whose title inspires the title of my introduction.

2. Cavitation and expansion are not necessarily joint operations: one might well occur without the other. That this transformation of human bodies is founded on cavitations and decorporealizations that quite literally threaten the possibility of being will, I hope, make clear that this process is not in any sense a simple and celebratory expansion of the human being as equivalent to all of nature. In "The Nature of Fear," *American Literature* 84, no. 2 (2012), Matthew Taylor argues that a nascent imperialism lurks in recent posthumanisms that ultimately expand the conceptual and bodily reach of the human and in so doing eliminate the rest of the world.

3. I use the term "Afro-American" instead of "African American" so as to avoid the national and continental geography often implied in African American.

4. John Locke, *An Essay Concerning Human Understanding,* ed. and abr. A. D. Woozley (New York: Meridian, 1974), 210.

5. Ibid., 207, 210.

6. Spinoza is perhaps the most notable exception to this tendency. His effort, in the *Ethics,* to treat "human actions and appetites just as if it were an investigation into lines, planes, or bodies" institutes a geometrical method that governs his conceptualization of both thought and extension and that shifts his focus from the body and its organization to the relation of parts. Baruch Spinoza, *Complete Works,* trans. Samuel Shirley (Indianapolis: Hackett Publishing, 2002), 278.

7. Here, it was as though the Lucretian swerve, which is properly a quality of atoms and not of bodies, becomes a quality of bodies.

8. In the long middle section of the *Dream*, Mademoiselle L'Espinasse imagines an anarchy of forms that counters the vitalist Doctor Bordeu's faith in the despotic organization of bodies, whether natural or political. This discussion of the relation of matter and forms is brought to the colonial question in the final section of the dialogue, where Bordeu and L'Espinasse address the problem of slavery and the brutalization of slave bodies only to immediately conclude their conversation, a conclusion so abrupt as to give the impression that the relation of the formation and deformation of the body and its matter must not be thought in too close a relation to the colonial question.

9. On early colonial efforts to chart the influence of colonial phenomena (particularly astrological phenomena) on human bodies, see Jorge Cañizres Esguerra, "New World, New Stars: Patriotic Astrology and the Invention of Indian and Creole Bodies in Colonial Spanish America, 1600–1650," *American Historical Review* 104, no. 1 (1999): 33–68.

10. J. Hector Crèvecoeur, *Letters* (New York: Oxford University Press, 1997), 43.

11. Jim Egan, "The 'Long'd-for Aera' of an 'Other Race': Climate, Identity, and James Grainger's *The Sugar Cane*," *Early American Literature* 38 (2003): 189.

12. Ibid., 197.

13. Chris Iannini, *Fatal Revolutions: Natural History, West Indian Slavery and the Routes of American Literature* (Chapel Hill: University of North Carolina Press, 2012), 233–34. Iannini's analysis of Jefferson and other late eighteenth-century North American naturalists traces their fraught and often unsuccessful efforts to assert a North American identity that was distinct from the West Indian networks of knowledge that were so central to the genre of American natural history and that rendered North America an extension of the West Indies. For Iannini's discussion of *Notes*, see *Notes on Virginia*, in *Jefferson's Writings* (New York: Library of America), 219–251. Here Iannini develops the fascinating argument that Jefferson adopts the posture of the degenerate Creole in order to avoid working through the contradiction between his republican principles and his investment in broadly West Indian planter (and natural historical) interests. Thus, even as Jefferson assays a continental geography for the United States, he also consistently fantasizes an extra-continental United States.

14. Sean X. Goudie, *Creole America: The West Indies and the Formation of Literature and Culture in the New Republic* (Philadelphia: University of Pennsylvania Press, 2006), 8.

15. This term is indebted to Goudie's notion of *paracolonialism,* a term he develops in the introduction to *Creole America.*

16. Vodou is typically associated with Haiti and to a lesser extent other French colonies; Santeria typically developed in Spanish colonialisms; Obeah typically developed in English plantation societies and is especially associated with Jamaica. All of these cosmologies were linked with slave resistance. As Vodou and Santeria are both typically understood as communal practices, while Obeah is not, Elaine Savory links Obeah to community formation. For more on this point, see Elaine Savory, "'Another Poor Devil of a Human Being . . .': Jean Rhys and the Novel as Obeah," as well as Margarite Fernandez Lomos and Lizabeth Paravisini-Gebert's "Religious Syncretism and Caribbean Culture," both in *Sacred Possessions: Vodou, Santeria, Obeah, and the Caribbean,* ed. Margarite Fernandez Olmos and Lizabeth Paravisini-Gebert (New Brunswick, N.J.: Rutgers University Press, 1997).

17. *The Tempest* (Hulme and Sherman), 2.2.1–3. On this point, consider Richard Grove's account of Black Carib resistance on St. Vincent in *Green Imperialism: Colonial Expansion, Tropical Island Edens, and the Origins of Environmentalism, 1600–1860* (Cambridge: Cambridge University Press, 1996).

18. Thus, while existing colonial, anticolonial, and postcolonial readings of the play have tended to divide Ariel from Caliban, attending to the fantasies of environmental vengeance that circulate in Shakespeare's play reveals that from the earliest moments of colonization Anglo-Europeans imagined a tenuous and revolutionary alliance between tropical elemental forces and subaltern persons.

On Afro-Americans' historical and more modern uses of "nature" to resist colonialism, see Elizabeth M. DeLoughrey, Renée K. Gosson, and George B. Handley, eds., *Caribbean Literature and the Environment: Between Nature and Culture* (Charlottesville: University of Virginia Press, 2005), as well as George B. Handley, *New World Poetics: Nature and the Adamic Imagination of Whitman, Neruda, and Walcott* (Athens: University of Georgia Press, 2005). The introduction to the former work proposes that the Caribbean natural world "served as vital repositories of indigenous and African beliefs and assertions of rebellion against plantation capitalism. This is most evident in the history of indigenous and slave resistance in which mountain ranges, mangrove swamps, provision grounds, and other sites of environmental opposition to the plantocracy provided vital alternative communities" (3). On colonized persons' relations to nonhumans, see also Helen Tiffin and Graham Huggan, *Postcolonial Ecocriticism: Literature, Animals, Environment* (New York: Routledge, 2010).

19. For a classic articulation of this thesis, see M. H. Abrahms, *Natural Supernaturalism: Tradition and Revolution in Romantic Literature* (New York: W. W. Norton, 1973). I should also note that, because my main interest here is not in periodization, I paint in broad strokes and overlook subtleties in both the Enlightenment and Romantic intellectual traditions, neither of which is under attack here.

My point is not to suggest that either the Enlightenment or the Romantic era did not exist, or that they did not exist as they have been ably described by generations of intellectual historians, but rather that a number of other possibilities were also in circulation. As Jonathan Israel argues, and as Susan Scott Parrish's and Marjorie Levinson's works make clear, there were many enlightenments and many romanticisms. Attending to this plurality changes our sense of history, periodization, and the political possibilities that circulated in and might be reclaimed from this era. To indicate the multiplicity of co-emerging and overlapping sciences and philosophies of the period, in the pages that follow I do not capitalize the terms Enlightenment and Romantic when I am not referring to the dominant understandings of those terms. Instead I will use lowercase and, where grammatically possible, pluralize: enlightenment(s), romanticism(s).

20. Although Nancy Ruttenburg, *Democratic Personality: Popular Voice and the Trials of American Authorship* (Palo Alto, Calif.: Stanford University Press, 1998), first proposes this terminological shift, Ruttenburg does not pose the person as an alternative to the subject but instead as a way of amplifying the performativity and contradictions she takes to be inherent to subjectivity. Drawing on Raymond Williams, *Keywords: A Vocabulary of Culture and Society,* rev. ed. (New York: Oxford University Press, 1976), and Lydia Ginzburg, *On Psychological Prose,* trans. Judson Rosengrant (Princeton: Princeton University Press, 1991), Ruttenburg argues that "the tension comprised by [and the interest inherent to] 'personality' inheres in the performative aspects of personhood" (8). I have gained a good bit from Ruttenburg's magisterially historicized analysis of North America's entwined ecclesiastic, political, and literary cultures. However, my geographical and economic focus (the American tropics and the plantation form) and my archive (travel writers in the Americas and Afro-American poets, writers, storytellers, and artifact makers) are quite different from hers, which leads us to quite different theorizations of the person. Ruttenburg's use of the term *person* tends to emphasize the ambivalence central to performances of American personality like those of Abby Putnam and George Whitfield, which are at once protodemocratic and deeply repressive. I am more interested than Ruttenburg in how the shifting and traversed boundaries of human bodies inflect understandings of the person. Moreover, given that my archive is not New England–focused, my analyses are not especially focused on Calvinist notions of the body, the mind, and the divine.

21. John Locke, *Second Treatise on Government,* ed. Thomas P. Peardon (Indianapolis: Bobbs-Merrill, 1952), 69.

22. Thomas Hobbes, *Leviathan,* ed. Edwin Curley (Indianapolis: Hackett: 1994), 101, 111. In fact, in Roman law the term *person* was also a juridical word for any entity (including things) that could be legible before the law; however,

Hobbes's focus on the theatrical genealogy of the term shifts from these capacious suprahuman and subhuman potentialities. See Yan Thomas, "Le sujet de droit, la personne et la nature: Sur la critique contemporaine du sujet de droit," *Le débat* 100 (1998): 85–107.

23. Locke, *Essay*, 219.

24. William Blackstone, *Commentaries on the Laws of England, 1765–79*, 15th ed. (London: T. Cadell and W. Davides, in the Strand, 1765), 123. As Stephen Best points out, Blackstone's concept of the artificial person became a cornerstone of free-market capitalism, which he proposes moved from a thingly to an abstract conception of property. While Best interprets the person within an Anglo-American legal tradition, I will suggest a mutation that wrests the person from this tradition, in part to move the person from the capitalist genealogy that Best points out is intimately linked with the concept of personhood in English common law. See Stephen Best, *The Fugitive's Properties: Law and Poetics of Possession* (Chicago: University of Chicago Press, 2004).

25. The reason that the discrete and individual body is necessary to capitalist property rights is because if a person had shifting boundaries—if its boundaries could not be clearly identified, or if it were conceived as a collectivity instead of a unitary entity—it would not be possible to claim that this was the sole entity that could claim any given property. If these boundary issues were not resolved, it would also be impossible to determine where a person's inalienable right to possess his own body began and where it ended. This would not only raise problems in determining the extent of a person but also would raise problems in determining at which point one could understand a substance as a nonperson and thus legitimately alienable property.

26. Blackstone, *Commentaries*, 130. In arguing that the parts of bodies must not be severed from the body proper, Blackstone idealizes the consolidation of parts into wholes far more than Locke did. Locke does consider what would happen if a leg or another appendage were to be lopped from a body and determines that a body so disfigured now simply organizes itself as an identity without a leg. The matter and parts of a body were never all that important for Locke, as it was only the body's drive to organize matter and parts into an identity that counted. As long as the desire for organization particular to an identity is not violated, the loss of a leg or an arm is not a conceptual problem for Locke as it is for Blackstone. Locke discusses this point in book 2, chapter 27 of the *Essay*.

27. Richard Price, *First-Time: The Historical Vision of an African American People*, 2nd ed. (Chicago: University of Chicago Press, 2002), 32–37.

28. Price notes present-day Saramakases's tendency to "transform conceptually Creole forest-born [maroon] leaders of the mid- and late eighteenth-century into late-seventeenth-century runaways" (ibid., 101), which suggests an ongoing

tendency to build a history and sense of self that preserves these three distinct scenes of (non)origin.

29. On free black men's revaluation as property, see Best, *Fugitive's Properties*, as well as Charles Foy's forthcoming work on black sailors on the eighteenth-century Atlantic.

30. For an account of how slavery challenges conventional psychoanalytic stories of subjectivity and origin, see Hortense Spillers, "Mama's Baby, Papa's Maybe: An American Grammar Book," *Diacritics* 17, no. 2 (1987): 64–81, later included in her book *Black, White, and in Color: Essays on American Literature and Culture* (Chicago: University of Chicago Press, 2003).

31. In his 1855 autobiography *My Bondage and My Freedom*, Douglass offers a far more positive account of Sandy and the power of his fetish root. It is not at all surprising that as black counterpublics gained more power and autonomy (in no small part through Douglass's own efforts) it became more possible for Douglass to give credence to Afro-American fetishism as something other than superstition. In *The Life and Times of Frederick Douglass* (1881), Douglass again gives greater attention to conjure as an intellectually significant and politically substantial black counterculture. However, here Douglass also suggests that it is Sandy who is responsible for betraying his and other slaves' effort to escape and thus continues to oppose his route to freedom (literacy) with the conjurer's.

32. Zora Neale Hurston, *Go Gator and the Muddy Water* (New York: W. W. Norton, 1999), 66–67. Of course, it might be possible to read this phrase as evincing Hurston's "feminization" of folk culture; however, in light of the Afro-American tradition more broadly, I suspect her phrase works to mutate the assumption that reproduction is a discrete, biological, and feminized event. I first learned of Hurston's pluralization and displacement of the womb from the female body in Susan Scott Parrish's wonderful chapter "Zora Neale Hurston, Folk Dynamics, and Ecological Modeling," in Joni Adamson and Kimberly Ruffin's "Ecological Citizenship and Belonging in a Transcultural World" (unpublished manuscript). My thanks to Susan Scott Parrish for sharing this work with me before it has appeared in print.

33. Wilson Harris's *Palace of the Peacock* (London: Faber and Faber, 1960) as well as *Womb of Space: The Cross-Cultural Imagination* (Westport, Conn.: Greenwood Press, 1983) suggest the impossibility of single genesis, or even of birth or death in the tropics where Afro-Americans, Native Americans, and even Anglo-Europeans often passed from the plantation order to marronage. For Harris, the plantation space gives rise to multiple beginnings and tragedies that are endlessly and carnivalesquely cross-pollinated and returned.

34. Paul Outka, *Race and Nature from Transcendentalism to the Harlem Renaissance* (Hampshire, U.K.: Palgrave 2008); Tiffin and Huggan, *Postcolonial Ecocriti-*

cism; Rob Nixon, *Slow Violence and the Environmentalism of the Poor* (Cambridge, Mass.: Harvard University Press, 2011).

35. Natania Meeker, *Voluptuous Philosophy: Literary Materialism in the French Enlightenment* (New York: Fordham University Press, 2006), is among the first works to develop this new materialism, although to be sure there are important predecessors such as John Rogers, *The Matter of Revolution: Science, Poetry, and Politics in the Age of Milton* (Ithaca, N.Y.: Cornell University Press, 1998). See also Jonathan Goldberg, *Seeds of Things: Theorizing Sexuality and Materiality in Renaissance Representations* (New York: Fordham University Press, 2009); Jane Bennett, *Vibrant Matter: A Political Ecology of Things* (Durham, N.C.: Duke University Press, 2010); Stephen Greenblatt, *The Swerve: How the World Became Modern* (New York: W. W. Norton, 2011); and Amanda Jo Goldstein's forthcoming work.

36. Indeed, I think we could push the point farther to argue that one of the goals of sentimental discourse is to produce this metaphor of the body that protects the sentimental self from its worlds. If this is true, then the most important work of sentimentalism is the consolidation and protection of the subject that is effected through the metaphorics of the body that is its first and foundational movement.

37. Lawrence Buell first proposed reading early American writing as postcolonial in 1992, but it was not until the first years of the twenty-first century that colonial and postcolonial analyses of late eighteenth- and early nineteenth-century American literature, culture, and politics were substantially developed, often by scholars with strong expertise in non-Anglo colonial histories and a focus on American transcolonialisms and transnationalisms (David Kazanjian, Kristen Silva Gruesz, Sean X. Goudie, and Elizabeth Maddock Dillon). My theorization of the personhood that develops unevenly from the American tropics contributes to the new American colonial studies' efforts to rethink the politics and geopolitics of the eighteenth- and nineteenth-century Americas. After all, if the most basic unit of political life might be seen to have a body and relation to the nonhuman that is different from that which we have often supposed, this changes our sense of the political possibilities available in the eighteenth and early nineteenth centuries.

38. Srinivas Aravamudan, *Tropicopolitans: Colonialism and Agency, 1688–1804* (Durham, N.C.: Duke University Press, 1999), 14.

39. Susan Scott Parrish, *American Curiosity: Cultures of Natural History in the Colonial British Atlantic World* (Chapel Hill: University of North Carolina Press, 2006), 260.

40. Jurgen Habermas, *Structural Transformation of the Public Sphere*, trans. Thomas Burger (Cambridge, Mass.: MIT Press, 1991); Benedict Anderson, *Imagined Communities: Reflections on the Origin and spread of Nationalism*, rev. ed. (New York: Verso, 1991).

41. My own study does not challenge the central theses of this body of work, powerfully conceptualized first by Michael Warner, *The Letters of the Republic: Publication and the Public Sphere* (Cambridge, Mass.: Harvard University Press, 1992), and then by critics looking to the role of orality in early national political cultures (Looby, Fliegelman, and Gustafson) or to Anglo-American performances of civility in literary cultures (Shields). I entirely agree that the massive increase in the production and consumption of print artifacts (often in strong relation to the oral cultures of property-owning classes) as well as the popularity of the relatively new genre of the novel shaped how persons conceived themselves, conceived political possibility, and understood the relation of public to private cultures. Some of Warner's work also explores how nonelite Afro-Americans participated in post-enlightenment publics and counterpublics. See, for instance, Michael Warner et al., "A Soliloquy 'Lately Spoken at the African Theatre': Race and the Public Sphere in New York City, 1821," *American Literature* 73, no. 1 (2001): 1–46. On print and oral cultures in early America, see also Chris Looby, *Voicing America: Language, Literary Form, and the Origins of the United States* (Chicago: University of Chicago Press, 1998); Jay Fliegelman, *Declaring Independence: Jefferson, Natural Language, and the Culture of Performance* (Palo Alto: Stanford University Press, 1993); Sandra Gustafson, *Eloquence Is Power: Oratory and Performance in Early America* (Chapel Hill: University of North Carolina Press, 2000); David S. Shields, *Civil Tongues and Polite Letters* (Chapel Hill: University of North Carolina Press, 1997).

42. Frederic Jameson, *Marxism and Form* (Princeton: Princeton University Press, 1974); Ed White, "Captaine Smith, Colonial Novelist," *American Literature* 75, no. 3 (2003): 487–513.

43. A good bit of early Americanist scholarship engages in debates about whether a work is or is not a novel or a secret history or a travelogue, and while these arguments importantly contribute to understandings of then-regnant genres, the very fact that it is so often difficult to agree on the genre of an early American text suggests that one of the features of this body of writing is that it is often extrageneric.

44. Price, *First-Time*; Annette Gordon-Reed, *Thomas Jefferson and Sally Hemings: An American Controversy* (Charlottesville: University of Virginia Press, 1998) and *The Hemingses of Monticello: An American Family* (New York: Norton, 2009); Colin (Joan) Dayan, *Haiti, History, and the Gods* (Berkeley: University of California Press, 1998); Joseph R. Roach, *Cities of the Dead: Circum-Atlantic Performance* (New York: Columbia University Press, 1996).

45. Cathy N. Davidson, *Revolution and the Word: The Rise of the Novel in America*, expanded ed. (New York: Oxford University Press, 2004).

46. Édouard Glissant, *Poetics of Relation*, trans. Betsy Wing (Ann Arbor: University of Michigan Press, 1997), 6.

47. Orlando Patterson, *Slavery and Social Death: A Comparative Study* (Cambridge, Mass.: Harvard University Press, 1985).

1. Swamp Sublime

1. William Bartram, *Travels* (1791; New York: Library of America, 1996).

2. Ibid., 78.

3. Edward J. Cashin, *William Bartram and the American Revolution on the Southern Frontier* (Columbia: University of South Carolina Press, 2000); Gregory A. Waselkov and Kathryn E. Holland Braund, *William Bartram and the Southeastern Indians* (Lincoln: University of Nebraska Press, 2002); Gordon Sayre "The Mound Builders and the Imagination of American Antiquity in Jefferson, Bartram, and Chateaubriand," *Early American Literature* 33, no. 3 (Fall 1998): 225–49; Christopher Looby "The Constitution of Nature: Taxonomy as Politics in Jefferson, Peale, and Bartram," *Early American Literature* 22, no. 3 (1987): 252–73; Thomas Hallock, *From the Fallen Tree: Frontier Narratives, Environmental Politics, and the Roots of a National Pastoral* (Chapel Hill: University of North Carolina Press, 2006).

4. I am not the first critic to note the aqueous quality of *Travels.* In his discussion of the manuscript's often competing drafts, Thomas Hallock suggests that the final version "swims within the paradoxes that were defined by the western ordinances" and describes an earlier version as having an "aquatic" "pulse." Hallock, *From the Fallen Tree,* 155, 158.

5. Bartram, *Travels,* 97, 265.

6. The term *zone* designates a political configuration that includes many different state powers but remains regional. The term resists nationalism because it recognizes that plantation spaces were shaped by multiple colonial states, and it also resists cosmopolitan universalism because it recognizes that regional practices and modes of connection were transformed as they moved out of the tropics and into other places.

7. My thinking on ecology draws on the work of Lawrence Buell, *The Future of Environmental Criticism: Environmental Crisis and Literary Imagination* (Malden, Mass.: Blackwell, 2005); William Cronon, *Changes in the Land: Indians, Colonists, and the Ecology of New England* (New York: Hill and Wang, 2003); Bruno Latour, *Politics of Nature: How to Bring the Sciences into Democracy* (Cambridge, Mass.: Harvard University Press, 2004); Timothy Morton, *Ecology without Nature: Rethinking Environmental Aesthetics* (Cambridge, Mass.: Harvard University Press, 2007), and *Poetics of Spice: Romantic Consumerism and the Exotic* (Cambridge: Cambridge University Press, 2000), chapter 4; and Dana Phillips, *The Truth of Ecology: Nature, Culture, and Literature in America* (New York: Oxford University Press, 2003).

8. My account of the relation between subjects and agents develops from Latour's *Politics of Nature*. Latour uses the term *actant* instead of *agent;* I use *agent* because it strikes me as more legible in contemporary academic discourse. I also draw on William Cronon's foundational effort to give life to "a cast of nonhuman characters which usually occupy the margins of historical analysis" (*Changes in the Land,* xv) as well as Marjorie Levinson's analyses of subjects and objects: "Object-Loss and Object-Bondage: Economies of Representation in Hardy's Poetry," *ELH* 73, no. 2 (2006): 549–80, and "Pre- and Post-Dialectical Materialisms: Modeling Praxis without Subjects and Objects," *Cultural Critique* 31 (1995): 111–27.

9. Bartram, *Travels,* 14.

10. Warner, *Letters of the Republic.* Warner's work focuses most closely on print cultures and public spheres and less on the emergence of postrevolutionary subjectivities. Benedict Anderson, *Imagined Communities: Reflections on the Origin and Spread of Nationalism,* 2nd ed. (New York: Verso 1991), who focuses on similar themes if mainly in the Latin American context, comes to similar conclusions and attends more closely to questions of subjectivity. The focus on subjectivity intensified in the work of Americanist critics whose work followed on that of Warner and Anderson.

11. My reading of print culture's materialities and immaterialities draws on Michael Moon's *Disseminating Whitman: Revision and Corporeality in* Leaves of Grass (Cambridge, Mass.: Harvard University Press, 1993).

12. Hofmannsthal's fictitious letter (1901) in *Selected Prose,* trans. Mary Hottinger, Tania Stern, and James Stern (New York: Pantheon, 1952), reveals Chandos as a man whose rapturous experience of the physical world stalls representation, which depends on the subject's separation from the physical world. Chandos's letter is addressed to Francis Bacon and, among other things, makes clear that there can be no further letters. Like Chandos, Bartram anticipates that proximity to the natural world presages the dissolution of the subject and of the representational projects associated with subjectivity. In my account of ecological agency, developed in the second part of this chapter, I suggest that this dissolution and attendant weakening of representational schematics occasions an alternative mode of action instead of the rhapsodic (but terrifying) cessation of action that Chandos and Bartram anticipate.

13. Bartram, *Travels,* 47.

14. Cabeza de Vaca, *The Narrative of Cabeza de Vaca,* ed. Rolena Adorno, trans. Patrick Charles Pautz (Lincoln: University of Nebraska Press, 2003), 41; see esp. chapters. 6–8.

15. William Byrd, *Histories of the Dividing Line betwixt Virginia and North Carolina* (New York: Dover, 1998), 56–80.

16. Ibid.

17. The difficulty of integrating swamp spaces into national structures is particularly evident in the controversy over Thomas Jefferson's selection of a marshy wilderness (now Washington, D.C.) as the site for the future U.S. capital (see Constance M. Green, *Washington Village and Capital: 1800–1878* (Princeton: Princeton University Press, 1962); John B. Ellis, *The Sights and Secrets of the National Capital: A Work Descriptive of Washington City in All Its Various Phases* (Ann Arbor: University of Michigan Press, 2006)). For George Washington's efforts to cultivate swamp spaces, see Charles Royster, *The Fabulous History of the Dismal Swamp Company: A Story of George Washington's Times* (New York: Knopf, 1999). For a broad account of swamps in American culture, see Anthony Wilson, *Shadow and Shelter: The Swamp in Southern Culture* (Jackson: University of Mississippi Press, 2006); David Miller, *Dark Eden: The Swamp in Nineteenth-Century American Culture* (Cambridge: Cambridge University Press, 1990).

18. Chateaubriand's *Atala* (1801) and his lesser-known *Les Natchez* (ca. 1790s; pub. 1826) both draw heavily on Bartram's work. In fact, the Mississippi vista that opens *Atala* is obviously indebted to Bartram's *Travels* (92–93). Other colonial writers who use the verb *vegetate* to refer to human beings include the narrator of the anonymous *My Odyssey: Experiences of a Young Refugee from Two Revolutions* (Baton Rouge: Louisiana University Press, 1959), who instructs French "philanthropists" (abolitionists) to "behold them [Africans] vegetate at your side" (93); and General Desfourneaux, who complains that Saint-Domingue's white Creoles were "vegetating with an insouciance that was as revolting as it was unacceptable," as quoted in Laurent Dubois, *Avengers of the New World: The Story of the Haitian Revolution* (Cambridge, Mass.: Harvard University Press, 2004), 150.

19. Bartram, *Travels,* 17.

20. Ibid., 18.

21. Ibid., 17, 22–23.

22. Ibid., 17.

23. It is significant that Bartram's juxtaposition of persons and plants develops through a simile ("as if"). Unlike metaphor, simile places clumsy markers—*likes* and *as ifs*—between the things it puts into association, thus marking difference while also calling attention to the negotiation through which associations emerge. Thinking carefully about the figures through which likeness emerges is important to ecological analyses, which need to grapple with the question of how they conceive the relation between things.

24. Bartram, *Travels,* 17.

25. Ibid., 73.

26. Edmund Burke, *Philosophical Enquiry into the Origin of Our Ideas of the Sublime and the Beautiful* (1757; New York: Oxford University Press, 1998), 61.

27. Ibid., 36.

28. Bartram almost certainly read Burke's treatise, but he probably did not read

Kant's work, which was unavailable in English when Bartram was writing. The subject and the object world became even more rigorously separated in Kant's account of the sublime. Unlike Burke, Kant does not locate the sublime in objects; rather, it is an exercise in reason and so ultimately the province of the subject; Immanuel Kant, *Critique of Judgment*, trans. James Meredith (Oxford: Oxford University Press, 2007), 83–89. Although Bartram did not read Kant, the reading of the sublime I offer could also be extended to Kant, whose work I have in mind when I speak of Anglo-European aesthetic practices.

29. Bartram, *Travels*, 126.

30. For more on how the aesthetic project of the sublime contributed to colonialism, see the account of Burke by Sara Suleri, who proposes that "the operation of the sublime is continually represented as parallel to the structure of colonialism, until it becomes more the property of the colonizing world than the aesthetic one." *The Rhetoric of English India* (Chicago: University of Chicago Press, 1992), 38.

31. Bartram, *Travels*, 228.

32. Quoted in Thomas Slaughter, *The Natures of John and William Bartram* (New York: Knopf, 1996), 159–60.

33. Bartram, *Travels*, 94, 259.

34. Ibid., 379.

35. See Jean Fouchard, *The Haitian Maroons: Liberty or Death*, trans. A. Faulkner (New York: Blyden, 1981); Richard Price, *First-Time*; Richard Price, *The Guiana Maroons: A Historical and Bibliographical Introduction* (Baltimore: Johns Hopkins University Press, 1976); Richard Price, ed., *Maroon Societies: Rebel Slave Communities in the Americas*, 3rd ed. (Baltimore: Johns Hopkins University Press, 1996); and Sally Price and Richard Price, *Maroon Arts: Cultural Vitality in the African Diaspora* (Boston: Beacon Press, 1999).

36. Bartram's tract against slavery is archived in John Bartram's effects in the broadsides collection of the Historical Society of Pennsylvania.

37. Quoted in Slaughter, *Natures*, 233.

38. That Bartram's account of loss verges on the elegiac is not incidental. As Peter M. Sacks has argued in *The English Elegy: Studies in the Genre from Spenser to Yeats* (Baltimore: Johns Hopkins University Press, 1987), the elegiac form often works to shore up—or, rather, produce—lyric subjectivity. I would argue that the elegiac form's subjectivism, like that of the sublime, is precisely what makes it appealing to Bartram as well as what ultimately makes it impossible for him to hew successfully to the conventions of the form.

39. Ronald Paulson, *Representations of Revolution, 1789–1820* (New Haven, Conn.: Yale University Press, 1983).

40. Edmund Burke, *Reflections on the Revolution in France*, ed. J. C. D. Clark (Palo Alto, Calif.: Stanford University Press, 2001), 188, 239.

41. Ibid., 240.

42. Glissant, *Poetics of Relation,* 70.

43. Of course, Bartram's failures register only in a certain political and metaphysical tradition. One might also argue (and I do argue) that the mutation of vision and practice inspired by swamps has a good deal of transformative potential. On this point, I draw heavily on Gilles Deleuze and Félix Guattari, *Kafka: Toward a Minor Literature,* trans. Dana Polan (Minneapolis: University of Minnesota Press, 1986), and *A Thousand Plateaus: Capitalism and Schizophrenia,* trans. Brian Massumi (Minneapolis: University of Minnesota Press, 1987).

44. Most plantations were in tropical and subtropical regions by the close of the eighteenth century, but it is certainly not true that there were no plantations in more northern climes, as John Jea's narrative (discussed in chapter 4) makes clear. Whether on tropical plantations or not, slaves and especially maroons did manipulate ecologies, a term that does not simply designate the collection of entities typically gathered under the concept of nature but instead a collation of systems that was certainly in effect in cities, for instance.

45. Emilia Viotti da Costa, *Crowns of Glory, Tears of Blood: The Demerara Slave Rebellion of 1823* (New York: Oxford University Press, 1994), 118.

46. Ibid., 16.

47. For instance, Winthrop Jordan writes offhandedly of "the [familiar] story of initial French success, [the] treacherous seizure of Toussaint, and eventual defeat at the hands of yellow fever and a British blockade"; *White over Black: American Attitudes toward the Negro, 1550–1812* (Chapel Hill: University of North Carolina Press, 1968), 377. The point is not that yellow fever was not a factor in the defeat of the French troops but that Louverture and Dessalines used to their advantage their knowledge of differential immunity as well as the climatological factors likely to cause the fever to spread.

48. Edward Bancroft, *An Essay on the Natural History of Guiana, in South America* (London: T. Becket and P. A. De Hondt, 1769), 40–41.

49. Ibid., 52–53.

50. John Gabriel Stedman, *Narrative of a Five Years Expedition against the Revolted Negroes of Surinam,* ed. Richard Price and Sally Price (1790; Baltimore: Johns Hopkins University Press, 1988), 396.

51. Ibid., 85.

52. Wim Hoogbergen, *The Boni Maroon Wars in Suriname* (Leiden, the Netherlands: Brill, 1990), 96.

53. This shift is in no sense simple, because eighteenth-century Anglo-European texts often contribute to the landscape tradition that enabled colonialism and at the same time to an emergent ecological tradition that compromised it.

54. Michel-Rolph Trouillot, *Silencing the Past: Power and the Production of History* (Boston: Beacon Press, 1995); Susan Buck-Morss, "Hegel and Haiti," *Critical Inquiry* 26, no. 4 (2000): 821–65; Sibylle Fischer, *Modernity Disavowed: Haiti and*

the Cultures of Slavery in the Age of Revolution (Durham, N.C.: Duke University Press, 2004).

55. Buck-Morss, "Hegel and Haiti," 849.

56. It may not be possible, or even desirable, to imagine a revolution that eliminates all forms of hierarchy. In any case, it would not be historically accurate to say that in Haiti revolution shifted from a vertical to a horizontal phenomenon. As Hegel followed events in Saint-Domingue, he presumably noticed this. Starting with Jean-Jacques Dessalines, and even more clearly with Henri Cristophe, the Haitian state became organized hierarchically, although, as Trouillot's work suggests, monarchial ambitions did not have the same meanings in Haiti as elsewhere.

57. Buck-Morss, "Hegel and Haiti," 848 (emphasis mine).

58. My readings of Glissant and of Atlanticism more generally draw on Ian Baucom's *Specters of the Atlantic: Finance Capital, Slavery, and the Philosophy of History* (Durham, N.C.: Duke University Press, 2005).

59. Glissant, *Poetics of Relation*, 7.

60. Ibid., 205.

61. Ibid., 205, 206.

62. Ibid., 206.

2. Plant Life

1. Alexander Humboldt, *Personal Narrative,* abridged and trans. Jason Wilson (New York: Penguin, 1995), 12, 248.

2. Ibid., 84.

3. Ibid., 58, 210; 76, 233.

4. Alexander Humboldt and Aimé Bonpland, *Essay on the Geography of Plants,* trans. Sylvie Romanowski (Chicago: University of Chicago Press, 2009), 65, 74. Jefferson's argument that heat and humidity are the conditions of vitality is in opposition to Buffon's argument that heat and aridity are the conditions of vitality. At stake in the difference is whether life-forms in the Americas are more or less vigorous than those in Europe and Africa. See Jefferson's *Notes on Virginia,* in *Jefferson's Writings* (New York: Library of America).

5. Humboldt and Bonpland, *Essay,* 118. Humboldt believed Natives' bodies had adapted to the tropics' charged atmospheres (ibid.).

6. Ibid., 118; Humboldt, *Personal Narrative,* 25, 94.

7. For these earlier readings of Humboldt, see Mary Louise Pratt, *Imperial Eyes: Travel Writing and Transculturation* (New York: Routledge, 1992), and Peter Hanns Reill, *Vitalizing Nature in the Enlightenment* (Berkeley: University of California Press, 2005). Although neither focuses on disharmony in Humboldt's early accounts of the tropics, I do not, in the main, disagree with either of these studies. Pratt's exemplary work has been central to my own efforts to consider how Anglo-

NOTES TO CHAPTER 2 · 201

European travel writers continually, often inadvertently though sometimes expressly, betray the imperial project they also push forward. And Reill's careful historicization of vitalist science in the eighteenth century proves immensely useful to the analysis of vitalism I develop in this chapter. See Aaron Sach, *The Humboldt Current: Nineteenth-Century Exploration and the Roots of American Environmentalism* (New York: Viking, 2006), for one of the most important (and explicitly ecological) recent revisions of Humboldt's work and legacy.

8. Foucault's understanding of vitalism and biology as nineteenth-century and modern organizations is evident in *The Order of Things: An Archaeology of the Human Sciences,* trans. Alan Sheridan (New York: Vintage, 1994). In the fifth chapter, "Classifying," Foucault focuses on eighteenth-century natural history as a system and method that attempted to build a language adequate to representing the visible world and that had no sustained interest in life as such. As he famously put it, "life itself did not exist" in the eighteenth century (128). In focusing on a vitalist materialism that preceded a vitalism focused on biotic organisms, or vitalism proper, I mean to trace an earlier moment in which liveliness was not the property of organized bodies but a general attribute potential or expressed in all matter. This eighteenth-century exploration of life as a general principle gave rise to questions about where life originates and what constitutes its smallest units. On this point, see Denise Gigante's *Life: Organic Form and Romanticism* (New Haven: Yale University Press, 2009). The questions that came from locating liveliness in the material world and not in biological organisms proper gave rise to a number of theological anxieties as it undercut the centrality of the human being and it also gave rise to political anxieties as it suggested that parts had power outside their organization in structures. Thus, if the eighteenth-century is, as Foucault suggests, a period obsessed with grids, classifications, and structures, a number of the thinkers who constructed these grids, classifications, and structures were interested in materialisms that confounded this systemization and method. The tropics that were central to the classificatory projects of Linnaeus and Buffon were also regions in which the agency of matter was understood to complicate this taxonomical effort.

9. If over the course of this book I focus mainly on transformations and changes of agency that occurred in tropical spaces and sometimes passed into Philadelphia, in this chapter I show that the metropole of Philadelphia was suffused with scientific and political theories that came from the tropics, from continental thought, and from its own academies and public health concerns. These vitalist materialist theories presumed conceptions of agency and politics that have been little explored by subsequent generations of Americanists. The contribution of this chapter to the larger study is to show how the destabilization occurring via Anglo-Europeans experiences in the tropics circulated in the premiere metropole of the early United States. Philadelphia has often functioned as the center that grounds Americanists' sense of an emerging national culture. I want to offer a natural

historical and political genealogy that diversifies this center, and in so doing diversifies our sense of what the Americas might have been.

10. Benjamin Rush, "Address to the People of the United States," *American Museum,* January 1787, 8–11.

11. In fact, by the 1790s, it would be hard to argue that Rush's thought was particularly conservative. He was staunchly anti-Federalist and also generally believed that African Americans, Native Americans, and white women were all reason-bearing persons capable of participating in public and even political life. Perhaps in part because of the criticisms leveled against him because of his treatment of yellow fever (more on this later), he became increasingly supportive of the rights as well as the intellectual and political contributions of those whose were elided or overlooked by capital-backed majorities. For instance, in his *Medical Inquiries and Observation: Containing an Account of the Bilious remitting and intermitting Yellow Fever, as it appeared in Philadelphia in the year 1794* (Philadelphia: Thomas Dobson, 1796), Rush claims that "the denial of events, or a general silence on the subject of them, is no refutation of their truth, where they oppose the pride or interests of the learned or the great" (74). Although this incipiently populist position is entirely self-serving (Rush, not without reason, believes himself among those persecuted by interests with a good deal of financial power), in this work he represents himself as genuinely open to the importance of heterodox opinions. He also repeatedly notes that he spends a good deal of time treating poor and immigrant patients in Philadelphia, unlike other doctors who preferred to treat more well-heeled patients.

12. Benjamin Rush, "Lectures on Animal Life," in *The Selected Writings of Benjamin Rush,* ed. Dagobert D. Runes (New York: Philosophical Library, 1947), 174–75.

13. See Colleen E. Terrell, "Republican Machines: Franklin, Rush, and the Manufacture of Civic Virtue in the Early Republic," *Early American Studies* 1, no. 2 (2003): 100–32. See also Terrell's PhD dissertation, "To Make a World: The Discourse of Mechanism in the Early American Republic" (University of Pennsylvania, 2002). Although I will depart from Terrell's assessment of Rush and early American natural history, my own analysis owes a good deal to her extraordinarily lucid and timely study, which, along with Joyce Chaplin's work (discussed later), is among the few recent Americanist studies to rigorously assess the interrelation of science and politics in the Early Republic.

14. As Peter Hanns Reill proposes in his intellectual history of the emergence of "Enlightenment Vitalism," mechanistic systems "assumed a substance-filled universe [in which] matter was never active, never an *agens.* It served as a medium, transmitter, carrier, or analogue . . . of a force. Late eighteenth-century [vitalist] naturalists rejected this position and reactivated matter, ascribing to it the anthropomorphic properties of striving, aversion, sympathy, penetration" (81). For Rush's effort to distinguish himself from animist and vitalistic thinkers, see

Lectures, 174; for Rush's argument that life is potential and not inherent to matter, see ibid.

15. Eighteenth-century vitalism vacillated between locating this agency in all matter or in certain configurations of matter. On this point, see Lester G. Crocker, *Diderot's Chaotic Order: Approach to Synthesis* (Princeton: Princeton University Press, 1974), and David Auerbach, "Moi and Lui and a Beehive: Denis Diderot's Philosophical Works," *Times Literary Supplement,* May 6, 2011, 12, as well as Auerbach's blog: "Diderot's Philosophy of Mind: Vitalist or Emergentist?" Waggish, May 21, 2011, http://www.waggish.org/2011/diderots-philosophy-of-mind-vitalist -or-emergentist.

16. For Rush's education, see the introduction by editors Eric T. Carlson, Jeffrey L. Wollock, and Patricia S. Noel to *Benjamin Rush's Lectures on the Mind* (Philadelphia: American Philosophical Society, 1981). See also Rush's own account of his education, especially in his 1796 *Account.* For more on Boerhaave's materialism and Spinozism, see Jonathan I. Israel, *Radical Enlightenment: Philosophy and the Making of Modernity, 1650–1750* (New York: Oxford University Press, 2002).

17. See Elizabeth A. Williams, *A Cultural History of Medical Vitalism in Enlightenment Montpellier* (Burlington, Vt.: Ashgate, 2003).

18. Reill, *Vitalizing Nature,* 122.

19. Ibid.

20. Joseph Priestley, *Hartley's Theory of the Human Mind, on the Principle of the Association of Ideas with Essays Relating to the Subject of It* (London: J. Johnson, 1775), xvii.

21. Ibid., xx.

22. Ibid., xix (italics original).

23. Ibid. (italics original).

24. Ibid., xxi. Natural scientists who argued for vegetables' power of sensation and volition frequently defended themselves from the supposed religious ramifications of these positions. The anonymous author of "On Vegetable Life," published in the Federalist journal *The Port Folio* in July 1814 argued, apparently seriously and not satirically, that attributing sensation and a striving to vegetables did not mean that he imagined vegetables possessed free agency, obligation, accountability, and a future state, all of which he suggests are the exclusive privileges of men (65). The author of this essay implicitly posited two forms of life: first, a general and earthly power of life that would extend to vegetable matter; second, a more specific and immaterial life only possessed by human beings. Thus, life is both immanent and transcendent in this reading. See T. C., "On Vegetable Life," *The Port Folio* 4, no. 1 (July 1814): 59–74, 176–191.

25. Joyce E. Chaplin has argued that Franklin should be interpreted as a materialist and that he continued in a materialist orientation even after he disavowed the *Dissertation.* See Chaplin's *Benjamin Franklin's Political Arithmetic: A Materialist View of Humanity* (Washington, D.C.: Smithsonian Institution Libraries, 2006).

To my mind, Franklin's satirical mode makes it difficult to name his position with the precision Chaplin believes possible.

26. Benjamin Franklin, *A Dissertation on Liberty and Necessity, Pleasure and Pain* (New York: Facsimile Text Society, 1905), 61.

27. Rush, *Account*, 75.

28. Ibid., 65; on swamp and marsh exhalation, see 59, 63, 65, 68, 71, 113.

29. For Rush, yellow fever could be either noncontagious or, under the right climatological and environmental conditions, contagious. By his theorization, contagion was not an inherent property of a disease but a point at which environmental factors allowed a disease to spread voraciously. For more on contagion in American culture, particularly in the late nineteenth and twentieth century, see Priscilla Wald, *Contagious: Cultures, Carriers, and the Outbreak Narrative* (Durham, N.C.: Duke University Press, 2007).

30. Rush, *Account*, 71.

31. On Rush's influence by theories focused on vibration, consider his reference to the diagnosis by "French physicians" of "laxite vabratile, by which they mean a liableness in the system to be thrown into vibrations or motions by the predisposition of debility" (*Account*, 129). He also directly notes Hartley's influence, particularly at the close of his *Account*.

32. For Rush, the human body was an environment whose matter and habits could, through careful regulation, reach optimal functioning. And if the human body was an environment, it participated in other environments, including homes and cities, that Rush believed should also be observed carefully so that their rhythms might be made more as opposed to less life-sustaining. Charles Brockden Brown, *Ormond, or The Secret Witness, with Related Texts*, ed. Philip Barnard and Stephen Shapiro (Peterborough, Ont.: Broadview Press, 1999), repeats a series of Rush's assumptions. Read through the lens of Rush's environmentalism (which Brown certainly knew), *Ormond* becomes a novel about the corrupting agency of bad air (or the seeds of contagion carried in bad air): while the city of Philadelphia was in the midst of a yellow fever epidemic, the narrator speculated that the seeds of the contagion suffused all bodies in the city and only needed the right trigger in inner or exterior environments to cause the growth of the disease. For the duration of the epidemic, the heroine Constancia attempts to modulate her environments, whether through controlling the movement of air in the apartment she shared with her father, changing her diet, or moderating her temperament.

33. On Hamilton's dislike of Rush and his blocking of this appointment, see John Chester Miller and A. Owen Aldridge, *Alexander Hamilton and the Growth of the New Nation* (Piscataway, N.J.: Transaction Publishers, 2003), esp. 380–83, as well as Ron Chernow, *Alexander Hamilton* (New York: Penguin, 2004). On Rush's materialism and monism, see I. Woodbridge Riley, *American Philosophy: The Early Schools* (New York: Russell & Russell, 1907), esp. 421–50.

34. Rush, "Lectures on Animal Life," 133–80.

35. It is worth noting that during the last twenty years Americanist scholars have not particularly focused on Rush's involvement in debates about materialism and mechanism. (Terrell's study is an exception and really elides this debate to move to the conclusion that Rush is a mechanist.) In fact, in the first part of the twentieth century, Rush was classified as a materialist. I. Woodbridge Riley's study *American Philosophy: The Early Schools* (New York: Dodd, Mead, 1907) notes the difficulty of interpreting Rush's position, given his occasional mechanistic claims, but argues that Rush is mainly a materialist, albeit one who often departs from the monism that was more common to eighteenth-century materialism to espouse a sort of pluralism (421–53). Riley's classification offended T. James Taylor, who wrote a letter that appeared in the July 20, 1907, *New York Times Book Review* in which he argued that Rush was not a materialist but a mechanist and emphatically religious. Taylor's response makes clear that until the early twentieth century materialism was understood as refusing transcendental power and thus potentially a sort of atheism whereas mechanism, which allowed transcendental power outside of matter, preserved a transcendent God. In fact, as Elizabeth Williams's *Cultural History* makes clear, Taylor was incorrect in assuming materialism was necessarily equivalent to atheism, as quite a number of vitalist materialists were religious.

36. Reill, *Vitalizing Nature*, 99.

37. Ibid., 102–10.

38. Ibid., 82.

39. T. C., "On Vegetable Life," 69.

40. Thomas Percival, *Speculations on the Perceptive Power of Vegetables: Addressed to the Literary and Philosophical Society of Manchester* (Warrington, U.K.: W. Eyres, 1785), 8.

41. Denis Diderot addresses some of these philosophical conundrums in *La rêve de d'Alembert* (1769). However, he did not publish the dialogue in his lifetime because he had been warned that he would be imprisoned again if he continued publishing subversive texts.

42. Reill, *Vitalizing Nature*, 88–100. The first and guiding principle of theorists of elective affinity was that like attracts like, which Reill suggests was often modeled on family relation or a genealogical model of likeness. A second principle was that opposites attract. Although elective affinity is most strongly associated with chemistry, Reill, drawing on the work of Mi Gyung Kim, proposes that this model of attraction drew on natural-historical models that focused a good deal on the sorts of combinations possible through sexual and asexual contacts (ibid., 83–88). Although I will not develop this point here, if eighteenth-century chemistry drew on natural history to theorize the results likely to come from the combination of different material forms, it might also be possible to argue that the elaborate racial classifications of a natural historian like Moreau de Saint-Méry also influenced the

development of chemistry. If this is the case, chemistry might be conceived as an offshoot of the colonial effort to produce racial rapports and affinities from a situation of impossible flux. (It would be interesting to compare charts of chemical affinities with Moreau de Saint-Méry's elaborate charts of racial combinations.) For a discussion of Moreau de Saint-Méry's classificatory system, see Colin (Joan) Dayan, *Haiti, History, and the Gods* (Berkeley: University of California Press, 1998), 25–26. There is one significant difference between natural historical combination broadly conceived and chemical combination: only the latter insisted that combinations were effected primarily through genital sex.

43. Reill, *Vitalizing Nature*, 90.

44. Dahlia Porter, "Scientific Analogy and Literary Taxonomy in Darwin's *Loves of the Plants*," *European Romantic Review* 18, no. 2 (2007): 213–21. I would describe Darwin's *Loves* as at the juncture of both vitalism and mechanism because it gently satirizes the animate matter of the former and refuses the dead matter of the latter.

45. Carl Linneaus, *Philosophia Botanica*, trans. Stephen Freer (New York: Oxford University Press, 2005), 99, 105 (all italics and brackets in the original). François Delaporte, *Nature's Second Kingdom: Explorations of Vegetality in the Eighteenth Century*, trans. Arthur Goldhammer (1979; Cambridge, Mass.: MIT Press, 1982), notes that Linnaeus's as well as other eighteenth-century botanists' comparison of human and plant sexuality repulsed and also titillated Anglo-European readers of botanical science (136–48). Delaporte's study—while not attending to the tension between mechanism and vitalism, and not focusing on analogy in particular—makes quite clear the prevalence of analogical thought to virtually all eighteenth-century botanists. William Smellie (who produced the first English translation of Buffon's *Histoire*) strongly critiqued Linnaeus's argument that plant sex was like animal sex, citing both the "indecency" of Linnaeus's prose as well as his improper use of analogy; *Philosophy of Natural History* (Halifax, N.S.: W. Milner, 1845), 226.

46. Linneaus, *Philosophia Botanica*, 105.

47. Gilles Deleuze, *Difference and Repetition*, trans. Paul Patton (New York: Columbia University Press, 1995), 28–37; and Gilles Deleuze and Felix Guattari, *A Thousand Plateaus: Capitalism and Schizophrenia*, trans. Brian Massumi (Minneapolis: University of Minnesota Press, 1987), 252–56. Theologian John Milbank, in an effort to rehabilitate analogy from Deleuze's analysis, proposes that analogy does not only imply identity "but identity and difference at once, and this radical sense can be liberated if one relativizes the genera/species/individuals hierarchy in the face of a more fundamental equality in created being, and recognizes, *with* the nihilists, the primacy of mixtures, *continua,* and overlaps and disjunctions, all subject in principle to limitless transformation." *Theology and Social Theory: Beyond Secular Reason* (Malden, Mass.: Blackwell, 1993), 307 (italics in the original).

48. Porter, "Scientific Analogy," 215 (italics mine).

49. In focusing on genital being, Darwin and others cover over other research of the time that showed beings that were hermaphroditic or who used other creatures instead of genitals to replicate (plants' use of bees in pollination, for instance). A number of theorists have already meticulously documented that eighteenth-century science created an "order of things" that attempted to ossify a culture founded on sexual difference and heterosexual desire. See Thomas Laqueur, *Making Sex: Body and Gender from the Greeks to Freud* (Cambridge, Mass.: Harvard University Press, 1990); Foucault, *The Order of Things;* and Michel Foucault, *The History of Sexuality*, 3 vols., trans. Robert Hurley (1984; New York: Vintage, 1980–1990).

50. Erasmus Darwin, *The Botanic Garden: A Poem in Two Parts* (London: Jones & Company, 1825).

51. Theresa Kelley, "Restless Romantic Plants: Goethe Meets Hegel," *European Romantic Review* 20, no. 2 (2009): 187–95, traces the differences between Goethe's and Hegel's writings on plant life as well as the relation of matter to spirit. This study also suggests that by the early nineteenth century quasi-vitalists thinkers, particularly those with a strong interest in botany, had begun to turn from the analogical method. In the first part of *La rêve de d'Alembert* the character Diderot also expresses skepticism about the primacy of the analogical method.

52. Benjamin Smith Barton, *Elements of Botany: Or, Outlines of the Natural History of Vegetables* (London: J. Johnson, 1804; Philadelphia: Author, 1811): (1804), 197; (1811), 20. Barton also argues that Linnaeus's "specious language" is "ill adapted to the grave dignity of science" (1804, 184; 1811, 20).

My citations from *Elements* come from both the London edition published in 1804 (which is available on Google Books) and the Philadelphia edition published in 1811, which I read in its entirety. Barton significantly revises the text between these two editions, although his revisions are not mainly syntactical or conceptual but structural (thus, information that appears on page 178 of the 1804 edition appears on page 55 of the 1811 edition). As much as possible, I cite the more readily available 1804 edition. However, because the *Elements* is quite long—about 400 pages—I did not in every case cross-reference quotations. In those moments where I could not find the citation in the 1804 edition, I cite the 1811 edition only.

53. Thomas Percival, *Speculations on the Perceptive Power of Vegetables* (Warrington, U.K.: W. Eyres, [1785]), 16.

54. Percival, *Speculations*, 5. Percival's attention to American botanical work is evident in his reference to *Dionaea* or the Venus flytrap, first reported to Linnaeus by John Ellis in 1768 although perhaps known previously via John Bartram who cultivated the plant or William Bartram who was the first illustrator of the plant (an illustration dated ca. 1765–1775). The plant was not particularly known when Bartram drew it, which led to his London patron Peter Collinson chiding him for

drawing "imaginary plants." Thomas Hallock and Nancy E. Hoffman, eds., *William Bartram: The Search for Nature's Design; Selected Art, Letters, and Unpublished Writings* (Athens: University of Georgia Press, 2010).

55. Percival, *Speculations*, 15.

56. Griffith Hughes, *The Natural History of Barbados* (1750; rpr., New York: Arno Press, 1972), Figure 4.

57. In their correspondence, Barton, although occupying a more public and prestigious social position than Bartram, posed himself as subordinate to Bartram, who passed the younger Barton many of his observations and drawings about mid-Atlantic and tropical plant life and also sent him philosophical meditations. Regarding the intensity of their relationship, I'd note, first, that Bartram's letters to Barton are significantly longer than his letters to almost all other correspondents; also, in letters to Barton, Bartram comes closest to openly voicing speculations about a nonhierarchical organization of life that he mulled over in unpublished writings. This was also an intimate and erotically charged relation; for instance, the two men exchanged portraits via the intermediary of Bartram's nephew James, prompting Bartram to write Barton, "I now have your Image always present, either before my Eyes, or engraven on my Heart or both at once" (197). In the eighteenth and nineteenth centuries, this sort of highly charged homosocial exchange was not unusual. Still, critics speculate about Bartram's sexual orientation (sometimes simply by denying that he was homosexual). Whatever his sexual and social proclivities, Bartram certainly did not participate in the bourgeois family life then becoming increasingly normative. Humboldt, like Lewis whom I will discuss in chapter 4, almost certainly preferred male lovers. Although traveling and the genre of travel writing were generally popular at the time and certainly could not be classed as part of a protohomosexual enclave, the practice and the genre may have offered an acceptable remove from the bourgeois heteronormativity of the family.

58. Hallock and Hoffman, *William Bartram*, 160.

59. Barton, *Elements of Botany* (1804), 14. *Elements* frequently attends to the relation between environments and vegetable bodies. For instance, Barton notes that the plant's root structure "accommodates itself . . . to the climate in which it grows" and "that soil, climate, elevation above the level of the sea, and other circumstances, considerably vary the aspect of the leaves of vegetables" ([1811], 14, 44).

60. Ibid. (1811), 55.

61. Ibid. (1811), 62.

62. Linneaus, *Philosophia Botanica,* 106.

63. Barton, *Elements of Botany* (1811), 194.

64. Ibid. (1804), 195.

65. This leap was no doubt necessary to the eventual discovery that insects were vectors through which diseases could be spread.

66. Isabelle Stengers, *Cosmopolitics I,* trans. Robert Bononno (Minneapolis, University of Minnesota Press, 2010), 34, 35.

67. Alexander von Humboldt, *Cosmos: A Sketch of a Physical Description of the Universe,* vol. 1 (1845), trans. E. C. Otte (Baltimore: Johns Hopkins University Press, 1997). Reprint of Harper & Brothers 1858 edition.

68. For Humboldt's vitalism, see Reill, *Vitalizing Nature.* He assigns Humboldt a pivotal role in the emergence and decline of the vitalist movement, which Reill proposes was waning in the early nineteenth century and was a dead intellectual movement that Humboldt stubbornly stayed with in the production of his *Cosmos.*

69. "The Dignity of Human Nature," which in fact insists that human dignity is not greater than that of other life-forms, is collected in Hallock and Hoffmann, *William Bartram,* 340–46.

70. Bartram, *Travels,* 53.

71. Ibid., 19.

72. The secret that Bartram's God promises is, as Michael Gaudio puts it in his account of Bartram's botanical art, the intense "particularity" of every life-form and environment. See Michael Gaudio, "The Elements of Botanical Art: William Bartram, Benjamin Barton, and the Scientific Imagination," in Hallock and Hoffman, *William Bartram,* 426–39.

73. This terminological shift is important, as the term *part* presumes the existence of a whole that determines it as partial, while the term *microcosmos* presumes that the small is both adequate in itself (it is a cosmos in itself) and at the same time participates in systems larger than itself (it participates in the cosmos). While the part gains relevance because it points outside of itself to the whole, the microcosmos remains sufficient in itself even as it participates in totalities.

74. See Lauren Ode-Schneider in Hallock and Hoffman, *William Bartram,* 342.

75. For the uses of tropical plants, see Londa Schiebinger, *Plants and Empire: Colonial Bioprospecting in the New World* (Cambridge, Mass.: Harvard University Press, 2004), particularly chapter 2, "Bioprospecting," and chapter 3, "Exotic Abortifacients," which focuses on how women and men in the Americas and Europe used—and often suppressed—botanical knowledge that related to women's reproductive health.

76. In fact, Bartram's English patrons often requested live, dormant, and even dried plants both because they were the real thing and not representations and also because they wanted to see if it would be possible to grow American plants in English nurseries.

77. There are certainly exceptions to this tendency. For instance, consider Anita Cavagnaro Been, *Animals and Authors in the Eighteenth-Century Americans* (Providence, R.I.: John Carter Brown Library, 2004), which proposes that illustrations were presented in this way to conserve paper, which was then quite expensive.

78. Hallock and Hoffman, *William Bartram,* 75.

79. Virtually all of Bartram's most bizarre images are housed in the London Museum of Natural History's collection, which was culled from Fothergill's and Collinson's correspondence with Bartram. Virtually all the images now collected in American archives hew more closely to eighteenth-century conventions for botanical illustration. It is possible that Bartram's more bizarre images were weeded out of American archives, but this difference between the British and American archives also raises the fascinating possibility that Bartram only produced hallucinogenic images for his British audience.

80. Richard Grove's *Green Imperialism: Colonial Expansion, Tropical Island Edens and the Origins of Environmentalism, 1600–1860* (Cambridge, Mass.: Cambridge University Press, 1996) shows that seventeenth- and eighteenth-century colonials assiduously debated the virtues and hazards of clear-cutting. Some, arguing that clear-cutting caused drought, opposed it; others, arguing that clear-cutting helped moderate tropical humidity as well as the black and Indian resistance waged from the forests, advocated it (on this point see Grove's chapters "Protecting the Climate of Paradise: Pierre Poivre and the Conservation of Mauritius under the Ancient Regime" and also "Climate, Conservation, and Carib Resistance: The British and the Forests of the Eastern Caribbean, 1760–1800"). Although colonials debated how many trees were optimal, all sides agreed that the tropics were full of trees: the question was simply whether trees were beneficial or a threat to Anglo-European, Indigenous, and diasporic African communities.

81. On the importance of size and scale in eighteenth-century thought, consider the debate between Buffon and Jefferson about whether animals' health and vitality changed according to whether they were born in the Americas or in Europe and Asia. Consider, also, critics' readings of this debate, which tend to focus on the relation of small and large animals in the Americas, Africa, and Europe. For a fascinating alternative interpretation of this debate, see Michael Hardt, "Jefferson and Democracy," *American Quarterly* 59, no. 1 (2007): 41–78.

82. I discuss and move from Stewart more fully in chapter 3.

83. Susan Stewart, *On Longing: Narratives of the Miniature, the Gigantic, the Souvenir, the Collection* (Durham, N.C.: Duke University Press, 1993).

84. For a reading of this point, see Daniel W. Smith's introduction to Gilles Deleuze, *Francis Bacon: The Logic of Sensation,* trans. Daniel W. Smith (Minneapolis: University of Minnesota Press, 2003), xvii–xviii. Smith reads Kant's use of the body as the measure through which concepts emerge as evidence of his phenomenonologism. My thanks to J. Jennifer Jones for bringing this point in Smith's introduction to my attention.

85. Gilles Deleuze, "Four Poetic Formulas That Might Summarize the Kantian Philosophy," in *Essays Critical and Clinical,* trans. Daniel W. Smith and Michael A. Greco (Minneapolis: University of Minnesota Press, 1997), 27–35, notes a break between the earlier Critiques, which each foreground a specific calculative facul-

ty—be it reason or understanding—and the final Critique, which puts each of the faculties into play and shows that "it is now the undetermined unity of all the faculties (the Soul)" that constitutes the subject (34). The latter work may emphasize the free play of all the faculties, but it remains the case that scenes of calculation and measure remain a crucial part of this play, for they work to push one faculty to its limit and reveal the powers of the next.

86. My thinking on measure has benefited from and is in dialogue with J. Jennifer Jones's work in progress, particularly her chapter "Grasping a Rhythm: Meditations on Kant, Deleuze, and Wordsworth" in which she focuses on measure and rhythm in Kant and Deleuze's work. She presented an early version of this work at the 2008 North American Society for the Study of Romanticism conference.

87. Kant's sublime is also an effort to think outside of measure, but Bartram's position is distinct from Kant's in two ways. First, Bartram is interested in thinking of relation outside of measure whereas Kant is interested in thinking *subjectivity* outside of measure. Second, Bartram's images freeze an unmeasurable moment that precedes any harmony to speculate on the possibility of suspending the harmonious interrelation of modes of appreciation; in this sense, he departs from Kant's strongly narrative sequencing of the harmonies of the subject. Bartram's work even suggests that this suspension beyond synthesis is an expansive (perhaps even permanently ongoing) event instead of an exceptional limit event, as the sublime is for Kant.

88. Although *American Lotus*'s subtending theme is consumption, Bartram is not particularly interested in the merging of life-forms. That is, I do not think Bartram labored under the fantasy that proximity allows the merging of subjects and their objects (even if those terms are radically destabilized in the plantation zone). Rather, Bartram insists on the relation and intersection that allows a body to change its movements—which is to say, he imagines the possibility of a plant body moving in such a way as to alter its powers and intensities, in the process altering its relation to animal life without at any point becoming animal. Although some eighteenth-century vitalists may have imagined a sort of merging that dissolves all differences and all others, this is not Bartram's fantasy, although to be sure his work suggests a rethinking of the other as an immanent and not a transcendent other.

89. On Bartram's ecological orientation, see Thomas Hallock, *From the Fallen Tree: Frontier Narratives, Environmental Politics, and the Roots of a National Pastoral, 1749–1826* (Chapel Hill: University of North Carolina Press, 2003).

90. Francis Hallé, *In Praise of Plants*, trans. David Lee (Portland, Ore.: Timber Press, 2002).

91. Bartram's turn from the human is often quite explicit in his diaries, letters, and unpublished writings. In an unpublished essay, he refused to acknowledge "Man" as "the first order of Beings in this World," noting that "his formulation [as

the first order of Beings] enables him to subjugate, & even tyrannize over every other Animal" to the point that he would obliterate it (Hallock, *From the Fallen Tree*, 352–53). In this same essay, he noted that "some Animals possess Arts or programs of modification in Inginuity [*sic*], beyond the power of Human art" (ibid., 354).

92. Bartram, *Travels*, 393.

93. Ibid., 61, 388.

94. Ibid., 57, 389, 406–7.

95. Ibid., 25.

96. Ibid., 24.

97. Ibid.

3. On Parahumanity

1. Cited in Antoine Gisler, *L'esclavage aux Antilles françaises (XVIIe–XIXe siècle)* (1965; Paris: Karthala, 1981), 171–72. I first learned of this quotation in Maryse Condé, *La civilisation du bossale: Réflexions sur la littérature oral de la Guadeloupe et de la Martinique* (Paris: Éditions l'Harmattan, [1978]). Gisler's work cites the letter in its entirety. The translation is mine.

2. Again, my development of the term *parahuman* is indebted to the conception of *paracolonialism* that Sean Goudie offers in *Creole America*. Although it might well be possible to define these beings as *paranimal*, I have chosen to call them parahuman as it was Africans' and African Americans' relation to human beings that was most in question in colonial discourses and it is the term *human* that continues to be the most value-laden term in contemporary analyses of colonialism. It is true that the parahuman is in a particular proximity to animal life, and this is a theme I will occasionally take up later, but it is also true that the parahuman is proximate to but outside of the category of the human.

3. William Earle, *Obi; or, The History of Three-Fingered Jack* (Petersborough: Broadview, 2005); Ottobah Cugoano, *Thoughts and Sentiments on the Evil and Wicked Traffic of the Slavery and Commerce of the Human Species, Humbly Submitted to the Inhabitants of Great Britain*, in *Pioneers of the Black Atlantic: Five Slave Narratives from the Enlightenment, 1772–1815*, ed. Henry Louis Gates Jr. and William L. Andrews (Washington, D.C.: Civitas/Counterpoint, 1998); Frantz Fanon, *The Wretched of the Earth*, trans. Constance Farrington (New York: Grove Press, 1963); and Henry Louis Gates Jr., *The Signifying Monkey: A Theory of African-American Literary Criticism* (New York: Oxford, 1988).

4. For the dominant critical understanding of enlightenment, see Jurgen Habermas's *Structural Transformation*; Lynn Hunt, *Inventing Human Rights: A History* (New York: W. W. Norton, 2008). For analyses that extend to the colonies,

see David Brion Davis, *The Problem of Slavery in the Age of Revolution, 1770–1823* (New York: Oxford, 1999).

5. Matthew Lewis, *Journal of a West India Proprietor, Kept during a Residence in the Island of Jamaica*, ed. Judith Terry (1834; New York: Oxford University Press, 1999).

6. In his discussion of Haitian Vodou, Moreau de Saint-Méry notes that practitioners often asked to "control the spirit of their masters." See Laurent DuBois and John Garrigus, *Slave Revolution in the Caribbean: A Brief History with Documents* (New York: Bedford, 2006), 6.

7. Lewis, *Journal,* 96, 115, 220.

8. David L. MacDonald, *Monk Lewis: A Critical Biography* (Toronto: University of Toronto Press, 2000), esp. 205–10; Louis F. Peck, *A Life of Matthew G. Lewis* (Cambridge, Mass.: Harvard University Press, 1961).

9. Lewis's relatively liberal positions on slavery (he supported the first wave of abolition, for instance) mildly estranged him from peers in the plantation-owning elite, an estrangement evident in his relatively skimpy commentary on Jamaica's white creole cultures in comparison to his commentary on Afro-American creole cultures. In the years preceding his sojourns to Jamaica, Lewis was in increasingly volatile relation to his peers and frequently a target of ridicule in the letters of friends and acquaintances who found him boring, garrulous, pompous, narcissistic, and perhaps also overly fond of men (MacDonald concludes with "near certainty" that Lewis was, in contemporary terms, gay). The company of the British elite may have vexed Lewis, but once he arrived in Jamaica he could claim a (literally) captive audience who could not write biting letters about him and upon whom he could indulge his interest in male bodies. Regarding this last point, Lewis spent a significant amount of time in his plantation's new hospital, where he personally nursed at least one male slave. The most relevant point, it seems to me, is not to map out the sexual orientation of eighteenth-century figures but to note that that the plantation form offered a space in which a number of sexual desires (mostly but certainly not exclusively those of white men), including desires that might otherwise be termed perverse, could be played out.

10. See, for instance, Kamau Brathwaite, *Folk Culture of the Slaves of Jamaica* (London: New Beacon Books, 1970), and *Development of Creole Society in Jamaica* (Oxford: Clarendon Press, 1978).

11. See the introduction to Nalo Hopkinson, *Whispers from the Cotton Tree Root: Caribbean Fabulist Fiction* (Montpellier, Vt.: Invisible Cities Press, 2000). Zora Neale Hurston, *Tell My Horse: Voodoo and Life in Haiti and Jamaica* (New York: Harper & Row, 2008), also discusses the importance of the cotton tree (also called the "ceiba," which is the name she uses) in the West Indies. In *I, Tituba* (New York: Ballantine, 1994) Maryse Condé burlesques the ubiquity of silk cotton trees in Afro-American signifying practices. Archaeologists William Keegan

and Lisabeth Carlson, *Talking Taino: Caribbean Natural History from a Native Perspective* (Tuscaloosa: University of Alabama Press, 2008), make the fascinating argument that diasporic Africans learned mythologies of the cotton tree/ceiba from the Taino before they were exterminated. They also suggest that Vodou practices of zombification (a practice that did not occur in West African religions and which uses fish and botanical neurotoxins not found in Africa) might have been learned from the Taino, who seem to have used the porcupine fish in rituals (see 114–15).

12. Lewis, *Journal*, 253–61.

13. See Édouard Glissant, *Caribbean Discourse: Selected Essays*, trans. J. Michael Dash (1981; Charlottesville: University Press of Virginia, 1989), 130.

14. On the Barbados slave code, see Alan Taylor, *American Colonies* (New York: Penguin, 2002), 212–14, as well as Richard S. Dunn, *Sugar and Slaves: The Rise of the Planter Class in the English West Indies, 1624–1713* (1972; Chapel Hill: University of North Carolina Press, 2000). The French *Code Noir* is reprinted and translated in Laurent DeBois and John D. Garrigus, *Slave Revolution in the Caribbean, 1789–1804: A Brief History with Documents* (New York: Bedford/St. Martin's, 2006). Edward Long's panegyric for the advantages of British over French colonialism claims that the French did not properly execute the terms of the *Code Noir* (440). Later in his *History* he documents what he calls the Jamaican Code Noir, which he represents as inaugurated in 1696 and updated over the course of the eighteenth century to respond to emerging problems, including Obeah practice. The third article of the 1696 code stipulates that slaves who steal may be punished by dismemberment, although Long adds a footnote in which he claims that this "barbaric" punishment is not practiced anymore (even if it remains on the books) in the early 1770s when he was writing (485). See Edward Long, *History of Jamaica*, vol. 2 (London: Lowndes, 1774).

15. The practice of punishing slaves by forcing them to wear masks, muzzles, spiked collars, balls, nabots (iron weights riveted to the ankles), and other prostheses suggests a perhaps linked phenomenon of reconstituting or reforming slaves' bodies, this time by addition, making them prosthetic bodies, something other than "natural" human bodies.

16. *Lady Nugent's Journal of Her Residence in Jamaica from 1801 to 1805*, ed. Philip Wright (Kingston: Institute of Jamaica, 1966), 63. Elizabeth Maddock Dillon noted this detail in her conference paper at the 2011 American Studies Association Conference.

17. On the fact that masters were reluctant to murder slaves largely to preserve their labor power, see the letter from a French officer cited in Edward Long, *History of Jamaica*, 3:936.

18. Although I will not take up the theme of headlessness more generally here, I want to at least acknowledge this theme in the late eighteenth and nineteenth centuries, where it is generally meant to be macabre in ways that Imoinda's decapi-

tation is not meant to be to its contemporary audiences (to be sure, Imoinda's decapitation is horrifying, but the narrator makes clear that she understands the logic, even the nobility, of Oroonoko's act). The recoil from the (relative) egalitarianism of the Jacobin phase of the French Revolution involved a recoding of such democracy as an entirely irrational (if rationalized) passion for equality, whose excesses are emblematized by what Hannah Arendt calls Robespierre's "passion for compassion" as well as his role in sanctioning the widespread use of the guillotine (Arendt, *On Revolution* [New York: Penguin, 1990]). I suspect that the turn not from the guillotine as such but from but the rational egalitarianism it symbolized is one of the reasons that headlessness takes on a particular horror and thematic resonance at this time.

The idea of headlessness as a symptom of irrationality (an interpretation of headlessness that remains dominant in the present) might be linked to the conservative, or counterrevolutionary, response to the egalitarian phase of the French Revolution. Thus, in "The Legend of Sleepy Hollow" (1820), Washington Irving, who was rather allergic to the revolutionary moment into which he was born, associated headlessness with the linked themes of the revolutionary rationality of the Connecticut Yankee Ichabod Crane and the deep irrationality that Irving, at least, associates with this revolutionary rationality and that he attempts to ameliorate by supplementing the revolutionary moment with a series of prerevolutionary moments (the lore of the Lenape Indians and the Dutch colonization of New York). The tale's framing poses headlessness as a joke, but it is also a real specter haunting both the society that precedes and the one that inherits the revolution and that points to the passion for change and for egalitarianism as precisely what must be sublated.

This counterrevolutionary account of headlessness as indicative of the irrationality of revolution is not, however, the understanding of headlessness that circulates in the Creole stories I discuss here. Rather, in these stories of a quite different revolutionary provenance, headlessness is a symptom of a positively valued disruptive potential. I would not be surprised if the counterrevolutionary and the revolutionary significations of headlessness eventually came together, particularly in twentieth-century renditions of the tales.

19. Lewis, *Journal*, 112–13 (italics in the original).

20. The plantation then was marked by the conjunction of biopolitical and sovereign power that Foucault suggests were distinct epistemological moments but that Agamben gives a longer durée and proposes were given their paradigmatic modern form in the Nazi camps. See Agamben's *Homo Sacer*, trans. Daniel Heller-Roazen (Palo Alto, Calif.: Stanford University Press, 1998), 5–6.

21. Another of the Ananse stories Lewis records involved a girl who marries a devil but who herself can shapeshift. This story recurs, in varied form but with the same plot, in Caribbean folk stories collected in the nineteenth and twentieth

centuries, lending credence to the possibility that Lewis is recording the stories he hears with some accuracy. Another story involves a woman whose food is stolen. When a pregnant woman is revealed as the thief and drowned, the teller concludes to her listeners that the property of others should not be stolen and that it is best not to persist in lies. Interestingly, this story offers a communally focused "moral" that Condé's study *La civilisation du bossale* proposed was more common to West African than West Indian folk stories. For the later tale collections, see Patrick Chamoiseau, *Creole Tales*, trans. Linda Coverdale (New York: New Press, 1997), and Elsie Clews Parsons, *Folk-lore of the Sea Islands, South Carolina* (Cambridge, Mass., American Folk-lore Society, 1923), and *Folk-lore of the Antilles, French and English*, 3 vols. (New York: American Folk-lore Society, 1933–43).

22. This order of rewards is telling. The first responds to the girl's immediate need—she has broken a water jug that she must replace. The second suggests ownership of property and the means of production that signified wealth in an economy structured by Anglo-European slavery. The third provides movement away, or mobility that is not given any specific trajectory.

23. Lewis, *Journal*, 157, 158.

24. William Bascom, *African Folktales in the New World* (Bloomington: Indiana University Press, 1992). Published posthumously in 1992, Bascom's typologies were based on a decades' long, uncompleted research project devoted to identifying a series of "tale types" common to African and Afro-American cultures. Bascom constructs his typology by collating English, French, Dutch, Portuguese, Spanish, Swahili, and Yoruba tales as well as tales recorded in other lesser-known languages, all of which were collected between 1880 and 1970. Bascom's focus on the retention of African origins in the New World performs the important work of insisting on the centrality of non-European origins to American folk cultures and also implicitly counters the schools of anthropology and folk culture study that argued that folk stories evinced a limited number of universal tales: for Bascom, an African story is a specific cultural production, not an incarnation of a story that exists in altered form in all other continental traditions. However, this focus on the retention of African origins also leads him to imagine that culture and influence always move from Africa to the Americas, as though influence were unidirectional from "old" worlds and traditions to new ones. Bascom's descriptions of his tale types thus always begin with African stories then proceed to American incarnations, even though his sources for American versions of a type sometimes predate his sources for an African version.

25. This tale type is nearly exclusive to the Americas, although Bascom records four twentieth-century African versions of the story. Three of these African variants were collected from nations heavily settled by Afro-Americans who returned to Africa—Sierra Leone, Ivory Coast, and Benin. A Malian version was recorded in 1944, and although this nation was not, to my knowledge, as heavily resettled by

Afro-Americans, its proximity to these coastal West African states suggests a good possibility that these stories were transmitted inland. The preponderance of American versions of the story and the paucity of African versions (all of which are West African, the most heavily resettled geography) supports the hypothesis that the story moved from the Americas to Africa and not, as Bascom suggests, in the other direction.

26. Amos Tutuola, *The Palm-Wine Drinkard and His Dead Palm-Wine Tapster in the Deads' Town* (London: Faber and Faber, 1952). That Tutuola claims his story, written in the mid-1940s, and was inspired in part by Nigerian state magazines that advertised for "black" cultural forms makes it quite likely that the story is not simply inspired by the "traditional" Yoruba tales that are its ostensible sources as by the revaluation of folk cultures that were just about as often grounded in West Indian as in West African sources (consider the work of Elsie Clews Parsons, Zora Neale Hurston, and Melville Herskovits of that period). On the travel of Afro-American persons and cultural forms to West Africa in the nineteenth century, see Sandra Gunning's *Moving Home* (Durham, N.C.: Duke University Press, 2009).

27. Many of the tales were recorded in the United States. I would classify the United States as an imperial power that colonized Native American, Latino border regions, and Africans, Asians, and eastern Europeans and others imported into the nation as a workforce. Which is to say, the United States remains in the present a colonial nation.

28. Francophone literary scholar Lovia Mondesir has confirmed that tales of headlessness and fragmentation remain common in Haitian oral cultures (conversations and e-mail exchanges in May and June of 2010).

29. A. James Arnold discusses this poem at length in his 1996 essay "Animal Tales, Historic Dispossession, and Creole Identity in the French West Indies," in *Monsters, Tricksters, and Sacred Cows: Animal Tales and American Identities,* ed. A. James Arnold (Charlottesville: University of Virginia Press, 2006), 255–68, as well as in *Modernism and Negritude: The Poetry and Poetics of Aimé Césaire* (Cambridge: Cambridge University Press, 1981).

30. I use Clayton Eshleman and Annette Smith's translation of the poem. See Aimé Césaire, *The Collected Poetry* (Berkeley: University of California Press, 1983).

31. Chamoiseau, *Creole Tales,* 74.

32. Condé, *La civilisation du bossale,* 40.

33. Ibid., 40–45.

34. I do not imagine that these parahuman stories are the effect of early or middle or later colonialisms but a cultural form that existed in each of these moments.

35. See Glissant, *Caribbean Discourse,* 129–30; Arnold, *Animal Tales.*

36. Lewis, *Journal,* 242, 261.

37. Lewis spends a good deal of time in the *Journal* noting his disapproval of whipping and other physical punishments of slaves: "I am more and more convinced every day, that the best and easiest mode of governing negroes . . . is not by the detestable lash, but by confinement, solitary or otherwise" (ibid., 238). However, he also allows his agents to physically punish slaves (these agents give him "to understand, that the estate cannot be governed . . . without the cart whip") (87).

Significantly, it is in Lewis's nineteenth-century colonial apologia and not in Afro-American oral performances or earlier eighteenth-century colonialisms or Anglo-European writings more generally where we see the theme of headlessness linked to the lack of cogito. That this meaning of headlessness emerges most clearly in Lewis's writing suggests that this particular division of cogito from body was emerging in the late eighteenth and early nineteenth centuries and developed in part as a strategy for codifying colonial racism. For a broader account of this phenomenon, see Dierdra Reber, "Headless Capitalism: Affect as Free-Market Epistime," *Differences* 23, no. 1 (2012): 62–100, which shows how twenty-first-century theory continues to be structured by the mind–body dualism that crystallized not with Descartes but with (colonial) capitalism's attainment of global sovereignty in the late eighteenth century.

38. For Giorgio Agamben's discussion of Linnaeus, see *The Open: Man and Animal,* trans. Kevin Attell (Palo Alto, Calif.: Stanford University Press, 2002), 23–31.

39. It is this racialization of the space between the animal and the human that Agamben fails to see and that is my primary challenge to his interpretation. The second and related challenge I pose is against the implicit telos of Agamben's argument. Agamben advocates a philosophy that holds open the space between the animal and man in hopes of slowing down the anthropological machine. He does not answer the question of for whom and for what purpose this machine might be slowed down, but the answer is clearly for human beings (a category that is more or less taken for granted even if Agamben's argument occasionally troubles it) and to produce an ethics based on the (very human, by his account) capacity for producing divisions. That the anthropological machine should be slowed for the benefit of human beings (or perhaps for a divine force that sometimes seems at play in Agamben's rather eschatological work) suggests that there is indeed a telos that subtends the suspension of the space between the animal: the implicit end motivating the analysis is a fully realized humanity that can only realize itself by accepting its own particular form of suspension. The echo of a Christian evangelical tradition (to be saved one must recognize one's sinfulness) is strong and perhaps not incidental.

40. Ottobah Cugoano, *Thoughts and Sentiments on the Evil of Slavery and Other Writings,* ed. Vincent Carretta (1789; New York: Penguin, 1999).

41. Although I will not develop this point here, one of the implications of my argument, an implication that might be developed from more sustained attention

to early black abolitionism, is that the politicization of the human being that Lynn Hunt argues occurred in the late eighteenth century actually developed in relation to colonial problematics (problematics that she treats as to the side of her study but which I would argue must be made central if any sufficient periodization of "human rights" discourse is to be obtained). See Lynn Hunt, *Inventing Human Rights: A History* (New York: W. W. Norton, 2008). Moreover, black abolitionists such as Cuguano who based their critiques on the argument that persons of African descent are human beings who cannot be equated with beasts contributed to an emerging political philosophy that conceived a fundamental opposition between human beings and animals.

Thus, while I will argue that Creole tales often argue for holding open the category of parahumanity, it is also the case that some Africans in the diaspora, particularly those who participated in print cultures, argued that politics and personhood required a fundamental division of human beings from animal life. In short, colonialism gave rise to multiple conceptualizations of the relation of human life to nonhuman life, and these conceptualizations cannot be understood along racial lines (as though there were a "black" position) because Africans in the diaspora took part in the formation of most if not all of these conceptions.

42. See Jacques Lacan, "The Mirror Stage," in *Ecrits: A Selection,* trans. Alan Sheridan (London: Tavistock, 1977). Françoise Vergès, "Creole Skin, Black Mask: Fanon and Disavowal," *Critical Inquiry* 23, no. 3 (1997): 578–95, first pointed out that Fanon was working with this earlier and less refined articulation of the mirror stage and not the 1949 version later collected in the *Ecrits,* which is the version most often studied today. Vergès' argument, which I will not fully draw out here but which is quite relevant to my own conclusion that Fanon ultimately walks away from the mode of identity that would emerge in the midst of the plantation zone, is that Fanon's writing performs a "disavowal of the créolité of the Antillean family" and, moreover, that "his construction of a Creole masculinity and femininity, entirely subjected to the desire of the white, have supported a conception of manhood and womanhood along lines that have enforced heterosexual and modernizing norms" (594–95).

43. Frantz Fanon, *Black Skin, White Masks,* trans. Charles Lam Markmann (New York: Grove Press, 1967), 161.

44. In *Dark Continents: Psychoanalysis and Colonialism* (Durham, N.C.: Duke University Press, 2003), Ranjana Khanna offers a deft analysis of Fanon's restaging of Lacan's mirror stage that proposes that Fanon's attention to historical and material colonial formations divagates from both universalizing psychoanalytic and reactive postcolonial theorizations of subject formation. Revealing subject formation as a crisis played out in and over time and outside of oppositional dialectics, Khanna suggests that Fanon adumbrates a theory of nonoppositional difference in which the other "is irreducible and yet is created and sustained by the manner in

which the *historical and economic* shape the perception of the *biological*" (172, ital-ics original). Khanna's invocation of the biological, which refers back to Fanon's own use of the term, makes clear that histories of colonial power gave rise to alter-native productions and also representations of the body. Pushing Khanna's insight a bit farther, I would suggest that Fanon's note implies the mutuality of the histori-cal, the colonial, and the biological—the body does not belong to any one of these domains but is produced at their intersection.

45. Vergès, "Creole Skin," 587.

46. Fanon, *Black Skin*, 161–64.

47. Frantz Fanon, *Wretched of the Earth*, trans. Richard Philcox (1961; New York: Grove Press, 2004), 42, 43, 313. Thus, while Fanon's early work goes a good bit farther than Lacan in showing how the Americas' plantation and extraplanta-tion localities produced a personhood based on fantasies of fragmentation that preceded and cannot be reduced to either modern or postmodern valuations of fragmentation, his later work detours sharply from these insights and attempts, in Vergès's provocative analysis, to "reconstruc[t] the black male body," making it into "a tight body, erected and immune to any form of penetration" (Vergès, "Cre-ole Skin," 583).

48. Fanon, *Wretched*, 58.

49. See Arnold, "Animal Tales," 259.

50. One might argue that Lewis's addition of what he sees as an appropriate conclusion to Goosee Shoo-shoo's story indicates a latent awareness of, and a de-sire to suppress, this circumlocutory movement that he senses.

51. Glissant, *Caribbean Discourse*, 84–85, 130.

52. Ibid., 26.

53. Glissant, *Poetics of Relation*, 212.

54. Édouard Glissant, *La lézarde* (Paris: Éditions du seuil, 1958).

55. Glissant, *Caribbean Discourse*, 130.

56. For cakewalking, see Eric Sundquist, *To Wake the Nations: Race in the Mak-ing of American Literature* (Cambridge, Mass.: Harvard University Press, 1993). For reperforming blackface minstrelsy, see the works of David Chapelle, Spike Lee, and Percival Everett. It is worth noting that both Lee's film *Bamboozled* (New Line Cinema, 2000) and Everett's *Erasure: A Novel* (Hanover, N.H.: University Press of New England, 2001) are deeply critical of the proposition that black paro-dy of colonial valuations of blackness offers the possibility of the restructuring of the social and political spheres both deem necessary. The short-lived tenure of David Chapelle's television series *Chappelle's Show* (2003–2004) suggests to me that he reached the same conclusion.

57. I offer an overview of the strong anthropocentrism of *The Open* in note 40. For the humanism that structures Agamben's account of how to pass from the state of exception (the conflation of law and politics and law and life) that has, in

modernity, become the norm, consider the concluding move of *State of Exception,* where he urges forging a space between life and law that allows "for human action, which once claimed for itself the name of 'politics'" (*State of Exception,* trans. Kevin Attell [Chicago: University of Chicago Press, 2005], 88).

58. Fischer, *Modernity Disavowed;* Laurent Dubois, *Avengers of the New World* (Cambridge, Mass.: Belknap, 2005); Anne Gulick, "We Are Not the People: The 1805 Haitian Constitution's Challenge to Political Legibility in the Age of Revolution," special issue, *American Literature* 78, no. 4 (December 2006).

59. I use Fischer's translation of the Haitian Constitution; cited in Fischer, *Modernity Disavowed,* 275.

60. Max-Pol Fouchet, *Wifredo Lam,* 2nd ed. (Barcelona: Ediciones Polígrafa, 1989), 36. Also relevant is that Lam's godmother Mantonica Wilson was a sorceress who inducted him into Santeria (38).

4. Persons without Objects

1. Margaretta Matilda Odell, *Memoir and poems of Phillis Wheatley, a native African and a Slave* (Boston: Geo. W. Light, 1834), 16. Twenty-first-century readers who are familiar with trauma theory and with postcolonialism might well think of other reasons for Wheatley's apparent difficulty with historical memory. Such readers might also note the inadvertent irony of the two causes Odell proposes for Wheatley's weak memory.

2. All citations from Wheatley are from Phillis Wheatley, *Complete Writings,* ed. Vincent Carretta (New York: Penguin, 2001).

3. In chapter 2 I suggest that this dyadic understanding of the low and the high, the material and the spiritual was not the only one circulating in the late eighteenth century: most incipiently vitalist thought rejected these sorts of antinomies. However, Wheatley's poetry did not participate in this tradition, instead relying heavily on dialectical structures.

4. John C. Shields, "Phillis Wheatley's Use of Classicism," *American Literature* 52, no. 1 (1980): 97–111, and *The American Aeneas: Classical Origins of American Self* (Knoxville: University of Tennessee Press, 2001). On the African influences in Wheatley's poetry, see also Mukhtar Ali Isani, "'Gambia on My Soul': Africa and the African in the Writings of Phillis Wheatley," *MELUS* 6, no. 1 (1979): 64–72.

5. Although Shields's argument is apt and also plausible, it is more plausible still that Wheatley meant to subordinate such African and classical traditions, fused or not, to the Christianity that she took as her own. For instance, one of the poems Shields calls on as evidence, "Thoughts on the WORKS OF PROVIDENCE," opens with a ten-line encomium to the sun, only to begin its second stanza by subordinating the sun to "the God unseen,/ Which round the sun revolves this vast machine." This subordination of solar to Christian divinity and of visible

earthly systems to invisible divine ones is elaborated over the course of the poem, as is usually the case in Wheatley's oeuvre.

6. As Edward P. Thompson shows in his study of Blake, *Witness against the Beast: William Blake and the Moral Law* (London: New Press, 1995), a number of antinomian sects produced philosophies that resisted the divisions that often structured normative eighteenth-century science, religion, and philosophy. The Afro-American materialism I will be discussing might be counted another of these antinomians, although certainly its relation to the moral law or to normative law is so askew and often so skeptical as to probably require a new term (after all, the term "antinomian" preserves the centrality of the law that it also claims is transgressed).

7. Although Wheatley intends the poem to stop short of Niobe's petrifaction, "another hand" whose presence is registered in the asterisks that star the poems' final stanza, gives the poem a properly classical ending. Although Wheatley's version of the story is quite distinct from that given to it by this amanuensis, no critic that I know of has attended to this point in their readings of the poem. Jennifer Thorn, "'All Beautiful in Woe': Gender, Nation, and Phillis Wheatley's 'Niobe,'" *Studies in Eighteenth-Century Culture* 37 (2008): 233–58, focuses on affect in "Niobe" but does not attend to this detail, which makes clear just how much Wheatley preferred the narrative arc of sentiment that Thorn discusses to that of objectification, which I will take up.

8. It is of course the case that not all poetry is narrative; however, Wheatley's almost always depends on explicit temporal sequencing that gives it a strong narrative tendency.

9. In mid-modern Atlantic cultures, it was not only Africans who could be categorized as objects: white women, indentured servants, and Native Americans could also be so conceived. However, I think it is worth taking the objectification of black persons as a particular and exceptional case for two reasons: first, the sheer amount of energy and writing expended arguing that black life was categorically distinct from and more justifiably objectified than differently raced "kinds" of life; second, it was mainly African and Afro-American persons who were charged with the improper valuation of objects (fetishism) that I will discuss in this chapter.

10. Glissant, *Poetics of Relation,* 208.

11. Manuel de Landa, *A New Philosophy of Society: Assemblage Theory and Social Complexity* (New York: Continuum, 2006), 10 (italics original). See also Deleuze and Guattari, *A Thousand Plateaus;* Deleuze, *Difference and Repetition.*

12. The remainder of the book builds on the analysis of parahumanity developed in chapter 3. I will use the term *(para)human* to refer to Afro-American reconfigurations of the "human." I will use the term *human* to refer to normative Anglo-European accounts of the "human."

13. Captain John Adams, *Sketches taken during Ten Voyages to Africa, Between the Years 1786 and 1800; including Observations on the Country between Cape Palmas and the River Congo; and Cursory Remarks on the Physical and Moral Character of the Inhabitants* (1823; New York: Johnson Reprint, 1970); John Newton, *Journal of Slave Trader, 1750–1754*, ed. Bernard Martin and Mark Spurrell (London: Epworth Press, 1962); William Smith, *A New Voyage to Guinea: Describing the Customs, Manners, Soil, Climate, Habits, Buildings, Education, Manual Arts, Agriculture, Trade, Employments, Languages, Ranks of Distinction, Habitations, Diversions, Marriages, and whatever else is memorable among the Inhabitants* (1744; London: Frank Cass, 1967). My thanks to Marcus Rediker for sharing his notes on these and other sources.

14. William Pietz, "The Problem of the Fetish, I," *RES: Anthropology and Aesthetics*, no. 9 (1985): 5–17; "The Problem of the Fetish, II: Origin of the Fetish," *RES*, no. 13 (1987): 23–45; "The Problem of the Fetish, III: Bosman's Guinea and the Enlightenment Theory of Fetishism," *RES*, no. 16 (1988): 105–23.

15. Olaudah Equiano, *The Interesting Narrative of the Life of Olaudah Equiano, or Gustavus Vassa, the African* (1789; New York: Penguin, 2003), 42. For Aravamudan's discussion of Equiano, see *Tropicopolitans*, 233–88.

16. Pietz, "Problem of the Fetish, I," 7–8.

17. Aravamudan, *Tropicopolitans*, 273.

18. Pietz proposes that fetishism "represents the emerging articulation of a theoretical materialism quite incompatible and in conflict with the philosophical tradition" ("Problem of the Fetish, I," 85). Over the course of his three-part essay on fetishism, Pietz makes clear that this genealogy of materialism offers a fundamental challenge to the conceptions of self, personhood, and (human) form that would develop from the dominant Enlightenment tradition. As he succinctly puts it: "the fetish represents a subversion of the ideal of the autonomously determined self" ("Problem II," 25). This suggests that the conception and practice of fetishism will intersect with—and challenge—the normative understanding of *personification*, another term and practice that was emerging in the eighteenth century.

19. See Vincent Brown, *The Reaper's Garden: Death and Power in the World of Atlantic Slavery* (Cambridge, Mass.: Harvard University Press, 2008); Jason Young, *Rituals of Resistance: African Atlantic Religion in Kongo and the Lowcountry South in the Era of Slavery* (Baton Rouge: Louisiana State University Press, 2007).

20. Cited in Karol K. Weaver, *Medical Revolutionaries: The Enslaves Healers of Eighteenth Century Saint Domingue* (Urbana-Champaign: University of Illinois Press, 2006), 117, who is in turn citing William B. Cohen, *The French Encounter with Africans* (Bloomington: Indiana University Press, 2003).

21. Médéric Louis Elie Moreau de Saint-Méry, *A Civilization That Perished: The Last Years of White Colonial Rule in Haiti* (Lantham, Md.: University Press of America, 1985), 42.

22. Henry Louis Gates Jr., *The Signifying Monkey.*

23. Ibid. It is possible and also necessary to produce analyses of black-produced writing that pass outside of this teleological narrative arc and in so doing incapacitate the "evolutionary narrative so dear to early abolitionists, that of humanizing the African" (Aravamudan, *Tropicopolitans,* 270). Readings that imagine that black-produced texts follow rectilinear narrative trajectories—instead of recognizing their imbrication of past and present, materiality and culture, magic and rationality—reproduce a narrative that posits the Enlightenment (here in the singular) marked the historical juncture at which Africans (might) enter into the realm of human culture. In positing an implicit dialectic between nonhumans and humans, this narrative passes over the fact that the eighteenth century was the historical juncture at which Atlantic exchange motivated Anglo-Europeans' production of the human as a universal political category, which is to say, it passes over the fact that Africans, Anglo-Europeans, and Native Americans were indistinctly human at this point, and that the modern secular concept of the human as a universal category was itself constructed at this moment. On this point, see Lynn Hunt's *Inventing Human Rights,* which, if it fails to recognize the crucial significance of the colonies to intellectual history, also recognizes the politicization of the human as a key feature of the Age of Revolution.

24. On this point, see Theophus H. Smith, *Conjuring Culture: Biblical Formations of Black America* (New York: Oxford University Press, 1994).

25. John Jea, "The Life, History, and Unparalleled Suffering of John Jea, the African Preacher," in *Black Itinerants of the Gospel: The Narratives of John Jea and George White,* ed. Graham Russell Hodges (1993; New York: Palgrave / St. Martin's, 2002), 91.

26. Mary Prince, *The History of Mary Prince: A West Indian Slave, Related by Herself,* ed. and introduction Moira Ferguson (Ann Arbor: University of Michigan Press, 1997), 76–77. My thanks to Sean Goudie for bringing this passage of Prince's work to my attention.

27. John Marrant, "A Narrative of the Lord's Wonderful Dealings with John Marrant, a Black," in *"Face Zion Forward": First Writers of the Black Atlantic, 1785–1798,* ed. Joanna Brooks and John Saillant (Boston: Northeastern University Press, 2002), 57–58, 70.

28. This is not to suggest that idolatry and fetishism were the same thing: Pietz elaborates at length on the difference in "Problem of the Fetish, II."

29. In "Free Carpenter, Venture Capitalist: Reading the Lives of the Early Black Atlantic," *American Literary History* 12, no. 4 (2000): 659–84, Philip Gould offers a compelling counterpoint to readings of Marrant that presume the categorical difference between life before and after conversion: "the structural logic of Marrant's *Narrative* displays his socially transgressive self—and voice—long before his actual conversion. In this way, it subtly undermines the conventional structure of spiritual autobiography" (666).

30. Jea, "Unparalleled Suffering," 123.

31. Marrant, "Narrative," 77; "A Journal of the Rev. John Marrant, from August the 18th, 1785, to the 16th of March, 1790," in *"Face Zion Forward,"* ed. Brooks and Saillant, 112–13. On the bloodiness of Marrant's evangelicism, consider the following scene when Marrant attempts to convert a woman in Nova Scotia. Marrant knocks on a door, and the woman who answers calls him a pickpocket and beats him with tongs until he bleeds so profusely that his blood spills onto her; she then beats him with a broom, at which point he retreats to a barn. He again returns to her door, but this time the woman "retaliated with more violence than at first. I was met with the poke and tongs, but the Lord, who overrules all things, prevented her from hurting me. I caught hold of her two shoulders, and held her for some considerable time, but she raged like a lion; and the Lord furnished me with words, particularly out of St. Matthew's gospel . . . and she struggled hard as long as she could, till she was almost out of breath; she then set herself down, and I [was] continually speaking to her concerning the sufferings of Christ . . . and she seemed somewhat calm." Finally she stretches herself on the ground where she lies mute, causing her relatives to ask "what I had done to her." "Nothing," Marrant tells them ("Narrative," 112–13).

32. For instance, see Mae G. Henderson, "(W)riting *The Work* and Working the Rites," *Black American Literature Forum* 23, no. 4 (1989): 631–60.

33. Thomas R. Gray, *The Confessions of Nat Turner, the Leader of the Late Insurrection in Southampton, VA.* (1832 facs.; Ann Arbor, Mich.: UMI Books on Demand, 1993), 9.

34. Ibid., 9–10. This move from transcendence to immanence indicates a move away from an abolitionist tradition that, as Philip Gould puts it, "can envision equality only in the safely removed space of heaven" ("Free Carpenter," 664).

35. Moreau de Saint-Méry, *Civilization That Perished*, 22.

36. If the span of a person extends beyond the human being's physical body, then juridical-political categories such as "corpus" and "citizen" should attend to the natural world as something other than property or raw material. And if the person extends past the body, the sentimental project of connecting (supposedly categorically distinct) humans also needs revision. This revision of sentimental convention is certainly at issue in William Earle's *Obi*. Although Earle's novel often gives conventional enough sentimental scenes, it also includes, in its final chapters, a scene in which crying moves to a spectacular evagination of the black body (one maroon character, attempting to speak to another, vomits his insides onto the other and then dies). In accounting for the ways that diasporic Africans' practice of Obeah alters (conceptions of) the body, Earle also reveals the collapse of a sentimental trope of tears as a substance mediating between inside and outside, spirit and body, one body and the next. William Earle Jr., *Obi; or, The History of Three-Fingered Jack,* ed. Srinivas Aravamudan (Ontario: Broadview Press, 2005).

37. For an account of the fetish as an oath, see Bryan Edwards, *The History Civil and Commercial of the British Colonies in the West Indies* (London: B. Crosby, 1798), 157, 170.

38. Earle, *Obi*, 164.

39. Ibid., 69–70 (italics in the original).

40. Ibid., 104.

41. Significantly, George does not imagine Jack's person is bound up with material forms to which Jack himself is proximate and which Jack does conceive as fetishes (for instance, Jack's "obi"). Instead, he imagines that Jack has projected himself into any material form that recalls Jack. Thus, even as Earle recognizes and records actual fetishistic practices, through the character of George he also suggests that for a white man a fetish is anything that reminds him of a black man (which, in a plantation space, might literally be any and every thing). Here, belief in fetishes is presented as a sort of psychological effluvium of the guilt of white men.

42. Weaver's *Medical Revolutionaries* notes several of these names.

43. See Price, *First-Time*; Gordon-Reed, *Thomas Jefferson and Sally Hemings*, and *The Hemingses of Monticello*.

44. Wyatt MacGaffey, "Fetishism Revisited: Kongo *Nkisi* in Sociological Perspective," *Journal of the International African Institute* 47, no. 2 (1977): 172–84, quoted at 173. Wyatt MacGaffey and J. M. Janzen translated Isaki's text from ba-Kongo to English, and MacGaffey explains that Isaki's text "is one of a large number of ethnographic essays written about 1915 at the request of the missionary ethnographer K. Laman" (183). Accounts of African fetishism, including MacGaffey's, sometimes call fetishes by the Kongolese term *nkisi/minkisi*, to imply the autonomy of Africa and African political and aesthetic traditions. It is, on the one hand, crucially necessary to trace African practices, including regional linguistic and cultural forms. On the other hand, Isaki's account suggests that early twentieth-century Kongolese fetishistic practice is not a pure form but a diasporic one. After all, his narration, prompted by missionary anthropological efforts, indicates fetishism as a form that exists in relation to colonialism and diaspora.

45. Wyatt MacGaffey, "The Eyes of Understanding: Kongo Minkisi," in *Astonishment and Power*, 20–103 (Washington, D.C.: Smithsonian Institution Press, 1993), 63.

46. Ibid., 43.

47. MacGaffey, ""Fetishism Revisited," 173.

48. Here, Isaki's account is entirely in keeping with Pietz's claim that a fetish is a way of recalling and returning a historically specific arrangement of material forces ("Problem I," 7). In proposing that a fetish is a combination that follows an "original model," Isaki calls attention to the issue of originality. Although many who write on fetishes note that the production of a fetish references an original arrangement of botanical, animal, and inorganic materials, these accounts also re-

veal that any fetish also departs from those that preceded it. After all, the fetish is a combination of materials found in some place, and these materials need not be local; the only requirement is that they be available in some location, thus bottles that were not locally produced in the late nineteenth- and early twentieth-century Kongo were used in fetish making.

The combinations of materials in a particular place would necessarily be distinct at distinct moments and would certainly be transformed by the dislocations of the African diaspora. MacGaffey notes that the "names of the various leaves, seeds, and other materials" collected in a fetish often punningly reference the "attributes and functions" with which the fetish is "endowed"; Wyatt MacGaffey et al., *Astonishment and Power* (Washington, D.C.: Smithsonian Institution Press, 1993); see also MacGaffey, "Fetishism Revisited," 177. Yet if botanical, animal, and other terrestrial ingredients changed and if language changed, as it did in the diaspora, then any fetish's arrangement of ingredients and lyric would also change. If a fetish holds within itself a recollection and repetition of an anterior moment of combination in which ingredients and words were effectively combined, this anterior moment would itself be remade, and the origin would become not singular but multiple because of shifting environmental conditions. Thus, the fetish's relation to the specificity of the environments in which they are produced moves away from, instead of facilitating, unitary or Afrocentric concepts of origins.

49. Martin R. Delany, *Blake; or, The Huts of America: A Novel*, ed. Floyd J. Miller (1859–62; Boston: Beacon Press, 1970). Earlier black-authored works do make oblique references to fetishes: in addition to the description by Equiano (*Interesting Narrative*) of the implements used by African magicians, which I noted earlier, Ottobah Cugoano (*Thoughts and Sentiments*) alludes to the idolatrous practices of Africans, and Frederick Douglass (*Narrative*) relates the story of a root he was given by another slave who suggested it would protect him from danger. I turn to Delany's text as it is an explicit and lengthy black-authored meditation on the fetish, which the others are not.

50. This ambivalence probably partly results from Delany's effort to reject the passive and atavistic representation of African Americans offered by Harriet Beecher Stowe's *Uncle Tom's Cabin; or, Life among the Lowly* (1852). To write of black fetishism for a mixed-race audience, as Delany did in *Blake*, was also to keep open white American readers' desire for atavistic blackness.

51. Delany, *Blake*, 112–13 (italics mine).

52. Ibid., 115. I am not certain to which plant "mocasa" refers. The characters are speaking in dialect, so they could mean "moccasin" (*Cypripedium*, also called "lady's slipper," a member of the orchid family), which was common to the region and also had medicinal properties, as Huron H. Smith documents in *Ethnobotany of the Menomini Indians* (Milwaukee: Board of Trustees, 1923). This plant might also be a name for the pawpaw tree (*Asimina*, of the custard-apple family), which

is especially common to the Dismal Swamp and was used by Native Americans for medicinal purposes. One other possibility is log fern (*Dryopteris celsa*), also common in the Dismal Swamp and also used medicinally. On the ethnobotany of the Dismal Swamp, see Lytton John Musselman, "Paw Paws and Mastodons; Logferns and Pinworms," April 17, 2007, http://www.odu.edu/~lmusselm/plant/swamp /pawpaws.php. It is also possible that the plant refers to the Chinese medicinal herb *moxa* (a much closer homophone for "mocasa"), although I'm not sure how Delany might have known of this herb.

53. Ibid., 114.

54. Thus, as in some of Hurston's work on fetishes, the narrator who initially allies herself with the skeptical reader moves this reader toward something like a respect for fetishism.

55. Because I am attempting to consider the relation of black-produced fetishes to personhood, in what follows I will draw on fetish production and ritual in several locations across the U.S. South and Caribbean, in a sense following the expanding network of relations that Delany himself sketches in *Blake*. However, as Aravamudan, Olmos and Paravinsini-Gebert, and Dayan's work (among others) makes clear, indeed as my own discussion of fetish-production as linked to local ecologies makes clear, diasporic African practice must also be thought of in specific colonial and historical contexts, which means that it varied significantly across the Americas. In short, diasporic Africans did not collectively produce one kind of artifact and a single cosmology but instead produced a multiplicity of artifacts and beliefs, which often evince strong resonances but cannot be thought of as identical. Fetishes in New York City, Virginia's Great Dismal Swamp, northern Haiti, Havana, Cuba, St. Thomas Parrish Jamaica, and a Surinam maroon community do not perform the same kind of work (indeed, no two fetishes in any one of these locations perform the same kind of work). The work any fetish performs indexes specific places and personalities, although neither place nor personality—then or now—could be conceived as unconnected from larger Atlantic networks.

To attend fully to any specific fetish, it would be necessary to attend to the particularities of colonial history in the place(s) where it was produced (for instance, whether a locality was under Spanish, French, Dutch, Portuguese, or English colonial rule, or whether indigenous American populations were present or absent) as well as the particularities of a given terrain (whether fetishes were made using gourds from the gourd tree or other kinds of containers). It is only to develop a general concept of the relation of personhood to fetish production that in what follows I trace resonances between quite diverse traditions, which might well also be studied in each specific location.

56. Robert Farris Thompson, *Flash of the Spirit: African and Afro-American Art and Philosophy* (New York: Vintage Books, 1983), 122, citing Lydia Cabrera, *El Monte: Igbo Fina Ewe Orisha, Vititinfina* (Havana: Edicones C.R., 1954).

57. Susan Stewart, *On Longing: Narratives of the Miniature, the Gigantic, the Souvenir, the Collection* (1984; Durham, N.C.: Duke University Press, 1993), 61. In considering Stewart's book in light of critiques of the subject that were, in the main, taken up in American literary studies after it was published, we might ask why the model of human subjectivity she traces requires a metaphorics by which the large becomes small. Why, that is, does consciousness require metaphors of enclosure and of an infinite regress into insides? Two possibilities come to mind. The first is that this metaphorics betrays an anxiety that consciousness, far from being a private and "inside" state, is borne of a relation of exteriority. The metaphorics of interiority attempts to override this anxiety by locating consciousness ever deeper on some inside. The second possibility is that the miniaturization of consciousness works to protect it by making it so small as to be the imperceptible and unanalyzable kernel around which the subject develops.

58. On this point I follow Latour's account of the fetish/factish in *Pandora's Hope: Essays on the Reality of Science Studies* (Cambridge, Mass.: Harvard University Press, 1999), 266–292.

59. Dayan, *Haiti, History*, 68. See also Maya Deren, *Divine Horseman: The Living Gods of Haiti* (1953; Kingston, N.Y.: McPherson, 1983); Alfred Métraux, *Voodoo in Haiti*, trans. Hugo Charteris (New York: Random House, 1989); Wade Davis, *The Serpent and the Rainbow* (New York: Simon & Schuster, 1985); Reginald Crosley, *The Vodou Quantum Leap: Alternative Realities, Power, and Mysticism* (St. Paul, Minn.: Llewellyn Publications, 2000). Note the Spinozistic echo in Dayan's formulation. The mind is the double of the body, or an expression of the body through another attribute (thought/mind) that is only visible and conceivable through the body. Dayan, like the anthropologists Alfred Métraux and Milo Rigaud and the sometime-anthropologists Zora Neale Hurston and Maya Deren, notes that Vodou assumes a tripartite model of personhood (the *gros bon anj,* the *petit bon anj,* and the *ko kadav*). This tripartite personhood is similar to that offered in certain West African cosmologies, particularly Yoruba and Akan—on this point, see Didier Njirayamanda Kaphagawani, "African Conceptions of a Person: A Critical Survey," in *Companion to African Philosophy,* ed. Kwasi Wiredu (Malden, Mass.: Blackwell, 2004), 332–42—and informs other West Indian religious practices, including Obeah and Santeria. See *Sacred Possessions: Vodou, Santeria, Obeah, and the Caribbean,* ed. Margarite Fernandez Olmos and Lizabeth Paravisini-Gebert. (New Brunswick: Rutgers University Press, 1997).

60. Fred Moten, "Resistance of the Object: Adrian Piper's Theatricality," in *In the Break: The Aesthetic of the Black Radical Tradition* (Minneapolis: University of Minnesota Press, 2003), 233–54, quotation from 239.

61. Ibid.

62. Ibid., 239–40.

63. Fred Moten, "Resistance of the Object: Aunt Hester's Scream," in *In the*

Break, 1. It is worth noting that while Moten's concept of subjectivity is quite clear (a process of subjection and also a possessive individualism that he suggests is troubling when applied to African American persons or to Marxist theory), his concept of personhood is not as clear. For Moten, personhood seems like a phenomenon that emerges as the excess (and effect) of the vexed and always dialectical relation of subjectivity and objectivity in the black tradition. Still, his quite brilliant analysis does not (yet) lay out the actual properties of the personhood he adumbrates. Nor does he elaborate how this sort of personhood changes the way we might think of plantation-produced commodities more generally (his focus, after all, is generally on the specific category of animate objects called slaves).

64. One of the difficulties of Moten's study is that it draws on but does not always distinguish between what I see as two distinct poststructuralist lines of thought. First, Derridean deconstruction, which I think is his primary theoretical methodology, plays on and thickens the dualistic terms that have been opposed by Western metaphysics, in so doing yielding a multiplicity that remains linked to the duality that births it. Second, Deleuzian immanence attempts to produce a reformulation of the inside that obliviates the structures of identity and dualities that previously dictated the terms of "reality."

65. It is impossible to speak of a single cosmology even within a single strain of diasporic African practice such as Vodou as these practices, unlike Catholicism or even Protestantism, do not have centralized governing bodies. If practice of religious belief is invariably local, the lack of centralized administrative structures common to many Afro-American religious practices that developed in the plantation zone makes these practices particularly localized and difficult to associate with any single cosmology (Afro-American religion that developed predominantly outside of the plantation zone—most obviously the African Methodist Episcopal Church in Philadelphia—have more centralized organizations). The analysis I offer draws on a wide variety of accounts of Afro-American practice but makes no claim at having identified a single coherent doctrine pertaining to the relation of spirit to matter in Afro-American practice.

66. Mercedes Cros Sandoval, *Worldview, the Orichas, and Santeria: Africa to Cuba and Beyond* (Gainesville: University Press of Florida, 2006), 83.

67. Métraux, *Voodoo in Haiti,* 255; Crosley, *Vodou Quantum Leap,* 86. Métraux claims that he cannot quite understand the meaning of the word, which seems to be the name for the force or substance that moves or constitutes all things. He proposes that Haitians do not use the word *namn* to refer to human beings, but this is not everywhere the case. For instance, Wade Davis conceives "n'âme as the spirit of the flesh that allows each cell of the body to function" (*Serpent,* 181). Dayan suggests that *nam* means "spirit, soul, gist, or sacred power" (*Haiti, History,* 32–33). All these definitions are helpful, although it is also important to keep in mind that *namn* is not simply a property of humans but a force that constitutes all

things. It is also important to keep in mind that *namn*, unlike the French *âme* with which it is sometimes confused, has an explicitly material or corporeal significance (ibid., 33).

68. Although the African conception of the body could seem rather like Aristotelian notions, I interpret this cosmology as closer to Spinozism, a point I develop in more detail in the next paragraph. There is no reason to suggest that diasporic Africans had access to Spinoza. To be sure, they may have had contact with Cartesian and Spinozan ideas as the Jesuits, who were the dominant Catholic order in the French West Indies until 1764 when they were expelled from Haiti, were a population that was likely to be familiar the intellectual controversy between Cartesianism and Spinozism (Israel notes that one of Spinoza's tutors was a Jesuit who spent time in the French Caribbean). However, even if this connection could be proven, the point, it seems to me, is not to show that African modes of thought had origins in Anglo-European philosophy, but that they existed even outside of Western "origins," and that they existed for diasporic Africans who did not read or write, or who, like Jack, chose not to be included in the emerging intellectual tradition of the rights of man. If there are only so many stories, and they are endlessly retold and made new in this retelling, it is perhaps also true that there are only so many metaphysics, and that these too are constantly retold and made new. Which is to say, is it not possible that Spinoza's central insight, that there is only one substance and the bodies composed of this substance are rhythmic constellations that gain and lose power (or pleasure) through their relation with other bodies, could have had precedence in other places or other times?

It is also worth noting that there are significant differences between Spinozism and West Indian cosmologies. Most obviously, diasporic Africans' cosmologies do not constitute a system (thus, while many who practice Obeah or Vodou posit something like *namn*, different practitioners give different accounts of namn, of persons' capacity to control it, and so forth). One general difference between Spinozism and West Indian practices is that the latter do not typically recoil from anthropomorphizing gods, even if they also generally presume that these gods are knowable in and through the physical world. Also, in West Indian cosmologies, a part of a body is imagined to retain that body's attributes and rhythms, even after the division or death of that body. This, it seems to me, is incommensurable with Spinoza's sense of the body as a singular ratio of speeds and slownesses: in Spinoza's system, the severed part might well continue, but it would not retain the rhythms of the body with which it was once joined. West Indian cosmologies, conversely, seem to suggest any part retains a physical memory of former assemblages in which it participated, even as it joins new ones.

69. Spinoza's theorization of substance resonates with and helps emphasize the metaphysical significance of this Haitian concept that translators often only gloss,

even if they also admit it is a complicated and significant term linked to West Indian monisms that are often dismissed as animism.

There are important differences in Haitian and Spinozistic understandings of parts of bodies (see the previous note), but bringing relatively undertheorized Haitian conceptions of the body into relation with well-theorized Spinozistic ones helps clarify some of the essential attributes of the body in Haitian and other West Indian cosmologies. *Namn* and substance are both extensions of animate force, and this means that its constellation in bodies retains this inherent mobility, even as each body so constituted is singular and has its own, in Spinoza's terms, speeds and slownesses or, in West Indian terms, rhythms. Any body so constituted is in relation to other similarly constituted and similarly extended body-objects and thus, in Marjorie Levinson's wonderfully lucid explication, it "endeavor[s] to preserve a kinetic poise within a dynamic ensemble of relations, an ensemble that also composes them as individuals"; "A Motion and a Spirit: Romancing Spinoza," *Studies in Romanticism* 46, no. 4 (2007): 366–408, cited at 377.

70. I reference Gayatri Chakravorty Spivak's essay "Can the Subaltern Speak?," first published in Cary Nelson and Lawrence Grossberg, eds., *Marxism and the Interpretation of Culture* (Urbana-Champaign: University of Illinois Press, 1988).

71. One of the reasons that the diasporic African cosmology I trace is important to us in the present is because it requires we come up with a way to think of place and the range of entities that comprise place as part of the political as opposed to dead stuff that is adjudicated by human beings whose political power and nature depends on their separation from their surroundings.

72. On possession in Obeah, see Jenny Sharpe, *Ghosts of Slavery: A Literary Archaeology of Black Women's Lives* (Minneapolis: University of Minnesota Press, 2002).

73. On polyrhythm in Vodou drumming, see Harold Courlander, *The Drum and the Hoe: The Life and Lore of the Haitian People* (1973; Berkeley: University of California Press, 1986).

74. Métraux, *Voodoo in Haiti*, 178.

75. The plenitude, the expansion of both body and mind that occurs through possession, is evident in the fact that the person possessed does not typically "revert" back to a former bodily form but always afterward carries and moves with the rhythms and desires of the god in her own.

76. Glissant, *Poetics of Relation*, 206 (italics in the original).

77. Recently, several literary critics have suggested loss as the central theme of Atlantic criticism, proposing that in this context melancholia is not a pathology but an ethical orientation particularly capable of recognizing the incalculable losses occasioned by Atlantic colonialism. This thesis is implicit in Debbie Lee's reading of the obi artifact, or fetish, as a combination of "partial objects" whose power accrues precisely because they are fragments and not wholes ("Grave Dirt, Dried

Toads, and the Blood of a Black Cat: How Aldridge Worked His Charms," in *Romantic Praxis* (online journal), paragraphs 12, 14, 15). Lee's point is that the organic (or the whole), whether this term is applied to aesthetic form or the personhood that emerges through this formalism, becomes impossible in the plantation world built from the brutalizations of slavery, brutalizations that can never be sutured or adequately recognized and mourned. As she explains at the close of her essay, the "power of the obi bag" is that it testifies to a "brokenness that longed for the no longer attainable whole" ("Grave Dirt," paragraph 16). Here, fetishes and the personhood to which they are linked evince a power that comes from "brokenness" while at the same time fixating on the holism, of objects or persons, that has apparently been destroyed by Atlantic colonialism. This analysis enfolds the fetish in an Atlantic melancholia that registers how the losses of the Middle Passage haunt all subsequent productions.

The ethics of melancholia that remains implicit in Lee's analysis is explicitly articulated in Ian Baucom's *Specters of the Atlantic* (2005). While Lee's analysis implies the melancholia of Afro-American fetishists, Baucom's analysis focuses on the melancholia of the critic. For Baucom, the proper ethical response to the brutalities of modernity is a "melancholy realism" whose "key unit" is "the sentimental, romantic, or melancholy case, scene, or fact" (222). In Baucom's study, melancholic witnessing departs from Freud's classic psychoanalytic conception of melancholia in which a subject invests her ego in a not fully recognized but intensely cathected object whose loss incapacitates subjective functioning. For Baucom the cathected object of psychoanalytic melancholia is replaced by the event of the Middle Passage. Replacing the impossible object with the impossible event, Baucom transforms Freud's theory of subjective dysfunction into a historical orientation, in so doing converting a pathology into an ethics. For Baucom, it is impossible to ever fully witness the event of the Middle Passage, and the ethical position is to put the tools of history, literature, and literary criticism to the impossible project of witnessing this event, in the process constituting a personhood founded not on detachment from this event but on a continually renewed attention to it

5. Involving the Universe in Ruins

1. Leonora Sansay, *Secret History; or, The Horrors of St. Domingo and Laura*, ed. Michael J. Drexler (1808; Toronto: Broadview Press, 2007). With Zelica [Leonora Sansay], *Zelica, the Creole*, 3 vols. (London: W. Fearman, 1920; rpt. Wildberg, Germany: Belser Wissenschaftlicher Dienst, 1998).

2. Sansay, *Zelica*, 1:18.

3. Ibid., 1:180–82.

4. Ibid., 1:132.

5. In the translator's glossary to Glissant, *Poetics of Relation*, xxiii. Bernardin

de Saint-Pierre's *Paul et Virginie* (1787) offers an early usage of the term, which also appears in Chateaubriand's oeuvre. Émile Littre, *Dictionnaire de la langue française*, vol. 3 (Paris: Librairie Hachette, 1878), suggests the nominative form of "morne" derives from the Spanish "*morro*, [hill or mountain] et son augmentatif *morron* [big mountain]" but that it might also come from the French "monticuli, [hill] qui s'est altéré dans la bouche des créoles français" (3:630). However, the Spanish word for Moor is *moro*. The proximity of the terms *morro* and *moro* and both terms' proximity to the creole words *maroon* (English), *marron* (French), *cimarrón* (Spanish) as well as the fact that maroons did often take refuge in the hills makes it possible that eighteenth- and early nineteenth-century Anglo-Europeans like Sansay as well Afro-Americans understood the term *morne* to carry with it a linkage to marronage and Afro-American resistance, a linkage I will develop further in the analysis that follows.

6. Sansay, *Zelica*, 1:20. As we have already seen in Bartram's *Travels*, travel narratives focusing on tropical landscapes obsessively turn to the terrain's capacity to literally destroy human beings. Thus, the practice of spectating that grounds both the picturesque and the sublime is not possible in these accounts. On spectatorship, the picturesque, and the sublime, see Alan Liu, *Wordsworth, the Sense of History* (Stanford, Calif.: Stanford University Press, 1989).

7. On Christophe's setting fire to the town and his house, Sansay writes: "Loud yells of joy evinced the pleasure with which this command [to set fire to the town] was received by the negroes, and the chief himself gave the signal for its execution by seizing a torch and setting fire to the superb palace he inhabited" (*Zelica*, 1:16).

8. Ibid., 1:17, 20–21. The burning of the town and destruction of the mountain that opens *Zelica* is also among the first events narrated in the earlier *Secret History*. That Afro-Americans' incineration and atomization of place is quite important to Sansay is evident not only in this repetition but also in the fact that this scene is narrated again about midway through book 1 of *Zelica*, where Sansay again offers a description of the scene, concluding that "on all sides, the burned and blackened walls presented melancholy proofs of the opposition of the people of colour to the establishment of the ancient order of things" (1:139).

9. As I discuss in my introduction, Roach's conceptualization of surrogation verges on a theory of history whereby the performances and styles of the Afro-Americans and Native Americans whose lives and productions only fleetingly passed into official records remain in the performances, including the literary writings, of those who consciously or not surrogate their performances.

10. For Deleuze's account of the actual and the virtual, see especially *Bergsonism*, trans. Hugh Tomlinson and Barbara Habberjam (1988; New York: Zone Books, 1990), as well as *Difference and Repetition*, trans. Paul Patton (New York: Columbia University Press, 1995). For a critique of Deleuze's configuration of the relation between the actual and the virtual, see Peter Hallward, *Out of This World:*

Deleuze and the Philosophy of Creation (New York: Verso, 2006). Deleuze uses the term *virtual* more than the term *potential,* but I will use the latter term as I think it helps hold at bay the questions (for instance, those relating to virtual reality) that the use of *virtual* suggests in English

11. Deleuze distinguishes sharply between the virtual and the possible. The possible is an image projected from, and thus determined by, the real. The potential is not an image of the actual (the term that Deleuze pairs with the virtual/potential) but a field of potentialities that remains undefined and that will be manifest in a life or an agency and not in reality as such.

12. Although the counterfactual could be associated with either the potential or the possible, I am here interested in it insofar as it is associated with the potential. On the counterfactual in American literary study, see also Myra Jehlen, "History before the Fact; or, Captain John Smith's Unfinished Symphony," *Critical Inquiry* 19, no. 4 (1993): 677–92.

13. On this point, consider her frequent counterfactual reference to Afro-Americans in Saint-Domingue / Haiti during the years 1802–5 as slaves, a misnaming that indicates an investment in superimposing onto the scene of antislavery a return of the scene of slavery.

14. Fischer, *Modernity Disavowed.*

15. Unsurprisingly, it is a lot easier to track Louis Sansay though the historical record than Leonora Sansay. Although he may have spent some time in France after leaving Saint-Domingue and was declared an insolvent debtor by 1806, by 1807 Louis Sansay was in New York City where he opened a dancing school and sponsored balls with a female partner. Newspaper archives indicate that the school remained prosperous through the second and into the third decade of the nineteenth century. In fact, Louis Sansay attempted to expand his dancing school into New Jersey and even Washington, D.C.

16. On Sansay's involvement in the Burr conspiracy, see Michael Drexler, "Brigands and Nuns: The Vernacular Sociology of Collectivity after the Haitian Revolution," in *Messy Beginnings: Postcoloniality and Early American Studies,* ed. Malini Johar Schueller and Edward Watts, 175–202 (New Brunswick, N.J.: Rutgers University Press, 2003). Drexler's essay, which offers an outstanding analysis of the ways Sansay's Haitian experiences led her to contemplate women's communities, roles, and desires, imagining configurations that were not possible in the early U.S. Republic, set the precedent for a good deal of recent scholarship on Sansay, including Elizabeth Maddock Dillon, "The Secret History of the Early American Novel," *Novel* 40, no. 1–2 (2006/2007): 77–103; and Gretchen Woertendyke, "Romance to Novel: A Secret History," *Narrative* 17, no. 3 (2009): 255–73.

17. On this point, see Jennifer van Bergen, "Reconstructing Leonora Sansay," *Another World Is Possible,* January 3, 2010, http://www.a-w-i-p.com/index.php /2010/01/03/reconstructing-leonora-sansay.

18. Bennett, *Vibrant Matter,* 54. Recent work in early American literary studies tends to focus on this dynamism, attending closely to the ways it recalibrates long-accepted ideas about nationalism, sociality, commodity exchange, and literary form (the latter often used as the microcosm through which the former are traced). The most recent Americanist work of Elizabeth Maddock Dillon, Leonard Tennenhouse, and Michael Warner, although distinct in its deployment of archive, method, and theory, all emphasize the dynamism that comes to the fore when the Americas are recast in an Atlantic geopolitical frame. Although I agree with the general moves of this body of work, in drawing on Bennett's and Deleuze's analyses I aim to suggest that an even greater plurality characterized this historical moment and am particularly interested in how this plurality impacts how we understand the linked but not equivalent concepts of *agency* (a power to affect and to animate that is broadly distributed and possessed by inorganic and organic forms and forces), *personhood* (a term I use to indicate an agency directed toward a political and social end and legible, at least to some extent, within political and social systems), and *subjectivity* (a term I associate with humanism, particularly a humanism grounded in the life of the mind or consciousness as an internalized operation that precedes and closes off the empirical world).

19. Some recent critics, most explicitly Elizabeth Maddock Dillon ("The Secret History of the Early American Novel"), have read *Secret History* as a novel. More recently still, Gretchen Woertendyke ("Romance to Novel") reads the work as a secret history along the lines charted by Michael McKeon. My own analysis is not focused on the genre of the text, although given that Sansay admired Germaine de Staël's writing I suspect that, insofar as she attempted a genre, it was something close to Staël's own fusions of travelogue, novelistic, and autobiographical forms. Most readings of genre focus on the ways genre contains the seeds of, and comments on, a particular historical moment, which is itself often linked to earlier historical moments. The payoff of these arguments generally has to do with the relation of the genre to emerging economic, spatial (or geographical), and social forms, particularly capitalism and nationalism and the ways they impacted how sociality and subjectivity were imagined and experienced. I am not convinced that reading the book as a novel as opposed to a travelogue or a secret history significantly changes how critics have interpreted the forms of sociality and subjectivity circulating in it. To be sure, arguing for one reading or the other might well impact critical periodizations, and generic considerations are also important to what Gretchen Woertendyke has described to me as the play between storylines, which pushed far enough might well indicate a shift from regnant modes of sociality and subjectivity, although in the main early Americanists agree—perhaps too much—in their descriptions of sociality and subjectivity, despite their attention to different generic forms. However, I am not focused on traditional periodizations or traditional accounts of sociality and subjectivity (indeed, I propose the *person*

as an alternative to the subjectivity generally imagined in early American studies), and it is for this reason that, even as I choose the term *travelogue* to distinguish *Secret History* from the more obviously novelistic *Zelica*, I remain agnostic on the issue of the work's genre. I am indebted to Gretchen Woertendyke for discussing this point with me.

20. On the reasons why scholars have been slow to attribute *Zelica* to Sansay, see Drexler's introduction to the Broadview Press edition of *Secret History* as well as Simone Vauthier, "A propos de l'image du noir aux Amériques dans la première moitié du 19e siècle," *Recherche anglaises et nord-américaines*, no. 3 (1970): 67–126.

21. Sansay, *Zelica*, 3:3.

22. *The Atheneum; or, Spirit of the English Magazines*, May 1, 1821, 132.

23. *Zelica* structurally replicates Mary's narrative function of serving as a counterpoint for and confidante to Clara; that *Zelica* recasts some of the musings that Mary offers in her letters as effusions of Zelica's consciousness makes even clearer the link between these two characters. For instance, consider that Mary's desire to "build a dwelling on the bosom of the waters, where, sheltered from the storms that agitate mankind" (*Secret History*, 61) returns in the character of Zelica, who, gazing at the sea, exclaims "Oh! that I was floating on that ocean . . . freed from the horrid fate that awaits me" (*Zelica*, 1:128).

24. Although twentieth- and twenty-first-century historians do not believe Dessalines was born in Africa, many early accounts assume this to be the case. While Glaude is probably meant to be a character type who recalls Dessalines, Dessalines himself is an occasional character in *Zelica*, so it is by no means the case that they are equivalent. Rather, the novel describes them as being in profound sympathy with each other (*Zelica*, 3:271). Still, one of the general preoccupations of the novel is to imagine what might happen to white (or white-looking, in the case of Zelica) women who, instead of repatriating to France or the United States, were to become wives or mistresses to Haitian leaders. Glaude, after all, is a general in the Haitian army. What, the novel speculates, would happen if white women were to throw in their lot with the Haitian Revolution instead of the U.S. Revolution? The former in many respects offered many more rights and possibilities to women, even if both were profoundly patriarchal as is evident in Dessalines 1805 Constitution, which explicitly considers the role and rights of women but understands Haitian citizenship as a strictly masculine enterprise.

25. Sansay, *Zelica*, 3:202. While both works criticize the fact that the possibilities available to women were so little changed by revolutionary movements, neither proposes a society, postrevolutionary or otherwise, in which autonomous women are given the rights of men. To be sure, *Secret History* traces Mary's growing acceptance that women should break from marital contracts when they prove abusive or even unsatisfying; however, Mary consistently imagines women need

the patronage of powerful men and does not allow the possibility of a mixed sex, postrevolutionary society in which women have any real degree of autonomy. As Michael Drexler first noted, Sansay does imagine the convent might be a space in which women might be autonomous ("Brigands and Nuns"). However, in her idealization of the convent, Sansay turns to homosociality as if to emphasize that no freedom is possible in eighteenth- or nineteenth-century heterosocialities. In Zelica, even the convent is not safe from the depredations of men, who attempt to rape the nuns. On gender in Zelica, see also Caroll Smith-Rosenberg, "Black Gothic: The Shadowy Origins of the American Bourgeoisie," in Possible Pasts: Becoming Colonial in Early America, ed. Robert Blair St. George, 243–69 (Ithaca, N.Y.: Cornell University Press, 2000).

26. In both works, the United States is often presented as though it were the best option because it allowed a female agency predicated on happy marriages and domesticity, but the focus of both works on bad marriages makes clear that domesticity offered a poor basis for women's agency. Which is to say, the U.S. option is not really an option.

27. Sansay, Zelica, 3:286. This position draws on an orientalist tradition then gaining ascendency in Anglo-European writing. Thomas Moore's novel Lalla Rookh (1817) clearly influenced Zelica, which borrows Zelica's name and many epigraphs from that work.

28. On this point, see both Drexler's essay "Brigands and Nuns," and his introduction to the Broadview Press edition of Secret History.

29. On the ways white women are objectified in Secret History, see Woertendyke, "Romance to Novel."

30. On the history of El Cobre, particularly its Marian tradition, which I will discuss in more detail presently, see María Elena Díaz, The Virgin, the King, and the Royal Slaves of El Cobre: Negotiating Freedom in Colonial Cuba, 1670–1780 (Palo Alto, Calif.: Stanford University Press, 2000).

31. Ibid., 11, 13.

32. Sansay, Secret History, 140.

33. Dillon, "The Secret History," 93. Dillon's argument draws on world systems theory, Marxism, and genre theory to propose that Secret History offers "an astute analysis of the relations of production and social reproduction that stand at the core of colonial politics" (78). One of Dillon's points is that Sansay's work requires that critics recognize colonialism did not end with the revolution and the emergence of U.S. nationalism. Working "both within and without the frame of the nation state," Sansay's text focuses on a "geopolitics of European colonialism and developing world capitalism that preceded and accompanied the national revolutions in the Atlantic world" (79). Social reproduction is, Dillon proposes, not possible in the colonies, which were entirely spaces of production. Because the novel is bound up in "mapping social reproduction," Dillon proposes that "there can be

no such thing as a creole [colonial] novel" (88). Yet Dillon concludes her essay by proposing that Sansay produces precisely this impossible form and in so doing offers alternate geopolitics and a quasi-utopian feminist community characterized by "cross-racial alliance" and the valuation of resourcefulness. In short, while mapping cross-racial sociality is not the overriding point of Dillon's analysis, this mode of sociality along with other modes of positively valued collectivity that emerge from creole relations (for instance, women's communities) is the point toward which Dillon's analysis drives.

34. To put this in simpler terms, one of the limits of Drexler's and Dillon's studies is that they give scant attention to Sansay's racism, which is not at all incidental to her project. My point in attending to her racism in this section is not only to more fully work out the dynamics of racism in early nineteenth-century Anglo-European writing but also to contemplate the modes of reading that twenty-first-century critics use to access these earlier texts, which require that we consider how to negotiate race and racism in the American tradition.

35. A number of critics have noted the 1805 Constitution's resignification of race. See, for instance, Sibylle Fisher, *Modernity Disavowed: Haiti and the Cultures of Slavery in the Age of Revolution* (Durham, N.C.: Duke University Press, 2004) as well as Anne W. Gulick, "We Are Not the People: The 1805 Haitian Constitution's Challenge to Political Legibility in the Age of Revolution," *American Literature* 78, no. 4 (2006): 799–820.

36. Sansay, *Secret History*, 124. This anecdote reappears in volume 2 of *Zelica*. Thus, while I will suggest a difference between *Secret History*'s investment in racial distinctions and *Zelica*'s exploration of white women's incorporation into a generalized blackness, it is by no means the case that the works develop sharply distinct racial ideologies.

37. Ibid., 125.

38. Ibid.

39. On this point, see Dayan, *Haiti, History*, esp. 16–29. See also David Nicholls, *From Dessalines to Duvalier: Race, Color and National Independence in Haiti* (New Brunswick, N.J.: Rutgers University Press, 1996), 38.

40. Although from a twenty-first-century perspective this advocacy of companionate marriage might seem a conservative position, that this was precisely the position advocated by Mary Wollstonecraft indicates that this was not the case in the eighteenth and early nineteenth centuries. While Wollstonecraft's position could be linked to a certain tradition of liberal radicalism, Sansay's text makes clear the insufficiency of this liberal tradition.

41. Sansay, *Secret History*, 153.

42. Surrogation involves an imagining of an other, but it is a material performance and thus distinct from Adam Smith's sentimental social ethics and their investment of imagining and feeling for another. While Smithian sentimentalism

involves a sense of the other as a bounded being that the subject can feel for, surrogation, in performing an other in the self, pushes against the boundedness and interiority that structures Smithian sentimentalism.

43. Here, I follow Dayan's argument that Vodou is a performance and process of memory that recalls the history of those who would seem to be excluded from history and that also meditates on processes of historicization. I am certainly not arguing that racial surrogation alone can be linked to forgetting while Vodou surrogations are tools of memory. All performances are necessarily processes of forgetting and recollecting. That said, Sansay's racial surrogation has a particular investment in forgetting relationalities, dissolving identities, and proliferating materialities that were common in the tropics. So racial surrogation works toward forgettings that allow the belief that New World identities are discrete and racially demarcated, and they also protect the genealogical and fiduciary systems grounded on these identities. If Vodou possession would necessarily involve forgetting, it is nonetheless a performance that recalls the cross-racial and cross-species relations, deviant materialisms, dissolved identities, and fragmented bodies that emerged in the tropics under colonialism.

44. Sansay, *Zelica*, 3:241

45. Antonio Benítez-Rojo, *The Repeating Island: The Caribbean and the Postmodern Perspective*, 2nd ed., trans. James E. Maraniss (Durham, N.C.: Duke University Press, 1996), 12.

46. Ibid., 16.

47. Sansay, *Zelica*, 3:139.

48. Ibid., 3:277–80.

49. Père Nicholson's *Essai sur l'histoire naturelle de St. Domingue* (1776) devotes an entire chapter to slavery, in which the main argument is a critique of the abuses of slaves under colonialism. In short, the chapter focuses on and is a critique of Anglo-European colonial practices and policies as they impact slaves. Nicholson was not entirely uninterested in the agency of slaves. He noted instances in which slaves had poisoned and in other ways killed their masters. However, for Nicholson Afro-American agency was part of a cycle of violence and retribution, and he seemed uninterested in Afro-American cultural forms or in the ways that they might allow responses to slavery that move from this cycle of violence and retribution.

50. The American Philosophical Society probably acquired its copy of Nicholson's *Essai* in the eighteenth century. Given that the book remains relatively common in libraries and special collections in Philadelphia and New York, it is likely that the book was not obscure in the early nineteenth century. Although I have no knowledge of the book's existence in Haitian archives, that there are several copies in French archives and that this was a book about Saint-Domingue makes it likely

that the book was available in Le Cap's library or in private collections in the late eighteenth and early nineteenth centuries.

51. As may be evident to readers grounded in American literary studies, my discussion of the fetish's office references and attempts to post an alternative to Bercovitch's reading of the "office of the scarlet letter," which he proposes as a paradigmatic example of the movement of submission and assent that has been constitutive to American culture since the Puritans. See Sacvan Bercovitch, *The Office of the Scarlet Letter* (Baltimore: Johns Hopkins Press, 1992), and *The Rites of Assent: Transformations in the Symbolic Construction of America* (New York: Routledge, 1992). My analysis does not simply push against Bercovitch's by posing a diversified political geography that does not allow the centrality of Puritans or New England, or permit us to stay with the supposed ubiquity of a hegemonic United States; I am also arguing against the model of the subject, the relation of part to whole, and the political structure that Bercovitch traces (and laments) across his tremendously influential oeuvre. For Bercovitch, the subject is fundamentally and constitutionally submissive. The office of the scarlet letter is to impart this knowledge to would-be dissidents. This means that for him the part (the individual subject) is always in subordinate relation to the whole (the public) to which it joins itself. Politics, then, is a hegemonic enterprise in which any alternate agency and forms would seem impossible.

My study, which focuses on persons instead of subjects, suggests that the person, while not in any sense free and undetermined, develops and can attain agency through relations with other proximate forces. The chameleonlike property of this person as well as the pleasures and powers gained through entwinings with a series of outsides does not presume submission to any one exterior force; rather, it is a process of relation through which a body is able to more or less well actualize its potential. None of these series of relations emerges as a definitive and all-encompassing enough to constitute the sole totality for that singularity. Thus, I am attempting to challenge both the expectation that the person is a subordinate part of some whole greater than herself and the expectation that the political is a unitary whole that has the power to co-opt all difference. Finally, I am proposing that politics might be linked to the resulting play of difference (on this point, I am simply repeating a point made previously by other theorists, most notably Michael Hardt and Antonio Negri in *Empire* (Cambridge, Mass.: Harvard University Press, 2001), *Multitude* (New York: Penguin, 2005), and *Commonwealth* (Cambridge, Mass.: Belknap, 2011).

52. This is not to say that Clara or that Afro-American cultural forms, in pushing against the bifurcation of life and death, have no concept of finitude. One formation of the body may well end, but endings also give rise to new assemblages. Certainly these new forms do not return what is lost, and certainly they might not prove to have good effects, so this is not in any simple or general sense a celebratory process, even if it is not melancholic.

53. Sansay, *Zelica*, 3:294. Indeed, this nuptial language as well as the way Clara's body is penetrated and opened as Glaude holds her in his arms suggests a sort of displaced consummation of the cross-racial love plot that drives the novel. If the close of the novel suggests Clara's becoming Haitian, this scene suggests it is a transformation linked to sexual penetration and marriage.

54. Colin (Joan) Dayan discusses this mythology in *Haiti, History, and the Gods*, 16–38.

55. See Timoléon Brutus, *L'homme d'airian*, vol. 2 (Port au Prince: Presses Nationales d'Haiti, [1946]).

56. As Gulick ("We Are Not the People") as well as Doris Garraway has shown, it is not the case that Dessalines and his Haitian government were in fact democratic, particularly insofar as women were concerned. My point then is not about Dessalines's actual politics and their likely outcomes but about how Dessalines, his conception of materiality, and his position on property were mythologized at the time. See Garraway, *The Libertine Colony: Creolization in the Early French Caribbean* (Durham, N.C.: Duke University Press, 2005).

57. *Zelica*, 3:309.

58. See Sansay's July 1812 letter to Burr, reprinted in the Broadview Press edition of *Secret History*.

Epilogue

1. Edgar Allan Poe, *The Narrative of Arthur Gordon Pym of Nantucket*, ed. Frederick Frank and Diane Long Hoeveler (Toronto: Broadview Press, 2010), 217.

2. Leslie Fiedler, *Love and Death in the American Novel*, rev. ed. (New York: Stein and Day, 1966), 391–29.

3. Gilles Deleuze and Felix Guattari, *Kafka: Toward a Minor Literature*, trans. Dana Polan (Minneapolis: University of Minnesota Press, 1986), 16, 18.

4. Ibid., 18.

5. Poe, *Arthur Gordon Pym*, 133–34.

6. Ibid., 155.

7. Ibid., 220.

8. Ibid., 222.

9. Sharon Cameron, *The Corporeal Self: Allegories of the Body in Melville and Hawthorne* (New York: Columbia University Press, 1991); and *Impersonality: Seven Essays* (Chicago: University of Chicago Press, 2007).

10. Colin (Joan) Dayan, "Poe, Ladies, and Slaves," in *Subjects and Citizens: Nation, Race, and Gender from Oroonoko to Anita Hill*, ed. Cathy Davidson and Michael Moon (Durham, N.C.: Duke University Press, 1995).

11. In fact, by the close of "Monos and Una," Poe was describing a monism in which the "autocrats space and time" assert their capability to produce difference,

thus counteracting the "bad" monism that he also fears and seemed, earlier in that same story, to ally with democracy. On Poe's materialism, see Maurice S. Lee, "Absolute Poe: His System of Transcendental Racism," *American Literature* 75, no. 4 (2003): 751–81.

12. Poe, *Arthur Gordon Pym,* 201.

13. Wilson Harris, *Womb of Space: The Cross-Cultural Imagination* (Westport, Conn.: Greenwood Press, 1983).

14. Ibid., 26 (italics mine on "between"; on "partial" in the original).

Index

Page numbers in italics refer to illustrations.

United States: American Revolution and, 30–32, 130; colonialism and, 29; Constitution of, 11–12, 53–54, 111; relationality and, 180–81; slavery in, 4–8, 12; tropical climates of, 3–5; vitalism in, 51–63. *See also* slavery

vegetation and vegetable life, 32–37, 42, 50–70, 74–82, 171, 175, 234n6. *See also* botany; ecology; natural history
Venus flytraps, 34, 74, 75, 78–79, 207n54
Vergès, Françoise, 105
Vessey, Denmark, 130
La Vie de J. J. Dessalines (Dubroca), 161
vines, 34–36, 42, 44, 67
Viotta de Costa, Emilia, 43
vitalism, 22, 51–66, 69, 71–73, 77–81, 171, 203n15
Vodou, 7, 23, 106, 134–39, 147, 157, 165–69, 213n11, 230n65, 240n43
Voltaire, 90

Walcott, Derek, 145
Warner, Michael, 32, 49, 194n41, 196n10
West Indies, 31, 60, 87–89
Wheatley, Phillis, 24, 115–17, 122–23, 128, 140, 221n5
whiteness, 5, 20, 23, 147–57, 159–62, 165
Wieland (Brown), 160
Williams, Elizabeth, 61
Wilson, Richard, 117
Wing, Betsy, 108, 144
Wollstonecraft, Mary, 170
women, 147, 149–53, 155–57, 159–65, 170–71, 192n32, 202n11. *See also* gender; *specific women*

yellow fever, 44, 59–60, 204n29

Zelica (Sansay), 23, 145, 147, 149, 151–56, 161, 165–66, 171

MONIQUE ALLEWAERT is assistant professor of English at the University of Wisconsin–Madison.